Upside In

Upside In

Upside In

An Interactive Introspective

SCOTT A235 HUGHES

Matador
9 Priory Business Park,
Wistow Road, Kibworth Beauchamp,
Leicestershire. LE8 0RX
Tel: 0116 279 2299
Email: books@troubador.co.uk
Web: www.troubador.co.uk/matador
Twitter: @matadorbooks

ISBN 978 1800463 622

British Library Cataloguing in Publication Data.
A catalogue record for this book is available from the British Library.

Printed and bound in the UK by TJ Books Ltd, Padstow, Cornwall
Typeset in 11pt Minion Pro by Troubador Publishing Ltd, Leicester, UK

Matador is an imprint of Troubador Publishing Ltd

1

Arrival

Robert Louis Stephenson once mused, *"I travel, not to go anywhere, but to go."* This didn't chime with my sentiments stepping onto the prison bus that rolled into court back in May 2019, to pop my cherry. A claustrophobe would consider the experience sentence enough. Unlike a police station or court cell, there is no toilet available at the press of a button either; my only real gripe considering the circumstances. There is, however, the novelty of being able to stand freely whilst on the motorway. This soon runs its course. It did become somewhat of a necessity, too, as I am a long-time owner and sufferer of a set of knees that like to conform to the rules even less than I did to find myself in this situation. I was especially thankful on a later excursion, which involved crossing countries.

1

On-board entertainment for that ride was provided by someone cursing away in one of the cells behind me – muffled and largely indecipherable, but I did just about make out: *"I'm going to WALES; that's the fucking **worst of it!**"* – not the fact he was about to be locked up over Christmas, then… or the latest addition(s) to his criminal record. Honestly it lifted the journey no-end.

From a neighbouring lane, unless you recognise a 'Serco' or 'GEOamey' logo on the side, you wouldn't necessarily glance at one of these vehicles and realise what it was. The small square tinted windows could have anything behind them, and really they are the only other clue, as, being a private firm, they are not kitted out with the familiar 'go-faster' blue and yellow chequered decals.

For me, these journeys were the best opportunity for reflection on exactly what I did to get myself there. I've done that to my satisfaction, but don't worry I shall do it here for your exposition.

My three different experiences in two different jails (predominantly over one incident) were actually wildly different at times, but I will not always specifically refer to one or the other, as there's plenty of cross-over. *Yes Minister* and *The Thick of It* never explicitly revealed who was who, and I always liked that.

These buses, though, always appeared to be exactly the same, and I assume always are. Things only take on a different feel when *"You have reached your destination…"*. Rather than the dulcet tones of a TomTom or Garmin, the words are bellowed by someone up front who has clearly lost the love for their work, and ends up actually sounding more robotic.

Our bus then goes through a modernised portcullis and awaits further instructions. For a while we are sandwiched between this gate and another whilst checks are performed. It's essentially an airlock or a border, sporting 19th century brickwork. It can be a long wait, particularly on one occasion when we were told there was an incident in reception and emergency services were still in attendance. If you didn't already have your guard up, you will after hearing that.

This brings me then on to reception. I'm sure, like myself, you have always associated this word with places like hotels, workplaces and schools. The irony is that jail is a combination of these, but their reception is like none of them. You immediately see things on the wall like *"You are going to be OK"*, but this won't stop you feeling a tad dehumanised from everything else, as you are herded through a series of holding rooms and in no particular order treated to the following:

Front desk

Again, not quite your old High School, or the Burj Al Arab. You are asked if you know exactly why you are there and how long for, then various questions concerning your mental state, and propensity to harm yourself or others. On one occasion this felt like breakneck box ticking, and on the other they genuinely seemed to care. The irony again is that they corresponded to totally the opposite in both cases. Where one had suggested everything was fine, it ended up being a largely unsafe and terrifying stay, and in the other case where they showed true care and concern, life beyond was actually

3

much safer in comparison. Not a breeze, and certainly not a holiday camp like some people would have you believe, but safe enough.

Reception front desk also involves taking an inventory of your possessions, most of which you will not see before your release. If you are on remand (awaiting sentence), you are allowed your own clothes provided they meet certain stipulations, chiefly not being certain colours or carrying any slogans. If you are sentenced, then you must make do solely with prison clobber, which we'll get to shortly. Valuables like phone, keys and wallet go to a vault somewhere (I like to think of Gringotts), in ownership of the cashier (again I like to think of Gringotts). All other items are bagged, signed for, and stored elsewhere. In one particular barbaric instance, I had my pouch of Amber Leaf jettisoned because it had been opened, literally the day before. I still hold a vigil every Sunday.

You are then given your ID card with your mugshot, date of birth, and prison number (see 'dehumanisation'). This number is going to be who you are and more or less all you are. The waltz of the front desk is complete.

Search

You didn't think you were going to get in without this, did you? At this stage, though, you are well versed in the proceedings, from the police station several times, and court, several times. In jail, as far as I understand, there's a randomisation process for bringing a sniffer dog or plastic gloves to the party. I avoided both on both occasions.

The first time round, I was ordered to drop my boxers but allowed to cradle the jewels from their vision, and this was sufficient. The second time, I was given a robe, initially for privacy, but then ordered to open it and offer my gennies to a studious middle-aged man. A barrel of laughs. I did try a chuckle to myself though, wondering how this must have felt for those in on indecent exposure charges. Confusing, I imagine.

Equipment issue

You are then given a large clear plastic sack, containing mainly clothes. If you're thinking orange, then you need to stop watching American television. Over here, it's all grey, baby. They will adopt an 'all sizes fit one' philosophy, and so you'll get what you're given. Luckily most of mine were Small or Medium, and the tracksuit bottoms fitted nicely. Sadly, though, no pockets, and so very quickly you get used to the feeling of stowing important items in your socks when you're out and about.

Although I was in grey from head to toe, if I was holding a MacBook I would have probably looked quite debonair. There's also a few pairs of boxers, which are about as you'd expect. No Egyptian cotton, but definitely the feeling of sand. The remaining contents of the sack are as follows:

- **Bedding**: a simple single sheet and pillow case, both in a garish pale green, the likes of which you would normally see on a Californian golf course. The duvet is essentially a thin orange throw, which is surprisingly good at retaining body heat, and so, for someone like me – always too hot – hardly used. I did manage to acquire a second green sheet which I used as a duvet instead. Anyway, I'm veering, let's get back to the important stuff.

- **Cutlery**: a white plastic selection, and not half bad. Accompanied by a plate, bowl, and mug, either in one of the other 49 shades you'll find in this place, or an equally soulless blue. Blue has long been my favourite colour, but I have to say it looked shit here. You'll find the same blue again in a pair of towels, and now we're on to the toiletries: your standard white travel toothbrush and a generous tube of paste, which doubles as an excellent adhesive for posters. I didn't get involved but I saw plenty of other's handiwork. A bar of soap, if you're lucky (or unlucky), a roll-on deodorant and a few sachets (yes, sachets) of shower gel. As someone who enjoys a daily shower and sometimes a cheeky second, this was a trifle insufficient, but I soon learned that these sachets are quite easily available on the wing.

Medical

So, we have our bag of goodies. Are we done now? No, no we're not. Next up is a trip to the nurse, which is a piece of string in terms of how long you're going to be in there. Although prison will ultimately get access to your GP medical records, this is not immediate. Nothing is immediate. You are expected to know the exact details of your prescription(s), but ultimately this is a fairly futile exercise as you won't see it for days, by which time your GP has provided the info anyway.

This proved quite a blessing to me. I will be quite open about the struggles between my ears, and I have been medicated for this for some time, in particular for anxiety. The time spent without this medication, albeit a short one, told me that I may no longer be as dependent on it as I thought I was. I know what you may be thinking, but the particular prescription I was on does not take weeks to take effect, nor does it take weeks to leave the system. I was more or less immediately aware that I was without it, and this didn't affect me like I thought it would. One of my stays was a pretty hostile and intimidating one, and I surprised myself at how I stood up to it. *"If I don't need it here, where and when do I need it?"* This was the start of me tapering down, and I'm delighted to say I now write this prescription-free.

Anyway, enough about medication for now (meds are a huge deal in here). As well as admin, there are routine tests to be done, such as checking weight, height, and blood pressure. Blood is then taken from a prick to the finger and dotted across some paper and sent off to someone for the wonderful occupation of checking for hepatitis. This is the last you'll see of a nurse for now.

I am also pleased to write this hepatitis-free.

Listener

The next encounter is with an inmate whose sentence is long enough to qualify for a choice of 'Peer' jobs (working with and helping other inmates), one of which is a Listener. The clue is in the title, and their role is to sit you down and outline what you can expect of your time there, and field any questions or concerns you may have. They will tell you in no uncertain terms that you need to be able to look after yourself, and not to ever leave your cell unlocked – because nothing will happen in the certain event that you get raided. It is not a case of *if* but *when*; do *not* do it. The Listeners wear an identifiable shirt and can roam the wings freely. Don't expect Frasier Crane, but rather someone who knows how it all works and will tell you what you need to know to get by. They are not quite the same as Samaritans, who are also present.

Now that's out of the way, there's one person left to speak to, and it's the one you've been waiting for:

Phone call

You are restricted to two minutes. You have certain vital information to disclose such as your prison number, which is essential to anyone outside. Like I said, this is who you are now, and things like this will occupy a bigger chunk of those two minutes than you think, by the time they've gone off and found a pen. Also, you don't see the time counting down, nor are you bleeped at when it's nearly up. This is frustrating as it can be days before you get your phone PIN and anyone added to your contact list. And no one likes being cut off.

There is one final thing to take care of before reception is complete and to many it is the most important part of all.

"Are you a smoker or non smoker, sir?" They don't quite phrase it like that. If the answer is non smoker then as far as I'm aware you get a 'non-smokers pack' comprising of a bag of

crisps (Seabrook being the brand), an apple, and a chocolate bar (Penguin being the brand). Penguins are good, though, aren't they. I certainly never complained about seeing one. Seabrook... uninspired. A disappointment in every sense – pallid, miniscule, greasy, safely all the things you don't want out of a crisp. You can't compare them with Manomasa's Serrano Chilli and Yucatan Honey, or a Dorito's Cool Original, or even the humble Wotsit... you just can't. Again, though, I couldn't and didn't complain any time I saw them.

Although I do smoke, I have always been a very light smoker – one or two a day, if that. But when I want one, I want one. Usually after a few pints or a heavy meal. This was an occasion. I was pleasantly surprised then to receive a decent vape with x3 tobacco flavoured 18mg cartridges, better known as caps or oils, which was more than I was expecting. These are to last you seven days, before you can order more through the canteen system. It is no surprise for you to learn then that they are a highly precious commodity, and you keep them on you at all times. Really, they are the highest form of currency you'll find outside of contraband, and you'll be asked if you have any at least three times a day. There is an economy of sorts around these and other items, and if you've played video games like Metro and Fallout then you have an idea what to expect. No Death-claws to be seen though. The cutlery ain't *that* good. I doubt it could even fend off a small rad scorpion. (There's an image).

Finally, reception is done, and off you are led to your wing. This is a dedicated induction wing, and you'll be over there for at least a few days, until (stop the presses), induction is complete. The walk itself will depend on prison size and layout.

One I went to was in a city centre and quite small, holding 800 inmates at capacity, whereas the other could take 1800 and was an absolute labyrinth. If you've watched Ross Kemp visit Belmarsh, you'll have seen that they have 4 blocks and can house up to 900 in total. One of my destinations not only matched there in terms of hostility, but doubled it in size and capacity. So yes, a longer walk anywhere, but hey, remember what ol' Bobbie Louis said a few pages back.

When you arrive at your block, a screw (warden / usher / curator) will unlock the gate, and you'll take your first steps on to the wing, into proper prison, and get your first taste of what life is going to be like here.

2

Amy

Let's move away from jail for a little while though, and I'll explain how I first found myself in the situation. No old laundry about to be aired here for me, but rather for you to understand how a man with a decent enough soul and a moral compass was driven to the places he found himself in, and indeed found himself (eurgh).

A quick word on everyone that I will mention over the course of this book. I have met a lot of people in my life, and most of them have been wonderful spirits. I am blessed in that respect to have met as many as I have. You will learn about some of these folk along the way, as well as those that have caused me pain. And I am conscious when describing any of those particular folk, to only disparage or question the things that *can* be helped, such as certain traits or appearance choices. There's a world of difference between genetic and superficial makeup, of course. Facial features and height etc. are probably hereditary; new eyebrows and ill-fitting wardrobe choices are definitely not. Likewise with personality and behaviours, some are genetic, and others developed, which can be changed almost as quickly as they were learned. I would never tell a sufferer of depression to *"cheer up"*, nor would I tell someone with anxiety to *"chill out"*. I'm talking about disciplines, tact and manners, and other general choices which were made toward or around me. I hope you recognise the difference? I hope that I do, too.

Right.

In 2018 I turned 31, and had been working away all year fulfilling somewhat of a lifelong dream. I'll cover this in more detail later, but for now I'll just say that I was away working, and I ended it fairly suddenly in the build-up to Christmas, so that I could see the family and recharge. My mental health and general energy were running threateningly low, and I didn't know where I could or would have ended up had I continued with what I was doing. I felt I had no choice but to take some time out and consider my working options. Christmas came and went as ever, and before I knew it 2019 was on us.

I had moved back in with my father, in a wonderful little house on the river that had already been my residential address while I was away. I updated my CV and floated it on the usual sites, and before long had an interview lined up for a Product Management role (a realm in which I worked previously and had looked at returning to). One interview led to a second the following week, and an offer was made. This was the biggest salary so far for me, almost double on the year before (I had taken a huge pay-cut to achieve the lifelong ambition that I promise I am not being too coy about. I'll get to it). Things were on the up, and I felt ready, even though really I wasn't.

Let's rewind a tad though. On the day of the second interview, I had taken my time coming back, as they were based an hour or so's commute from me, way down deep in de middle of de country. Over lunch I had a notification on my phone to say I had a new match on shall we say a popular dating platform. She had a memorable aesthetic, and I remembered her bio as well as the face from a few days earlier. Yes, I do actually take the time to read these things. I'm sure many other guys do, too. She reminded me a lot of Amy from *The Big Bang Theory;* frumpy in an endearing way, and with a big face that was somehow stern even when smiling. In fact let's call her Amy.

One thing in particular had made her stand out to me though; she was a fan of cricket. Big box ticked there. And a few days after I'd seen her profile, she had arrived at mine, recognised the Lords shirt I was wearing in one of the photos, and well, the rest is the rest. She also particularly liked one of my photos during my blonde period, in which I was wearing a tuxedo t-shirt. A shirt that I had always loved, that sadly stayed with her. Presumably long since thrown out, and certainly not worth returning now – it's had nearly a year of being stretched, in all places. (Recognise the difference!)

In terms of the rest of my dating profile, I'll give you the same quick info she would have had: 31 years of age, average height and build, liberal, agnostic, no children but open to them in the future, green eyes, never content with the same hairstyle, and a big passion for sport and the arts.

I got back home and went for a meal with my parents that evening at the pub two doors down the road. Conversation naturally was on how the interview had felt – whether I covered what I had rehearsed and what I had read into their reactions and how it was left – all the usual affair one loves to overthink afterwards when they should be winding down. My mind was elsewhere, though, as by this point Amy had initiated contact and we were chatting. I'm not particularly one for the game of playing it cool and leaving it as long as possible – I've never truly understood *"Keep 'em keen"* and all that bollocks. If you like someone, and they appear to like you, don't dither on it I say.

As this was evening, messages were flying back and forth, much to my parents' disapproval. I decided I would stay in the pub after the meal and be on my own with my thoughts for a little while. Later that night we had our first phone call. My experience with online dating, is that speaking over the phone is considered somewhat an old-fashioned way of doing things, but I disagree, and it was nice to see it suggested here. We chatted for hours, way beyond last orders. I remember being sat in the garden by the river, with the staff gesturing as if to say *"Well, we're outta this joint, you know where the gate is."*

"Cheers".

One thing immediately struck me on the phone – her voice. She was originally from Buckinghamshire, and possessed much of the ostentation that typically comes from there. We'll get to that too. For now though, I loved her accent, but not just her accent; her voice. It was soft, comforting, and melted me into the chair. It was a voice that I'd be happy to chat anything with: Tesco's condiments selection… Under

14's hockey events… avocado plantations in South America… you name it. Our first conversation wasn't any of the above, but rather what mobile phone we had and on what tariff. I don't think it's what either of us had planned, but just naturally happened – and bizarrely, when I look back, our phones and type of contract were indicative of many superficial things that divided us.

Topics soon turned to other matters, like what we were doing with our lives. It was at this point I learned she was an accountant. This was most amusing really as I had struggled with debt over the years, and currently held a credit rating lower than Adam Lyth's test average. Amy would get the joke. She didn't see the humour in her job of course, and was proud of it. And rightly so, it must be said. For her age she had progressed well in her respective career, and her salary dwarfed my potential new one at the time. Now I can understand a certain pride in this for sure, but it is only one degree of success, and, to me, not a true barometer of someone.

"It's not the wage you earn,
It's about the things you learn… and the love that you
feel."

Steven Wilson is a brilliant singer, songwriter, guitarist, pianist, producer, artist. 'The Raven that Refused to Sing' in particular is one of the most beautiful songs ever written. Do check him out.

Anyway, I was very interested to learn all about Amy's job, her aspiration for the future, and the determination that had got her there. It was, and still is, something that I admire.

I enjoyed explaining my career too, and she appeared to enjoy hearing each word of it.

"Hearing without listening..."
(Simon & Garfunkel. I shouldn't need to tell you about them).

We continued to talk interests and passions, and a big one of mine, bigger than cricket in fact, is theme parks. As a nipper, I was taken to a place for the first time that has since held a special magic for me – every bit as magical as its name would suggest. That place was, and is, Chessington World of Adventures. Now I'm guessing most of you haven't heard of John Wardley? (Don't be shy, hands up. And if you have, revise or chew gum for a minute while I tell the others).

Do bear with me here. John first made a name for himself on set and prop design in the film industry, working on some very high-profile features. If you want to know which ones, buy his wonderful autobiography *'Creating My Own Nemesis'*.

John quickly established himself and was approached to overhaul the Ghost Train at Barry Island, of all things. This he would discover was a more fulfilling occupation, and he did quite the job. I know you might be thinking *"How much can you do with a simple ghost train"*? Well he used not only state-of-the-art special effects at the time, but also demonstrated an understanding of what thrills people on a basic human level, and in particular, what makes it marketable to other prospective riders. For example, right after an elaborate show-stopping sequence, he would have the ride temporarily leave the building before pirouetting back inside, so funfair-goers could see the awe on the riders' faces. It was ingenuity, and other similar touches added up to something special. This led to a discussion with a man who had just taken over Chessington and was after someone to come in and *"see what could be done with the zoo"*, which was more or less all it was back then.

At this time, big waves were being made across the Atlantic with places like Disneyland in California and the more recent Walt Disney World in Florida, and John, after conducting a thorough assessment at the zoo in Chessington, realised far bigger ambitions to give it the breath of life and commercial traction it needed. Thus began a significant overhaul, albeit cleverly, to add rides to the equation without messing around too much with the landscape, ergo keeping cost down.

Phase One was introduced, with a log flume and a few other attractions. This was done with the intention of introducing a grander Phase Two later on, dependent on success. The success from Phase One would be far greater than ever imagined.

A key to this success – a crucial one – was the theming. John had realised what Disney were doing so well; to create a true breathing world, one of full and pure immersion. Visceral right from the entrance. Somewhere that you could suspend your disbelief if you wanted to, and live in.

At this point, I should highlight the difference between a theme park and an amusement park. Well I may have already done the job. An amusement park is essentially just a collection of rides and attractions, and for the record there's nothing wrong with this. Cedar Fair and Six Flags do it well, and Blackpool Pleasure Beach is a good one that you may well have experienced over here in Blighty. A theme park, however, goes way beyond the attractions themselves, and invests as much again in its 'lands' or 'zones', or whatever they may wish to call them. Alton Towers and indeed any of the Merlin parks would be a prime example. In the States, you will see certain companies paying unfathomable amounts of money to acquire blockbuster IP franchises like Marvel, Jurassic Park and Harry Potter (all within the same park actually; Universal's *Islands of Adventure*). But John Wardley did not have this sort of money to play with, nor was the marketplace driven in such a way in the UK at the time, as it was the early 90s. Instead what he did was craft his own themed worlds around the zoo animals, and attribute the rides to those themes.

So, enter 'Phase Two', and enter a young Scottlet. I had no comprehension of any of the above at the time, I just knew I was going to a place called Chessington World of Adventures. Phase Two was now complete and open. My father had taken me, and no sooner than 20 minutes after we entered, we turned into one of the newly opened themed areas, and I was to experience two very different rides that would shape the theme park nerd that I am today.

First of all, *Professor Burp's Bubbleworks*. Just saying the name again gives me a warm fuzzy feeling (like you get when Bob Mortimer comes on the telly). *Bubbleworks* was a simple enough water ride, in which one sat in a barrel and floated leisurely through Professor Burp's factory, receiving at best (or worst) a mild sprinkling that would dry off even in the most English weather. But what made it so incredibly special, was the premise it was built upon, the lovingly-realised world that had been created, something akin to a Roald Dahl story.

Professor Burp was not too unlike Professor Weeto or Dr Emmett Brown; a well-meaning eccentric whose excitement for his creations was unpredictable and infectious. It was a true multi-sensory experience; a budget building transformed into a swirl of ambience; colour and music, sight and sound, and all-in-all an absolute riot, even for the parents. *"Burp and the world burps with you"* I remember being one of his mantras. Whoever the person is that you are now, back at the age of seven you enjoyed a good burp... admit it.

This was something the UK had not seen before in a ride, too; a well-rounded story and theme that swept you into something that only the best films had done before. The difference here, though, was that it was tactile – you *were* in that world; it was there not only to see or hear but to reach out and touch. I'd never felt anything like it.

This was to continue as we walked away and into deepest darkest Transylvania. The attention to detail everywhere we looked was a marvel. Even the fencing. This was somewhere I felt at home (not specifically Transylvania (or around fencing for that matter), but in a lovingly themed world). How much does this have to do with my disillusionment of the real one? Probably not that much, as it was happening back at the age of 7. I can't remember whether I had consulted a park map and knew what I was heading towards, but before long as we made our way through this Transylvanian town, I heard a roar in the distance. We turned a street corner, and BAM, it was there, flying above our faces. *Vampire.* It was to be my first ever proper roller coaster.

This, I would argue, is possibly John Wardley's zenith. It was certainly what put him on the map for subsequent larger projects. Vampire is what's known as a suspended coaster (one that hangs below the track, rather than gliding above it). Not only this, it was an Arrow swinging suspended coaster, which meant it wasn't locked into angle with the track, so when it turned a corner it swung out to the side, practically fully sideways when it had the velocity. Sadly, it doesn't swing like this any more. This was very much a family ride – it did not break any speed records, nor did it have any inversions (upside down), but it struck fear and awe into me.

To understand, you only have to look at my face. If you're unfamiliar with QR codes, use the camera on your phone which should automatically scan the code and give you the option to view the photo. If this doesn't work within the camera, there are countless free QR code scanner apps available.

Or skip it of course if you prefer.

It's safe to say that when I stepped off I was a different person. I immediately knew that if theme parks couldn't end up being some sort of career for me, they were at least something I wanted to be around as much as possible. I didn't realise just how much I was looking for this kind of experience, and it was to be the first in life that gave me goosebumps. The name "*World of Adventures*" in itself had signified something magical for me before I had even got there, and, to go back to Roald Dahl for a second, as he penned in his swansong The Minpins: "*Those who don't believe in magic will never find it.*"

I was very fortunate in later years to get the chance to visit California, home of the original Disneyland, and Ohio (home of the ultimate amusement park *Cedar Point*), and also Florida – arguably my favourite place in the world. In fact, check the back cover for a young gimp in front of his absolute favourite ride ever, The Twilight Zone Tower of Terror.

But enough of that, we need to get back to John, then back to Amy. Clearly, I was not the only one ready to be bowled over by this new experience, as Phase Two of Chessington was a roaring triumph. John went on to work with Alton Towers on many of the rides you know today. One of his first there was perhaps his most notable; Nemesis. Still arguably the best roller coaster in the UK for me and, if they ever try to remove it for ANY kind of project, I shall be the first to blubber and chain myself to it. John has since consulted on many of their other successful rides, like Oblivion, Air (now Galactica), and even The Smiler, which still gets a lot of coverage over a particular incident. This, whilst undeniably tragic, was proven in the end to be human error – overriding the very safety mechanisms of the ride that would have kept those poor people safe. I am not the only one whose heart still goes out to them, but who's also glad the ride itself is still operational. It wasn't its fault. It wasn't John's either.

That was a tangent wasn't it, or was it? The point is, I am incredibly passionate about theme parks and roller coasters. It's who I am. They don't have to be the tallest and fastest; far from it. A well-themed experience is the mother-load for me. Disney World spent $100m recreating Mount Everest for a family coaster, and a fantastic one it is too. And Universal recently tripled that, again for a family ride.

The *real* point is, the above would have formed the basis for half my output during those first phone conversations with Amy, when interests and the like were discussed. I love to learn all about the things I love, and talk about them (who doesn't?). And she seemed oh so happy with hearing it. On a recent trip to Florida I had vlogged my experiences and shared these with her, and she watched all 10 in the space of a week.

As well as watching my escapades, Amy had time for her job and also for more phone calls, which I seem to remember every evening that week. By this point I was having to keep myself grounded – I'd had lots of relationships that hadn't amounted to anything deep or special, but had a truly different feeling about this potential one. Everything her end seemed to reciprocate this, too. It was hard not to be excited about our first date. I wouldn't have to wait long.

Amy had her own house in a rather salubrious area of the country and a fair distance from me. She'd only moved in a few months ago, but was well on the way to making it her own. She had actually moved in with her ex, but they separated very soon afterwards. No fault of the house. I was invited over that weekend to pick her up and go for dinner in a nearby town of extensive restaurants and expensive cocktails. By this point we had spoken so much on the phone and she had seen so much of my face from the vlogs, there was little-to-no mystique left. This created its own fears; that our connection wouldn't transcend to face to face, or that we had simply already run out of things to talk about. Well this didn't prove to be the case, as before I even thought to check my watch, she advised we had missed our table.

I'll omit the next hour or so, and then we decided to dine on pizza for the evening instead. Not a takeaway, nor a ready-made frozen, but somewhere between. We walked to the local shop and grabbed ourselves two bases, and the toppings to make our own each. Now for the good of you, the reader, I should probably get this out of the way early on. I am a fierce lover, and defendant, of pineapple going onto a pizza. And the fact I had to say defendant upsets me greatly. If I had to put my finger on the pulse, I'd say it's less to do with the taste of pineapple itself and more the concept of fruit of any kind being added to something one wouldn't typically associate with fruit (yes I know the tomato is a fruit). It's just found itself fashionable to identify against through no fault of its own. I agree that the potential marriage of mozzarella and apple, or mozzarella and pear, strawberry, gooseberry, just about anything, could turn a stomach. But have these people ever tried pineapple on it for goodness sake? It's a holy communion, and frankly doesn't need the ham (was that ever even a thing in Hawaii?)

Still with me? There's a reason to all of this, as believe it or not a chunk of pineapple was about to be a loose thread that would threaten to unravel an entire tapestry. Not an argument over the above, but rather as I bit into a slice, a chunk made a break for it and settled upon her sofa. I, like most others

I would hope, sprung into action and darted for the kitchen to grab a cloth to clean any potential damage. There was no damage, to the sofa at least. I had apparently chosen the wrong cloth, and this was met with an air of disdain I was not prepared for.

Now I mentioned she was house-proud, and I've no qualms with that, but beyond this lay a system; a meticulous one that I would never quite manage to get a grip on. I also mentioned earlier that I won't have a go at anything that can't be helped, and this is sat in somewhat of a grey area, because I can understand what's known as Obsessive Compulsive Disorder. However, usually this doesn't manifest in the same way. For the record, I don't know whether Amy actually has OCD. For context though, my mother is probably somewhere on the scale – she won't mind me saying it – but if I were to place something in the wrong drawer, I wouldn't even know about it. It would be relocated; Mum would recognise a simple mistake, not for conflict. She would probably also appreciate that I had shown the initiative. Likewise, if I had been in a room and Mum entered later and could spot a cushion out of place, it would be corrected and that would be the end. With Amy, however, it was a fundamental issue to the point of wrath. Like Ted in *How I Met Your Mother*, I'd had my own pineapple incident, and with it my first hazard sign. There had been a line crossed, but it was most definitely she who had done so. Rather than politely informing me that there was a certain spray and cloth in a certain drawer, and thanking me for at least taking some ownership – she was about to say for the first time, a quote that proved to be a staple of hers, and one that echoes to this day… *"What is* wrong *with you?"*

I didn't really know how to react, but apologised profusely and proceeded her way, avoiding any escalation. And before we knew it, it was forgotten and we enjoyed the rest of our night. She was keen to show me a particular TV show which she believed to be something I would love for its positivity. She had clearly taken to the love I had displayed for the things I held dear, and it was apparently a ringing quality. I had never seen this show, and I must admit within 15 or so seconds I was starting to wonder where on Earth she had drawn any parallels to put something like this on. I should first say that I have no issue whatsoever with homosexuality, or indeed same-sex relationships and partnerships of any kind. It's something to be proud of in modern society, but more importantly something that never should have been taboo in the first place. However, I am sure I am not the only one that finds an over-the-top level of camp slightly uncomfortable. And this was a level I had not seen before.

It was a strange exercise, as I had to work to desensitize myself to the tone of what was being said, to register what was actually being said. Not fundamentally dissimilar to death metal vocals, albeit at the opposite end. It was totally worth it though for the subject matter, which was heart-warming to say the least.

We soon realised we had another thing in common, *Game of Thrones* – albeit again at different ends. I had started it once before and got about as far as a certain jovial marriage ceremony, whereas she had seen it all, and suggested watching it all together within the space of a couple of months, in time for the infamous final season to come out. Read on, and you might find that we ended more entertainingly.

(I joke, but I actually enjoyed Season 8. If you didn't, fair enough and I hope you've got past it by now). We watched the first couple of episodes and took to bed. Night #1 negotiated, after a brief wobble at the second hurdle.

We would go on to spend the weekend together, with the majority being lovely. It's only fair to highlight the positives, and there were plenty at the start. We enjoyed quite a lazy time of it, ploughing through Season 1 of *Game of Thrones*, and other lighter viewing. The thing with watching TV of course, is that all the attention is on that, with chances of an altercation being minimal. I'm not the type to waffle over anything, or commit the ultimate crime of "*Well I can tell you what's gonna happen 'ere...*" – I've never been one to predict or seek out a twist or ending, I sit back, enjoy the moment and let it happen. Partly why I revere shows like *Inside No 9* so much.

There was one thing that bothered me about watching television with her, but it was only minor in the grand scheme of things. Amy, I already knew, had plenty of time for her phone. She had the house and all the utility dealings that come with it, and a demanding job, and she was keen to point these out to me, but that's never what she was doing when I glanced over. Without being a serial poster, per say, she was entrenched in all forms of social media at all times, and, although I was aware of it, it was when we were watching something together that I especially noticed. I've mentioned two shows above; one of which was 'our' project to get through (and an enjoyable one at that), and the other being something that was picked out especially for me, with focus being largely on what I made of it. I could feel it as I watched. This didn't bother me too much, but when it was my turn to suggest something to view together I would have to push through a cloud of reluctance, with the best outcome usually being to get it pencilled in for some time later, with me having to politely chase, choosing the moment carefully as to not seem overbearing. Not exactly parity, but still nothing major.

Eventually, the time would come and I would load something excitedly to introduce her to. With a myriad of potential shows in my head, it was surprisingly taxing to narrow the choices down. But when I did, within I would say a matter of minutes of viewing, my peripheral could see her arm reaching for the coffee table... and then back... and that would be it.

It wasn't an attention issue, nor was it withdrawal symptoms, as she didn't have the same problem when it was something she wanted to watch. It was frustrating. If you know someone will like something, and you finally get the chance to introduce them to it, that's usually the battle won isn't it. It didn't take too much more of this for me to suggest to her that we form an agreement of sorts, that if we were watching something which the other party had especially chosen for us, we surrendered our phones to a shelf on the other side of the room. This was actually well-received. I had pitched it in a jokey manner even though deep down I was deadly serious, and it was agreed to. And even upheld for a while.

Anyway, no real horror story there (remember this had only been night #1, and nothing in Paranormal Activity happened until at least #10. (Who can forget 20)). The TV/phone situation was quite typical, I would say, of the mini warning signs that were starting to crop up. Amy had initially seemed so interested in the things I was passionate about, and so besotted with seeing me around them, it was sad and strange to see this dying out so quickly.

There's more to cover though before we get anywhere near Night #20. We're still on the first weekend here. Her neighbouring town was lovely and quite unlike any others in the area; certainly a nice one to explore. We went out and about, had a few drinks in the centre, and enjoyed what was quite a pleasant temperature for January. There were nice moments to be had at the house, too; we realised we had something else in common which I won't disclose, but it was especially fitting as she had reference to it on display and even in lights on one of her shelves in the lounge. When it was switched on and we first noticed, it felt a strange quirk of fate; that this was meant to be.

At this point we weren't officially an item, but I think it's fair to say that we had both stopped checking the app I alluded to earlier. I think we had both stopped that much earlier in the week. I even uninstalled it in front of her, which she didn't do in return – I wasn't asking her to – but I at least wanted to demonstrate that I felt serious about how this was going.

She didn't cheat on me to my knowledge, by the way. (Just in case you read the above and were expecting a few pages down the line to hear about me chasing a semi-naked man – or woman – through the countryside. Sorry to disappoint). She did later remove the app too.

Through the pleasantries that happened throughout that first weekend, mini hazard lights were continuing to flash, particularly in the kitchen. On Sunday morning Amy made pancakes with bacon and maple syrup – the breakfast of champions. As she was doing so, I was learning where she kept the various components, and I could see and indeed feel the irritation over trivial matters such as putting something back on the wrong side of the shelf, or the wrong section of the dishwasher. When I say the wrong section, I don't mean trying to ram a mug into a knife-holder, I mean picking a suitable spot which just happened to have been personally designated for something else. But like I say – minor irritation, that was all, as I was learning as I went. The same thing happened with an epic roast later in the day, about twelve times. Minor irritations though, that was all. Minor warning signs, no more.

Early on the Monday morning (5:30 to be precise), we woke to Amy's alarm, out came the phone for a quick social media sweep, and then she started readying herself for work. I had seen some of her kitchen routine, and here came the big one. It was simple enough to negotiate the first time, as I did not have to particularly ready myself for anything other than to drive home, so it was simple enough to keep out of the way and to have the time to assist where helpful. I was still waiting on feedback from my second interview, and was hoping to hear that day after they had chewed on it over the weekend. I asked what I could do as she got ready, and got a predictable and fair request for a coffee. This was managed without a hiccup and the remaining duty was just to sit and provide company, which I was more than happy to do. We had spent a long first date together, and an informal debrief of sorts was probably needed. Then, it was time for me to jump in my car (a 2002 maroon Fiesta, what else?) and head home. A kiss goodbye, sat-nav set, and away I rolled before she needed to get into her car and head to work. I'd passed.

The drive home was one of reflection. I doubt anyone's any different on exiting a first date – it's the first litmus test of whether absence will make the heart grow fonder. I'd had a mixed experience over the weekend, but teething issues were to be expected, especially when she had high standards around the house. I wasn't perturbed or concerned too much by these; it just meant there would be the initial period of learning and then it would hopefully cease to be of any friction. I also had time to look back on the preceding 4 or 5 days before we had met, and I remembered them fondly. This was going to work.

*

I arrived home full of beans, and WhatsApp messages. Amy was no ditherer either. She had clearly cherished the weekend in the way I'd hoped she had, despite some ambiguous signals, and before lunch we had already arranged to meet up again later in the week. This was even more exciting – we knew now that it wasn't just ships in the night, and that we both had no intention of taking what we'd got from the previous weekend and ghosting from here. Three days soon elapsed, and in that time I'd had a phone call.

A quick word on the company I was to start for. They are in the healthcare industry, something that resonated with me from 5 previous years of working in the NHS. I was to cover maternity leave for their only Product Manager, a senior one at that, and I was under no illusions that it was going to be tough asking. I knew I hadn't allowed much time over Christmas to recharge, but I felt ready.

I decided to wait to tell Amy until I saw her on the Thursday. It's always fun clutching on to a big piece of news like that, isn't it? It calls to the actor in all of us. I had brushed aside the alarm bells from the weekend and was enjoying the same excitement again. I do have a tendency to throw myself into these things, but it's always been with the purest intention, in the hope of what Meg Ryan attained in *Sleepless in Seattle* or *You've Got Mail* (not specifically Tom Hanks).

I arrived on Thursday evening, and by this point she had been pressing about the job, why I hadn't chased it up, and what I thought of the fact I hadn't heard anything. Well I was barely inside the door before I broke the news, and she nearly broke the door.

Career was an important thing to both of us, and after having spent a year out, potentially jeopardising my chances of returning to a more sustainable income, it was a relief to us both that I had got back on the freeway so quickly. As I had no notice period, it meant I could start the following week. It also meant that we had rather a healthy joint income to forge memories with. And the planning started straight away.

There was talk of visiting South Africa for the Test series, something happening as I type. But more immediate planning was to be made. I'm a man that likes a varied collection of clothes. I love a simple t-shirt and jeans combo, but I also like to look smart and for the occasion. Amy recognised that though I did have smart shirts and shoes etc., I was perhaps in need of a bolstering to my wardrobe. I agreed; always good to start work with the best impression, and so we went into town that weekend to look at the options. It was fun. In my eyes, this was mainly for perusal only, as I didn't really have any money until I got a pay cheque under my belt, but Amy had other ideas – belt included. I barely knew what to say; this was the first time anyone had ever bought anything impromptu for me, and I must state for the record that I was extremely grateful. Hundreds of pounds were spent, and we (well, she) followed it up with dinner.

You may be asking at this stage, how things came to go south with someone who in spite of a short fuse here and there, was willing to do things like this for me. Well, for starters, what if I told you that it wasn't really for me. Although it wasn't apparent at the time, I'll jump ahead for a moment and say that I don't think Amy ever loved me at all. She certainly seemed to love the idea of me, and the image of me, and that is what appeared to drive these spontaneous purchases – which were to continue into the year, sometimes in hilarious fashion.

She, unlike me, had been born into wealth, and schooled privately in upmarket surroundings. As I saw it, Amy had grown up with – and gone on to develop tenfold in her own way – an inflated idea of status being the crux of life. And when she saw me emerge from the dressing room, in a light blue shirt and navy blazer, I rightly mistook her smile at the time to be one of *"you'll look great at work"*. But what she was really thinking was *"you look great right now"*.

I know I just said it, and I'm keen to again – I was grateful. If I had known of any ulterior motive at the time, things might have been different. But how could I have known. I now had several nice outfits in which to impress at work, but there was one other thing she had in mind; that we should bake some cakes or brownies for me to take in on my first day.

I was right on-board with the idea, not least as it would make a good first impression, but also as it was the kind of thing I had always considered as being part of a successful relationship; a creative joint pastime that was a little less expensive than going out, a little more active than watching TV, and frickin' delicious.

Back to the kitchen then. Now I grew up predominantly with my mum, a wonderful chef amongst other things. I didn't show a great degree of interest in cooking until I was ready to be independent, but I like to think I'm a dab hand around the kitchen these days. I have some seductive little recipes in the proverbial locker, and I enjoy cooking them. One area that I had never really forayed into though was baking. I remember Mum and Nan making cakes, and I am sure they had involved me in it as a child, but it wasn't something that was tradition nor ingrained into my upbringing like it had been for Amy. This meant she took the mantle of master, with I, *"your humble apprentice, m'lady"* (Christ I've gone into *Thrones* mode just thinking about it). I recall an orange drizzle cake and chocolate brownie being the choices. This wasn't the last time we would bake, but it really should have been.

Going back to Amy's job for a second, she was in somewhat of a position of power in her role, with many of her tasks being delegated. She had a close relationship with her boss, and as far as I could see and hear, they made a good team. One thing she was apparently marked down upon in an appraisal though, was a lack of clarity when instructing. Constructively-speaking, perhaps an area in need of some attention. It's no surprise that her work's HR protocol didn't include coming to someone like me for additional feedback, but, had they done so, they may have learned as much and twice as much as they could have hoped for. Remember, I am of a nervous disposition, I have struggled with anxiety all my adult life; I am analytical of both the spoken word and tone. And not without a degree of intelligence.

Amy's kitchen… first there was the remembrance of where things were stored in the respective cupboards, and where they would go after use. Not just where, *exactly* where. I was doing alright with this. Then there was the added task of taking instruction on how much 'X' to add here, before zesting 'Y', and how long to set 'Z' for. Not too horrific, even for someone with the tendency to forget or to make mistakes when said anxiety is running wild. Even for me, it should have been simple enough. And it's safe to say it probably would have been, had I received the proper instructions.

An example: *"Stick this with this, over there."* Well that's two examples. Three in fact. I'll translate as we go. *"Stick this with this"*. My interpretation was to keep these two items together, ready for action down the line. A fair one? I don't know. What was actually meant though was *"Add all of this into this, and mix, now"*. So, not just combine the items, but to use the entire contents of one of them. Thirdly, *"over there"*. This was accompanied by a nod of the head over towards a bit of worktop that was by the back door. Surely this couldn't go wrong, too. I did as I thought was asked, and then returned to see what else could be done.

*"What is **wrong** with you?"*

Not being the confrontational type, I didn't rise or lower to it – I just apologised and continued. The next supposed instruction was one of similar grappling. And so forth.

By the end, we were both emotionally drained for different reasons. I was starting my new job the following morning, but I had barely even thought about it, as I had been caught up in each and every moment unfolding here, on the supposed day of rest. It was her ambiguity and temper that was informing my anxiety, not the other way round. And the two became quickly entwined in a kind of torturous tango. Symbiosis. The drizzle cake wasn't worth it – the brownie possibly was. I love a good brownie, and indeed a bad one.

I don't know what time it was that we went to bed, but presumably it was sensible, as we would wake again at 05:30. I could remember how things worked from before, but on this occasion I had my own work preparations to carry out. Of course, I could have gone home the night before and dealt with this with more freedom, but Amy was all too keen for me to stay, and I was keen to stay. I loved the idea of her seeing me off in the clothes she had gifted me; a memory to look back on. Sadly, all I remember of that morning was toil.

I knew my window of opportunity to use the bathroom, and I didn't exactly need long in there; a shower and a brush of the teeth, and then back a bit later on for my hair. The length of time in there wasn't to be an issue though, but rather the fact I had closed the door. Yes. Now there was some logic to this – Amy didn't have a working extractor fan at the time, but the window was still sufficient to take care of the situation. It wasn't just in the event of a hot shower though; I learned that this door was to be kept open strictly at all times. And innocently forgetting this would be every bit as much a problem as placing a fork in an unlabelled spoon section.

I moved on and downstairs to make us both a coffee. I remembered how she liked her coffee from last time, and surely was about to get a thank you at the least. Turns out she wanted a cup of Earl Grey and had neglected to specify this when I said I was getting us a drink. What was wrong with me. Then, as she was preparing to leave, I had opened her front door and gone outside to ready my car before hers, it being a rather intimate driveway. I did what I needed and returned, passing her the keys as she was getting ready to lock up. It transpires, that her preference is to leave the keys hanging off the inside of the door at all times, and, despite my need to use them, my failure to return them to their rightful home before seeing her had soured her entire routine.

You're starting to get an idea of things now. Here's another way of looking at any of the moments of that morning or the day before. Imagine if you will, an episode of *The Crystal Maze*. Now, let's make one or two adjustments. A contestant finds themselves locked into a room with a puzzle – typical enough – but let's take away most of the team members, so that only one is on the outside yelling instruction. Now let's take away the instruction element, so it's *just* yelling. Now, let's imagine the contestant inside already had anxiety problems. Then let's imagine there's no prize as such at the end, other than being able to get on with their life. And finally, let's imagine that *life*, in this case, was beginning a new job the next day.

This had been only my second weekend with Amy, and despite some of the highs we'd had, my first drive to work was concerned with the lows when it shouldn't have been concerned with any of it.

I arrived and met the rest of the team. This was a small

company with big ambition, and I had felt ready to be a part of it up until now. This may not have been Amy's fault; this could have been put down to first-day nerves, but it's safe to say that although I arrived in smart new clothes, orange drizzle in tow, these items were more present than I was. Thankfully I managed to cast her aside, and enjoyed getting to grips with life back in the product realm, and the healthcare industry.

This was still mid January – barely a month since I had left my previous occupation, and I was starting to fear that all this was going to catch up with me. This was worrying at such an early stage in both the job and the relationship. I did start to settle back into the routine of working and having time for myself in the evenings. This didn't just include Amy – I still lived reasonably far from her and was always happy to return home, not least because my father lived there and I wanted to update him on work as much as I did anyone else. I was rotating between three counties, often on a daily basis. And this continued throughout the remainder of January. All of the above did.

February came, and a fortnight continued in much the same trend. Work was providing the usual and enjoyable challenges, and as each day went by, I was continuing to learn more about Amy's house rules, too, negotiating them bit by bit, with a strange enjoyment for the complexity and punishment. Anyone who has played a game like *Dark Souls* will understand.

By this point I was nearly a month into my work probation period, and with weekly meetings being held, I already knew I was on a good path and certainly not in any danger. Amy, on the other hand, was still wildly difficult to understand;

continuing to tear into me over nothing, and minutes later looking lovingly into me as if I had cast her under the sort of spell that I was too stupid to realise I was under myself.

If you are the anxious and emotional type, these situations plagued with uncertainty are draining. Especially in love. One alone is quite enough. We need time to process these moments, consider the permutations, if necessary, and then discuss, if necessary. But this was all happening so quickly, in tandem with my work which I was taking into the evenings, I hadn't the chance to reconcile anything.

Now, remember I said we're into mid-February. Let me share with you one of the most humiliating moments of my life.

I had learned by this point, that Amy had quite an expensive taste. And if you're talking middle class then it's not long before you get to the subject of vino. I don't have an especially cultured nose for these things; if you want to know my opinion as far as I have experienced, anything red from South Africa seems to be nice, I prefer my white nice and dry, and either Lidl and Aldi have struck gold with both of these, or they're charging what everyone should be. Amy was an Ocado kinda gal. I came to learn her taste in wine, and naturally when it came to Valentines Day I thought this might be a nice example to show that not only had I taken notice, but equally wanted to put a calculated twist on the proceedings. Something she didn't have, but had inadvertently hinted she might go for.

We'll get back to wine though, for the real topic on my mind had been what meal to cook for her. I hadn't received a pay cheque yet, and so I wanted to make a mini statement with what I had, that highlighted the thought and effort. Even if I'd had the money, I don't think I would have defaulted to a fancy dinner out in town, especially this one. It's full of those types of restaurant, and, on Valentines Day, the type of wanker who will wait for the perfect moment to puff their chest and slap their plastic on the table. Not my crowd.

Anyway, all I had to play with was the remainder of some money I'd had to generate for myself over January and February. I'd had about enough to finance my commutes to and from work, but I wanted extra to get between home and Amy's house, and also to be able to contribute in some way to what we were eating and drinking. Only fair.

There was only one feasible way to do this at short notice with my credit rating, and it was to take my PS4 Pro into a second hand shop. Those things weren't cheap when I got mine (finally they're down to half price or so with the herald of the PS5). Anyway, I had received a predictably paltry sum for it, but it was the only option I had. I knew I could procure a replacement in the future, and was glad to cut my losses and be able to do something special for Valentines Day, albeit on small scale. Sticking with the PlayStation for a minute, I never ended up being able to replace it, with all that was to follow, and believe me there were times when I desperately missed it. I have only just this month finally bought a replacement, a standard PS4, and during my downtime from writing this I am ironically crawling my way through *Dark Souls: Remastered*. Call it research, or 'method', or whatever.

The day arrived, and I'd planned to get all items on the day, so that they hadn't been hidden anywhere in the house. Believe me it would have been impossible. After work I raced to the local supermarket. I must have looked like I hadn't planned any of it and had got through two thirds of the day before someone reminded me of the date. Either that or my bladder was about to burst. I got what I needed for the meal, and some roses (because they're always nice to throw into the mix. Don't ever *just* get roses though), and a bottle of wine. Now I know I said don't be a ditherer in love, but I agonised over the choice of this. I knew what reds were likely to go down well, but they were already in the house. Amy loved her red, and I didn't want to go with this, nor did I think it would compliment the meal I was doing. Nor would rosé. I had thought about what form of white to go for, and, being a fan of Chablis (who isn't), that was looking like the safe option. However, my eyes landed on a white Châteauneuf-du-Pape, which was nestling below the Chablis section and somewhere in the same region of £20 or so. Amy was a definite fan of a red Châteauneuf-du-Pape (who isn't), and perhaps didn't know it existed in white form. I didn't. A glance at the label seemed to indicate this would go perfectly with the meal too. I was running out of time at this stage and so I'm glad this told me what I was hoping to read – otherwise I would have had all of the Chablis to pick between.

A quick word on wine descriptions. Some of them amuse me no end. I don't know if it's snobbery or not, but when you read something like *"a rush of poached quince"* how can you not erupt with laughter. Beer isn't exempt from this either. Fullers Brewery, based in Chiswick (very much where I'm from and close to my heart) have a champion selection of beers, one of which, the arguable champion of them all, is ESB. One taste and you'll agree. (That rhymed and was undoubtedly cheesy, but still arguably better salesmanship than going for something like *"warm marmalade undertones"* on the back). Which they did. I mean you're not wrong Fullers, but honestly, did that work? I don't know. All I can say is I'm used to seeing London Pride and Honeydew on the shelves, but where is ESB? With a description like that, Buckinghamshire.

Anyway. I had what I needed, dead against the clock, and dived into the car for Amy's. I had several missed calls. She had finished work, too, and was checking that I had already arrived back so that the system of car placement on the drive wasn't tampered with. I told her where I was, about 500 yards further from the house than her, and explained the good reason why, and got nothing but flack. As I arrived at the junction where I knew I was likely to see her car, I did indeed see her car. Or, if not, the exact same model in the exact same colour. Couldn't make out the licence plate. I took a risk on turning right when I knew the typical route was left, knowing that if I caught the lights correctly then I could make up the time and actually get there first. This went beautifully.

I arrived at the house and let myself in (by this point I had been given a spare set of keys), and maniacally started setting the scene. When I say this, all I really had in mind was to get the food and wine in the fridge, the roses splayed attractively on the dining table, and the card. Now the card had been the simple part of the equation – I'd taken what we both considered to be "our photo", which didn't actually include our faces at all but rather looking down at us stood together in the same pair of white Converse. Again, fitting. It was a nice photo, though, and was always going to be my choice for the card. And I knew where I wanted to place it; on her shelf in the lounge, next to the illuminated quirk of fate that I mentioned earlier. I had previously spotted that the batteries for this were low, but not to worry – I had just bought some and replaced them just in time.

Before I could get everything else ready, I heard the door. I must have looked flustered, and I was. Of course I knew that her arrival was imminent, but I wanted it to be perfect. The card was placed, as were the roses, so I was happy enough with the ingredients for the meal still being left out on the kitchen surface. Let's get to those then shall we.

Now, we can talk about taste in wine, and food, and where those tastes came from. Personal taste for these particular things is something that you largely can't help. One might profess to a certain taste in something specific, like wine, but I think that can often be because of outside influence. Deep down everyone knows what they really like. Same goes for food in a wider sense. I don't understand how anyone can enjoy the taste of beetroot, anchovies, or fennel, but of course I accept it. And, even if I wanted to, I can't just decide to book and attend Beetroot 101 and emerge a singing advocate. But we're not talking about those kinds of taste here.

We're talking about the *idea* of certain food, whether you enjoy the taste of it or not. We're talking about looking downwards. Not like in our photo, but rather turning your nose up. Valentines Day can be seen as a number of things, and really it's all of them to me. Let's face facts, it's mainly an event designed and driven to commercialise the subject of love, and push the price up on respective things that we are told to use to demonstrate our love for someone. I am a cynic in that respect, but equally a romantic, and as we had only been together a matter of weeks, I didn't fancy my chances of pitching the aforementioned and saying something *"I'll treat you and I can't wait to do it, but why do we have to conform to the 14th? The 17th is a more suitable day as it's the weekend and I have the whole of the day to make it more special for us.* No, Amy both lived and worked in a world where the first question the next day would be *"So what did he do for you then?"* And there was an amount riding on it.

I should say Amy *was* aware I had sold my beloved PlayStation to finance seeing her over the month and to have something left to make this meal happen. The meal itself was something I had considered perfect for the occasion, as it would demonstrate thought, preparation, effort, time, and also something that was personal to me which I wanted to share with us.

I had been to Greece many times with the family, in particular the island of Andros that lies in the Cyclades isles (you may be familiar with Kos or Mikanos, the better known neighbours). Andros is a beautiful and largely unspoilt isle, maybe the size or so of Jersey. The capital is Hora (also known as Andros Town), but we had always stayed in the fishing town of Batsi, some 20 minutes away. My Mum had friends out there, with a son and daughter of a similar age to myself and my brother, and we had some times. In terms of dining, Batsi was restaurants-akimbo, often specialising in seafood that had been caught fresh from the bay. I didn't go with that. I love all things seafood, but it was a ballsy move, and not one I had ever considered for this occasion. One of the other dishes out there, that you could find more or less in any restaurant, but each with a fresh take and spin, was stuffed peppers or stuffed tomatoes. It was not something I had ever really tried back in the UK before our first visit, even though you'll see them in restaurants of more or less all levels, and I fell in love with both of them.

Something had sparked this in my memory when I was thinking about what I could cook for Amy, and I realised that it was a nice choice not only in bringing a part of me and some sentiment to the table, but also highlighting effort and time to make in equal measure. I was to do it similar to the Greek way; feta of course, with wild rice, tomatoes, caramelised onion, and a choice of meat. I managed to find the latter two combined and also on offer. Two birds with one sausage. I had researched how best to prep and cook this particular recipe, and it would take roughly 70 minutes.

Amy caught me dead in my tracks in the kitchen, and I had no choice but to explain the meal first, before getting to the other bits. I don't know how I would have looked explaining my thought process to her, but I fail to see how it could have shown anything other than love, thought, and a sprinkle of creativity.

Her reaction was one of "O*h*" – perhaps not the best first sign. It wasn't an especially ambiguous "*oh*" either. For once there was clarity, and not of a good kind. However, let's not panic yet, maybe I didn't convey the story behind this well enough. We'll try again. I got about half-way through before Amy had her phone out, and a smirk upon her face that cut me like a gateaux. This wasn't the worst of it – her phone was out because she was texting her friends (or at least one of them), to make fun of the fact she had come home to "*stuffed peppers*". I was being laughed at, not just by her, in front of my face, and she didn't seem to care how obvious it was.

She not only already knew about the PlayStation, but of my nervous disposition and sensitivity around these things.

Being a hopeless romantic and sufferer of anxiety is not a kind combo and this was like the World Cup Final for each of them alone. To see it go down like this, with an audience, was something that I won't ever forget. I didn't know whether to cry, walk out, storm out, or firefight. I just hadn't expected it, and although my feelings were still working themselves out, I was hurt and wound up as I venture you might have been, too. And I didn't particularly care that she saw it.

I made further attempts to explain the reasoning and thought behind it, which she appeared initially to change her tune to, but it turned out that this was no more than 'a rush of feigned compassion, followed by warm undertones of condescension'. This was confounded as I led her to the card and then the flowers, as it was obvious her mind was still on the peppers, and what the ding in her pocket had just said. For someone so typically on the ball with her work and everyday organisation, she suddenly looked completely vacant.

Not only this – the choice of wine was apparently not a good one. It would have been better to have gone with one that she already had in the house, or played safe and boring with something similar. Being such a fan of Châteauneuf-du-Pape, I thought she would have appreciated that I'd managed to find it in white, which complimented the food, but no. And talking again of the food, a better choice on a small budget would apparently have been to recreate our first date by getting DIY pizzas from across the road. Now I like the idea of this and it did actually cross my mind, but given that the first date had only been about 5 weeks before, I deemed it still a bit early for something like this. A nicer idea I thought would have been to wait and recreate that just before our 1ˢᵗ anniversary, and then do a proper celebration on the date.

Apparently I didn't know her at all, and maybe I didn't. This was still early days, but I thought I knew enough to know that taking a few small thoughtful risks wouldn't have yielded disastrous results like this.

In fact… what do you think?

I know stuffed peppers and salad doesn't exactly scream "belle of the ball", but given the thought, story and sacrifice behind it, would you have appreciated this? I'm intrigued. Perhaps you're intrigued to see what others think? Let's kill two birds again then.

- Green Pepper = **YES**
- Red Pepper = **NO**

If the red pepper prevails, then so be it and perhaps with it I'll learn another valuable lesson in life. Either way, I can take it this time. And this isn't about validation, it's just a bit of fun – a chance to interact with your good self, at my risk of embarrassment again.

Back to the evening. Due to the preparation of the meal, and Amy's growing disapproval across the kitchen as I made a start on it, I nearly pulled out on several occasions. Yes I don't mind saying I was virtually a wreck, and with every chop I didn't know whether to pull out of not just the meal but the relationship, for the good of both of us. I held it together, though, and kept going, and once it was in the oven and we sat with a glass of wine, I think she had warmed ever so slightly to the idea, or at least let go of the shock. I hadn't.

The peppers came out rather nicely if I may say so – she even asked for me to do them again – but this was the first and last occasion. It took me some time to recover from the humiliation I had felt that evening, and don't worry, she was reminded of it. Because things were not about to get any rosier from here. Pun intended.

February limped into March, and the job was now proving to be taxing too, albeit in a fun way. I was up for and up to the challenge. *Dark Souls*. Amy was a serial texter, throughout the day at work and also when I was driving, and so I still felt her presence in what should have been a nice period to myself in between work and her house. I was in a routine of feeling worn out before I had even reached hers, and then truly shattered by the end of the night, only to wake at 5:30 and start over, beginning with perhaps the most stressful part of it all.

With this I started to develop another routine, which was to stop by one of the pubs on the way home and plug my headphones in and get some true time to myself. Music being the better tonic. I am an introvert by nature and I very much value and cherish a bit of time to myself each day. I'd pass I would say 10 different pubs on the way back, and I got into the habit of picking a different one each day, the decision being made spontaneously on the journey (usually governed by my arsehole of a bladder). Thirty minutes or so with one pint, and headphones in, was proving to be vital in letting me recharge and ready myself for going back there. There's a reason that you don't see hurdles added to anything beyond a 200 metre event, and that's because regardless of stamina it would be a killer. That's what I was starting to feel like I was in, and so this little pit stop was paying dividends. It calmed me down in the event of confrontation later on, especially as I was getting increasingly worried that the next blow-up over something trivial could be the one that made me finally snap.

Little things were starting to irritate me with her, too. She had previously been a heavy smoker, over 20 a day, and had since replaced this with a vape and menthol liquid, always within a 3 foot radius, and never without a backup charged and readied in the handbag. This itself was not an issue, but I was finding myself becoming a VA (or vape assistant), knowing when to have things ready for the royal changeover.

You might be asking why I was such a damp squib or a push-around, but I was always aware that I was in her house and her rules, however perplexing, and though I was met with an expectancy and attitude over things like helping with this,

I always obliged. And the reaction was a bag of revels (not literally). At the best of times I felt like Caligula's horse.

I mention the handbag – Amy had a collection of them, each well over a grand in cost. A chest next to her sofa in the lounge was the storage for these, along with another exorbitant selection of candles on the coffee table. (Not having a go here – she had the money for it and why not – just painting a little more of the space we spent so often in). About the only thing I had which was more expensive and of a higher quality than hers was my TV (and we'll get to that too). For now we're talking about her items, and in particular, the status that supposedly came with them. Amy, as we know, was enamoured of her job, and pretty much all of her friends were her work friends. Without knowing any of them, they certainly already knew about me, and I never came to learn exactly who was involved in the laughter at my expense, but I was probably right to assume all of them, and I was about to finally meet them all.

I was first invited to join them at a bar round the corner from her workplace, and although I had just spent an hour with my new personal trainer at the gym (also a friend of Amy's and who likely knew more about me than just my name and lack of fitness), I leapt into something smarter and hopped off to meet her and her colleagues. This as I recall was pleasant – she actually worked with some nice people, even within her team, and they weren't being nice out of pity. They seemed genuinely cool. One particular colleague of hers lived close to where I did, and beyond the small-talk of the towns themselves, we found we got on well and had other things in common. One person absent from this event though, was

Amy's boss. Someone who I had heard an awful lot about by now. Let's call him Jonathan.

I had been told all about Jon in our very first phone call – Amy was keen to gush admiration for him and how tight they were professionally. This was of no concern; I had quickly captured a sense of how she was in business and from what she was saying I could understand why he was so important to her, not just in her career progression but to her in general. He was practically a deity figure.

At first I wasn't sure whether to look forward to or be petrified of meeting him, but in the end I couldn't wait. I know my strengths and weaknesses of character, and I was forewarned he was as sharp as a pin – someone who could spot and value someone's wedding ring much more quickly than someone like me would spot my fly undone. Despite my nervous disposition around new people, I was surprisingly keen to get in front of him and see what he would make of me.

Our first meeting was billed as an interview of sorts by Amy, and I was fine with that. I was invited out to dinner and to meet him and his girlfriend for the first time. It was their favourite pizza place in town and naturally I went for the Hawaiian. Curiously, we all did. Not only was it tasty, but it was consumed without fear of the pizza doing anything to destroy the situation. Of course, I was in full potential of doing this myself. I seem to recall my first comment to him being some quick-witted remark about the Prime Minister at the time (in retrospect, Christ, what a stupidly, brilliantly bold move). It went down well, and I think my character resonated with him to a degree. I did not possess the clothes, nor the cars that these guys did, nor the money, but despite feeling studied throughout, I could understand why, and I don't think I did anything to damage things between Amy and myself, or indeed between them in terms of the validity of her choice in me. The evening completed, and I had passed relatively well.

I would soon go on to meet Jonathan and the team again at a dinner party, hosted by Amy and *"your humble servant, m'lords and ladies"*. Now this was quite an amusing evening, in retrospect. The event itself was fine and more or less without a hiccup. Amy's cooking I have to say was divine, credit where it's due – she had cooked a chicken and leek lasagne dish which remains to this day one of the most delectable things I have eaten. My role as waiter was handled satisfactorily, and I was on form afterwards (her friends' words not mine), as we chatted over the meal. Bizarrely I can remember introducing everyone to a Russian folk band named Otava Yo, to great merriment. Both down to the wine, I imagine.

All good so far then. Well actually, the real drama happened before anyone had even arrived.

Now I was keen to state beforehand that I would not explicitly blame my anxiety for anything in particular, but I would like to risk hypocrisy for this occasion. Also, in the interest of parity and transparency, I know I have referred to one or two things that Amy does in and around the kitchen that I don't consider to be normal. Well, I was about to do something which was, whatever way you look at it, abnormal, idiotic, and if you were anyone other than Amy, laughable. She had passed me a large candle that had run its course, and my instruction was to dispose of it and the wax. No real ambiguity here – and really the two should have counted as one. But I, at this point in a fit of nerves around everything to do with the evening, chucked the wax down the sink without a second thought. Yep.

I will gladly present myself as a muppet when I was being a muppet. I immediately knew what I'd done but it was too late, it had hardened and was about to block the entire sink – just before everyone was due to arrive. This is the only real time that Amy raised her temper in a way which I can understand. By now, instances of red mist in ways I *didn't* understand were probably pushing triple figures. The only technique I had really managed to develop for this, which I considered the final available means of diplomacy, was to just walk away from it. She liked to call it running away, but trust me it was walking, and there's a considerable difference. I'm not going to get you to vote on that one. Ultimately it was proving time and time again the only way to diffuse things, and I stand by it. She even recognised begrudgingly that it worked. I would go for a long walk, ignore the calls and texts, and, more often than not, come back to an apology and sex. Not why I did it.

But, on this occasion, I had been an idiot primarily of my own accord, and I was about to run rather than walk for the first time. Amy's tirade of anger here was not without its merit, but, recognising I was about to crumble, I held my hands up as if to say *"nope, screw this for a laugh, I'm off, for good – you deal with it"*. I know this was wrong – I knew this was wrong at the time, but this was a man teetering on the edge of insanity, and I don't know whether it was the coward's way out or not, but it was certainly the only one I saw available. It's important to me that I show the worst of myself as and when it happened. And here I had undoubtedly caused the issue and just childishly left it to be dealt with by her literally 30 or so minutes before her guests' arrival. I ignored the calls and abusive texts that followed. I was totally done with her, with everything. I disappeared (you guessed it, to the pub around the corner), and that 20 or so minutes in which I was there, ignoring her, gave me a slim lifeline in my mental health. Amazingly, Amy then texted me offering a lifeline too, and, perhaps in revival of my own stupidity, I decided to return and patch things up.

She had googled how to deal with the wax, sorted it, and I returned and changed shirts etc. just in time for the arrival of her boss. No time for bed, and I didn't want it. We were on eggshells, but no one would have noticed, as in our own way we were both incredibly good at putting on a face.

Going back to Jonathan for a second, I have mentioned Amy's gushing admiration for him, and I believe it *did* go beyond professionalism... not in any physical sense, but in her head. He had just the material qualities for someone like Amy; it was as if Cupid had missed and hit a magpie. Jonathan earned well in excess of £100k a year, had a beautiful flat down-town, with a beautiful cat, and a girlfriend. Amy was keen to push me front and centre as an indication that she had found someone herself, but it became increasingly obvious to me as time went on that she was in unconditional love with Jonathan and was fighting it every step of the way. It was more than just a glint in the eye whenever she talked of him, and it was far more than a glint in the eye when she looked at him. I think everyone knew how obvious it was but her. But isn't that often the case.

Like I said , I don't think Amy ever truly loved me, and this was showing itself time and time again through March. There's one particular instance that sums things up perhaps far better than Valentines Day did. It was a throwaway comment from her, and just about the final straw. She had recently procured an expensive new seat in the lounge – not one that ever got used that I saw, but it was brought in as a precursor to replacing the main sofa in the same style, which was out of her financial reach at the time. Of all the things I had done to anger her, on one evening I was about to to blow all previous out of the water.

First, let's go back to me, and my passions. We covered theme parks, but there is another that has been both a love and hobby of mine for some 12 years or so now, and it was also something that had hugely attracted Amy to me in the first place. It's a possession. Not the TV – that's still to come – no, this was my guitar. One could argue that I was her favourite possession, and well, this was mine. Sometime in the past month or so, I had brought it over with me, and I always have a little lick that I play when checking it's tuned correctly. This apparently had her drooling before I had even played anything. Again, not boasting – her words. And I, the soppy romantic, thought there would be some nice little opportunities down the line to discover what she really loved music-wise, and to learn and play these for her at unexpected moments.

It proved quite hard to learn her musical taste. She did have a case of vinyls in her dining room, but the only one she seemed to particularly latch onto was Joy Division. She had a framed picture on the wall with perhaps their most famous lyrics, and the irony doesn't escape me for a second. Now I love many bands from the 80s, but these guys, and indeed New Order, never really did much for me. I was more a Talk Talk and Tears for Fears kinda man. But enough of me. Joy Division didn't exactly lend themselves well to the guitar. I went on to learn that she was also a fan of Busted, and I decided I would learn something of theirs one day and surprise her with it. I don't remember the song, but I learned it and waltzed into the kitchen one afternoon to surprise her. I had also learned another song for her; the name eludes me, but I recall it being from the *Twilight* soundtrack (yes, Busted and Twilight. But we'll skip that). The real issue was that I hadn't chosen my moment correctly for whatever reason, and instead of her showing any love or appreciation for the endeavour, I was hit with red mist again, for interrupting something in her routine that frankly was interruptible for less than this. She would speak lovingly of these moments to her friends around me (at the bar when I met them for one), but she and I know how these moments really unfolded. You can see what I mean when I talk about 'the idea of me' over me. Parading serenading.

That's not *the* moment though.

In terms of her music taste, I don't wish to have a go at the bands she was into. They cross into another grey area of something that you *can* help liking, but can easily condition yourself to without even realising. You hear it all the time, your friends are into it, ergo you persuade yourself you are too. Bands like these are so concerned with the image as well as the musical content, again it summarised the whole thing rather well. Also, Amy had studied music theory at school, which apparently rendered her an expert on everything to do with music. Now, I'm not going to say that knowing music theory forces you to think inside a box (even though it often can), but it can certainly detract from the *feel* of something. Few artists have a theoretical knowledge of the notes they're playing and then go on to play or write things that really tug the heart strings. Guthrie Govan as a guitarist would be a good example of how to do it. You're a bastard, Guthrie, a talented bastard, and I love ya.

Anyway. My beloved guitar is not something which cost anything close to what the new seat in her lounge did. But it's something deeply sentimental, and something which I look after. I decided one day that I would commit the unspeakable act of resting it upon this particular seat in the lounge. Just sat there – no weight strain, no fluff or dust upon it that would transfer. Let's take a quick moment to recognise that a seat is designed to take a human arse (and indeed the rest of a human with it). And hers was considerable, especially compared to a guitar. Her response was one of blind rage, and to *"get that* shit *off there at once – what is wrong with you?"*

For once, the latter quote isn't the one that stood out. Frankly, how dare her. This is another example of how the love for something of mine that had existed a matter of weeks ago had now wilted in spectacular fashion. Although I didn't snap back, or indeed walk out, the more I reflect on this the more I realise how disgusting a person she was capable of being. To me she was a control freak of the highest order, with astonishing anger issues, and, although, this wasn't quite the occasion yet, I was about to have enough. If you're in a relationship with someone, and you call perhaps their most beloved item *"shit"*, and fail to see the impact of that, then you're not what I consider to be a person in love. Or a decent person. And in moments where I had walked away, her retort was always that if you love someone, you stay and work through it. Well there was never any way of working through anything with her, and, again on this occasion, she wasn't exactly demonstrating an idea of what it is to love someone in the first place.

In case anyone's interested, here is the beloved item in question. An Ibanez Electro-Classical, pictured on a somewhat friendlier piece of furniture.

After that, I started to assert myself more. This by no means tipped the balance though. You may have asked several times by now why on Earth I stayed in this relationship as long as I did, given the stress it was causing. I still don't know to this day. I was slowly welcoming her to kill me. As I mentioned, though, I was now starting to stand up for myself, and on one particular evening of pillow talk I stated in no uncertain terms that I fantasised about leaving her on a daily basis. This was the truth, and regardless of how callous I might have sounded, she needed to hear it. I left her with that and slept more soundly than I had for some time, only to wake to her in tears, wrapping herself around me and begging me not to leave. More ambiguity.

I bought it though, thinking that maybe this time it had got through, that I was not prepared to take this sort of shit on a daily basis any longer, and that perhaps she would start to think before she spoke or acted (like I always had with the exception of Waxgate). Moments like this, albeit with tears, were not enough to indicate that she really did love me over the idea of me. This didn't seem like a fear of losing *me*, but rather a fear of what might come with it from her sphere of influence (nice little Black Mirror reference there, from a very equatable episode).

This was the first time that I had stated just how torn I was. And things didn't change a great deal. I was one minute getting the daily catchphrase (*sing it with me now!*), and the next being shown a ludicrously expensive engagement ring on the internet. I'm not joking. It's hard for me to take my head out of the sand and see which strands of this relationship were the most ridiculous, but I feel that's probably as presentable as any other. I was being told exactly which ring she wanted, and even on my salary which was respectable enough, we were talking years of savings. Amazingly, I still thought that I could get over the hump of these things and that two years on could be possible for us. To most people, the first months are the honeymoon period, but to me it was feeling more and more like 'the hump'; much like with Mark and Sophie in *Peep Show*. (Sophie... deary me).

By this point we have reached the end of March and the start of April, and my little breaths of life, my fleeting moments of sanctuary in the pub on the way home, were starting to escalate. Not in those moments themselves, but later on in the evening, I was finding reasons to escape again and seek refuge there. Or in evenings where I was not at Amy's, reasons to go there instead of to hers. Given the precariousness of the relationship, it's no surprise that showing up at hers less was causing suspicion, and conflict. Not to mention that drinking each evening was causing a strain upon my work, like everything else was. She was getting more irritable by the hour, and my first tipping point was finally about to arrive. And it wasn't over any particular incident this time. It was while she was at work.

I mention that I'd started ramping up the drinking, and I was about to ramp it up much further and do something unfathomably stupid. It was Monday and I had called in sick for work – we'd just had another torrid weekend together and I just did not have anything like the energy needed to drive 30 miles for a day's product management. This left me on my own at Amy's – I could have gone home, but I didn't want anyone else to know that I wasn't going into work. Well, it must have got barely past 09:30 when the desire to escape became too much. I walked round the corner and bought two bottles of white wine. Amy knew I was potentially up to something, as she owns a smart doorbell and so the detection of me in the porch, twice, would have alerted her phone at work. I don't recall what the discussion was, but I would presumably have made an excuse about needing something like antacid tablets (which I often do), and then shielded the bag from vision when letting myself back in.

By 11:30 or so, both bottles had been demolished, and by 12:00, they had both kicked in. Alcohol, I recently learned, is mainly absorbed by the small intestine – so it can take quite a while depending on what else is in your stomach. It certainly never goes *"straight to my head"*, cuz science sayz so. I had spent the morning fighting in my head over everything – the fact I was still in this relationship, the fact that it was now affecting my work, and the fact I was suddenly a wino. Eventually, it all became too much, and here we go then… the first time I lost control.

I knew I had to get far away from the house, from Amy, everything to do with her. I hurriedly packed my overnight bag and stormed out. She immediately saw this on her phone, and the calls started. I didn't care. Without even thinking about it, I was about to commit the first of the crimes you will come to learn about. Yes. And, before I knew it, I was half way up the motorway to get nearer to home. I remember it perfectly; I was thinking with an odd blend of insanity and clarity. I could also feel the car had a slow puncture, and that I needed to get straight off before it got any worse. Luckily the next junction was mine anyway, and I got off safely and to a friend's in a nearby village where not only could I inspect the damage, but also say a quick hello and burst up the stairs before my bladder did.

I'd had time to do a quick inspection of the tyre before I rang the bell. I knew the wheel had completely had it as I was rumbling through the village… but though I did cause damage to the axel etc., amazingly it didn't look all that bad. I spent my time in their toilet thinking frantically about what to do next. For once I hadn't thought of Amy in over an hour, but I wouldn't exactly call it liberating, due to what else was going on. I knew I couldn't drive anywhere, and would have to wait for the booze to leave my system before getting someone in to recover the car. Things were starting to formulate in my head, and I was starting to think more freely. I opened the front door to return to the car to get a few items, and all plans flew out of the window as two police officers parked up behind it and walked towards me. Shit.

Well I asked for it, obviously, but, nonetheless, *shit*. Everything was about to change, and rightly so – not only was it the right thing to happen, but I desperately needed things to change, too.

I was immediately arrested, breathalysed, and put in the back of their car for what felt like an eternity, awaiting the arrival of another vehicle. This is not the only police incident that would happen in the year, and I will skip over much of the rest of this one other than to give you the necessary detail. It was as you'd expect; I was booked into the station, breathalysed again (same reading if I recall), met with a duty solicitor, and finally interviewed around midnight. I explained the situation in full – none of it was any mitigation of course and I wasn't making a case for that either. I understood the full severity of what I had done and took full responsibility, even though they recognised there were aggressing factors. I was released pending investigation, amazingly still with my licence, as the police wanted to gather any dash-cam footage and speak again to a witness who had reported me driving down the road *"on three wheels"*. All in all I spent around 12 hours in police custody, and was kindly driven home by them around 01:30. My phone was dead, but I knew from making a call to my father in the station earlier that Amy wanted to talk to me. And I wanted to talk to her.

I got in, plugged my phone in and switched it on to a flood of missed calls, voicemail and other messages, not just from

Amy but most family members. This showed perhaps she did have some compassion somewhere, as when I had gone quiet she had taken a chunk of time out of her work to make calls to both my parents.

Everyone was relieved that I was safe, and, frankly, were being far too kind to me given the jeopardy I had put myself and others in. I didn't deserve one iota of this, and when I saw Amy a couple of days later I don't mind saying I burst straight into tears, and pretty much didn't stop for the rest of her visit. We appeared to be all the stronger for it; perhaps she had finally understood how close to the edge I had been all this time, and finally took a shred of the responsibility herself. The soft and comforting voice I'd long forgotten about had suddenly returned, and, perhaps for the first time, we appeared to be on the same team.

Over the following days, the car would be recovered and repaired, and as mentioned I still had my licence until the charge(s) were officially made. But there was one thing I had to immediately do: I knew it, Amy knew it, everyone knew it. I needed to see a GP and ask for help. This happened the following day (I called in sick again to buy the time to try and establish what was going to happen with everything).

As you will continue to see, I'm quite candid when it comes to discussing my personal problems. I certainly didn't hold back with the doctor. I explained I had struggled with social anxiety since peer pressure had first kicked in around the age of 12, but that I had never sought help over it. I also explained that I had typically self-medicated with alcohol and other drugs at different periods over the years, and explained in full the current situation I was in. A three-pronged attack was recommended; I would be referred to an NHS mental health programme, as well as an organisation specifically for the drug problems, and was prescribed Sertraline to see what effect it would have on my general anxiety. Sertraline is what's known as an SSRI, which are given out like mints these days for depression and/or anxiety. They are, like alcohol, a drug, and I'll cover them along with others later on. For now, I had done what I could, and would wait to hear back on these referrals. Amy suggested something else afterwards which hadn't occurred to me, which was to speak to the GP again about potentially being signed off work. This was not a bad idea as it would give me some time to rest and recover, as well as time for my car to be repaired ready for my return. I made the call and collected a sick note (for a week) later on that day.

My next port of call was to speak to my boss. As mentioned, she was due to go on maternity leave, and I had been appointed to cover this. We were now in the 4th and final month of her handover, a critical period, and certainly not an ideal time for any of this to be happening. I decided again to tell the absolute truth, all of it – and she was amazingly understanding and sympathetic. She was relaxed about not only the time off, but the impending loss of my licence for at least a year. I hadn't prepared for that; I was expecting this to be our last discussion. It was to be our penultimate.

I had no idea what was to come in the following month. There were certain things I was aware would happen, such as progression with the mental health treatments, my car being fixed, and potential news on my charges etc. Things were a little better with Amy – almost back to how the first week or so had been, but I was still on the edge and finding it difficult to relax during what was supposed to be a week of recuperation. There was one thing I wasn't aware of, though, that no matter how close to the edge I thought I was at the time, I hadn't quite made it yet, and Amy was to assist each remaining step of the way. Note I say *assist*.

I soon got my car back, which meant that I could start visiting her again more often. My relationship with my father was now under strain with everything that had happened, and in such a small house we were on top of each other all the time. I can't believe I was actually looking forward to spending more time again at hers, but I really thought we had turned a corner – that she understood how precarious my anxiety and general health had been around her, and, like I had practically begged during our fallouts, that she might now consider some of her mannerisms that had been triggering it at every turn. Within hours of being there, though, *The Crystal Maze* was back for a new and improved series. Clearly, she now felt I owed her big time, and that I was duty-bound to do anything and everything at the drop of a hat, before it even hit the floor. This went on for an hour or so, before the anxiety got its talons in, and I started repeating old 'mistakes' in the kitchen.

And this time and onwards, it was less red mist and more like that scene in *The Shining* with the elevator doors. Things had plunged right back to the worst of it, beyond in fact, and I was presented with all the same worries, not least including whether to stay or leave. I still felt that I loved her in spite of everything, but I have come to realise that I had mistaken love for a combination of fear and awe. We know from the start of the chapter that the ride *Vampire* struck fear and awe into me. Well at least, despite the name, that wasn't blood-sucking.

Earlier that week, I had been thinking what else I could do to show I cared, and this had now included upgrading her TV with mine. She then brought her original lounge TV up to the bedroom and sold the bedroom's predecessor to a colleague. She had profiteered from that and also essentially from mine. It was an LG 4K HDR bad-boy that I had previously bought to compliment the PS4 Pro. The Pro was long gone for her, and the TV had now moved in for her to use when I wasn't around. I was fine with this, though, plus I wasn't using it at home at the time anyway. It was now mid April, we had just about reached the end of *Game of Thrones*, and were lapping up any titbits of information we could about the imminent final season (series*).

The TV was really about the only thing that was keeping us from falling out, as like I said we could focus our attention on to that rather than each other. Now that *GoT* was on hold, there was time I had hoped for bringing some of my favourite shows to the table, but, alas, this was still all but forbidden. I remember watching certain films on her request, something I would never have chosen myself, only to sit in front of it with her buried in her phone (my proposal as good as dust at this point), with her often demanding a shoulder rub at the same time, too. So, no one's attention really on the film then.

One mini moment of comfort came during the film *Room*, which I'd had my attention largely taken from until one of my favourite bands suddenly made an appearance. The song was 'The Mighty Rio Grande' by the mighty This Will Destroy You – a band that are truly epic, though not perhaps in the way their name would suggest. They are a gorgeous post-rock band, arguably the best – and their songs are a cathartic swirl of ambient guitar that builds to a crescendo, as is often the way with the genre. The song suited the scene perfectly – one of the most impacting things I'd seen in a while – and I was quietly cursing the fact I hadn't been able to pay proper attention so far. Incidentally, the film was one of captivity, and this scene was one of escape. They are a band I'd seen live maybe 4 or 5 years ago, and it was a song I hadn't heard in ages, and it took me back to better times. It fell on deaf ears when I mentioned it. I'll come back to this band shortly.

Whilst we're also on the subject of films, I rewatched one this week which funnily enough had been a topic of conversation with Amy at some point in the relationship... I forget exactly when. The film is *Lost in Translation*. The premise itself is a well-trodden one: *"A chance meeting between two strangers forms an unlikely bond that will change their lives as they know it."* How many times have you read that on the back of something? But there's a reason we've seen stories like this so many times down the years, because they are not only uplifting and touching, but hint that a similar thing could happen to us if we ever found ourselves at a crossroad. In terms of execution, *Lost In Translation* does it masterfully. You forget it's acting, and you forget it didn't really happen.

The point is, Amy had seen this film before, and didn't care for it in the slightest. Her words, which I can only paraphrase, were either *"It's rubbish"* or *"I hate it"*. It was definitely one of the two – maybe even both. Now, whether you actually think the film was executed well or not, to *"hate"* the film or pronounce it as *"rubbish"* suggests an aversion to even the idea of it. And it sums up how I remember her; bitter and seemingly dead against the sort of ideals that I believe a good person hopes and strives for. This is the kind of attitude she was showing to me every waking moment, and, in polar opposite to the film in question, the coming together of Amy and I in life was one of unimaginable pain, negativity, and disastrous results, which I promise I'm getting close to now. We're into the final month now, and with it night #20.

In my time away from Amy, friction was continuing to develop at home with my Dad, and I was still waiting on news of the referrals. The Sertraline wasn't working, I had even changed prescriptions with the doctor, and the new one was proving more difficult. I was doing well one minute to avoid alcohol, and the next throwing it out of the window and being drunk before I had even realised what had happened. I know you might be thinking this hadn't given the medication a fair crack of the whip, but they had been causing problems of their own with a certain element of the relationship, which I understand is a very common side effect.

In my last appointment with the GP where I had changed prescriptions, I had also been signed off work for another two weeks. I had spoken again with my boss about this, and she wished me all the best as she was on maternity leave from the following day. Naturally I wished her all the best too. Her boss, who was to become mine, seemed a lovely fellow. I had a long conversation with him about everything, in which he reassured me that he had come across worse in his career, and to take the time that I needed. I would have easily been able to do so without the relationship down my neck.

Every little thing was now an issue, most of which were things that had unfolded before without being any kind of a problem. If she appeared to hate me so much, why on Earth was she still with me, and texting me every waking minute when she wasn't with me? And why was I still with her when my health and job were now so clearly on the line? I don't know. I don't know.

I had spent a typical couple of days over at hers, before she was due to visit the family for the weekend down in Bucks. I had gone back home so I didn't have the added pressure of a different morning routine before she set off. I was at my wits end and desperately thought this weekend might be a chance to get some time to myself. She was barely out of the door before levelling something at me over the phone, and I was about to assert some actual control over her for the first time. And believe me she wouldn't like it one jot.

I said that I needed a break – not the end – but that we should refrain from contacting each other over the weekend. I was about as ill as I had ever felt and I needed to distance myself not just from her but from everything, to get the rest that a medical professional had told me I should be getting. Not to mention it would be surely good for her to spend quality family time away from her phone. I explained this as best I could, and without wanting to block her I put my phone aside. After she realised the ticks weren't going to turn blue, she turned to my father instead. He replied further explaining the reason for this – with him now seeing first-hand how ill I was – and told her I would be in touch a couple of days later on Bank Holiday Monday, the day she was coming back, which predictably went down a storm. She replied flippantly and we were both blocked. She had enjoyed her control over me, but now the tables had turned, and Dad was happy not to listen to her thoughts on it either.

As the weekend passed and some clarity returned, I realised I needed to try a different approach to get through. I would write a letter, and it would be driven down with Dad's help and delivered through her door personally on the Sunday, the night before she was due back.

I had apparently been unblocked and re-blocked throughout the weekend, but I hadn't noticed. I knew, though, that to accompany the delivery of this letter I would probably need to message in some way to let her know what I was doing. Let's not forget her doorbell would inform her that I had been there, and yes, it crossed my mind to recreate that scene from *Love Actually* (not word for word, of course; far from it). In the end I dropped her a message explaining why I'd felt I had no choice but to do it. The reply again was predictable, demanding over and over that I reveal it all there and then. I knew she would fail to see the point of any of this, but hopefully the contents of the letter would break through when she got back.

Now in terms of fine details of the letter, and indeed our relationship in general, I do have to be mindful of privacy, and as such I have often passed the paintbrush sooner than I would have liked. Not that I don't trust you! Although technically I own the contents of the letter, I would prefer to keep it between her and I. Being honest I can't really remember a great deal of it anyway, and I'm sure you already have the gist.

I do remember one thing which I'll share. I knew she would skip straight to the final page, and I had planned for this. Whether it was a case of *"get to the point"* or *"I want to know if this is a break-up"*, or both, I just knew she would. And I made a joke about it, one which I knew would make her smile and show that perhaps I did know her a little bit after all.

Ultimately, the letter wasn't a breakup, but one that suggested it was right around the corner. Which it was. I didn't know that it was at the time, and I still cared deeply about making this relationship work. I still remembered the connection I had felt on many occasions, and all this pain would have been well worth it had we ever got there in sorting it out. What she didn't know whilst reading it, was that I had driven to her neighbourhood and was camped in a supermarket car park, on-call for her reply, ready to be there immediately.

The next thing I knew she had arrived home, read the letter minutes later, and I was in her hallway just minutes after that.

I really thought we'd fixed things this time. There was a mildly heated discussion to begin with, but a newfound feeling of parity – we were both making points and then sitting back and listening to the other's. *"Working through it together"*, finally. This was the first time I believe I actually told her that I thought she was a control freak, and this would be quoted back to me over the next week like a broken record. Must have been true, and hit a nerve.

Although I thought to begin with that this weekend had been a breakthrough, Amy was still working through it in her head and couldn't get to grips with the fact that she had no longer had the same tyranny over me. I should point out I was no angel at this point either – I was still on the verge of another breaking point and I was biting back in my messages. Talking of her family in Bucks, I had come to learn all about them, and one person in particular I had been warned of, even more so than her boss, was her mother. She sounded every bit her daughter's mother, too. Her job didn't seem enough to warrant the glamorous home and area and so I made the conclusion she had been married or inherited into the wealth. I don't want to get political but we usually know what happens there, don't we?

Also, I talked at the start about having a go at manners, or a lack of, and this was a big old deal in Amy's family. On our very first evening together, within minutes, I had been notified that my style of holding a knife was a problem. I have always leaned towards gripping it between the thumb and fingers as you would do a pen. I still continue to use it like a knife. It's just the naturally comfortable way for me to hold it, and I am sure others might agree. (*Yes*, pizza and cutlery by the way. Well remembered).

Now if I were to go on to swing the knife like Jaime Lannister's sword, then I'd understand a reaction, but not only was I holding it in a largely indistinguishable way, I still ate cleanly and courteously. But no, I would have to correct this long before even having a chance to meet her mother. This was not the only thing I would have to "*correct*", and that word in this context brings me back to *The Shining*, and one of the greatest if not the greatest scene in cinema history, between Jack Torrance and Delbert Grady in the ballroom bathroom. The only difference there being that Delbert's idea of "*correction*" had rather more serious connotations.

This all comes back to the class divide between Amy's family and I. When we think of love we often think of *Titanic*, *Romeo and Juliet*, or *Pride & Prejudice*, all tackling the issue of love and class divide – but this wasn't love.

That week, Amy's mother was to visit, and despite all the problems that were continuing to happen, she actually couldn't wait to introduce me to her, which was a little strange. But the night or so before she was due to arrive, Amy and I had another text conversation, that was to be one of our very last. She was struggling to get to grips with my TV, and rather than asking how to change the settings to her liking, or refrain from saying anything, opted instead to say she hated it.

This may not appear much on the surface, but it was a continuation of the attitude that was now causing as much anger as it was upset. I may not have had the emotional attachment to the TV that I did with my guitar, but again I found it being essentially referred to as a piece of shit; something that was mine, indeed one of the few things that was still mine at the time, and something that I had internally made a big deal of gifting. Yet another fallout followed, and communication blissfully ceased until the following day, the day we finally separated. (I say *finally*, remember this was only four months.)

I had been to a hardware store and stopped after for a late breakfast with Dad, and received a message from Amy, saying not to bother about coming over the following day to meet her mother. This, in itself, hardly bothered me, but the following did…

She had decided she was to bill me for the following:

- Rent, calculating every night I had visited
- Contributions to all food and drink
- Full cost of the clothes she had gifted me

To the tune of *"thousands"*…

I was in shock. She had a mortgage of something like £1300 a month, but she had always asked me to stay – I had never invited myself, and despite her conflicting behaviour towards the value of me, she had always maintained she was delighted to have me over. She had practically instructed me over on so many occasions, and I had certainly never done anything to skyrocket any of the bills while I was there. She would have been watching TV anyway, and my side of the bed never had the electric blanket on.

Then the subject of food and drink. I had contributed at various stages to this; tapping my card at the local shop, and had been glad to do it. Her taste in wine was on a scale that was not sustainable for my income, but I had still picked it up many times. She also knew that I was about to receive a miniscule pay cheque for the three weeks I'd had off work.

Then the clothes. These, she had been all too keen to impress at the time, were gifts, with no repayment necessary. I had treated her in my own way whenever I could, with the money I had at the time, but clearly this wasn't equal. In a monetary sense alone, no, it wasn't. I didn't have hundreds of pounds to fritter on her; the PS4 sale and Valentines Day told you that. In return she was still holding on to that bookmarked engagement ring she had shown me, something she had probably gazed at once a day at least, failing to realise that she wasn't and isn't worth 5% of it. If I didn't already think she wasn't, boy I knew now.

My retort was *"Piss off"*. I remember it well, as it felt good. Her reply was that the relationship was 10000% over, and well, that felt pretty good, too. This was enough. The conversation dragged on, throughout the day, if I'm being honest getting a bit pathetic on both our parts in terms of jostling over who was suddenly better off. Materialism seemed such a key part of her life, and her idea of wealth was very different to mine. I recently watched an interview with Tyson Fury. Now say what you like about him, he's a smarter man than you may believe him to be and knows exactly what he's doing. He is a man who has conquered mental health issues, and a man who has accumulated a vast amount of what you would call wealth. However, don't let his exuberant dress sense fool you, this is done for show in the build-up to a fight when he relishes stepping into that persona. Outside of this, he is a remarkably humble man, and has been sensible and charitable with his money. He knows that money is not what makes you a wealthy man. He said this again recently and you know he means it when you see and hear him say it. I've great respect for him as a person.

I had learned myself over the course of this quarter that money does not make you wealthy, and also, that manners don't always mean class. This had been by far the worst relationship I had ever been in, she echoed the sentiment, and we would never see each other face to face again. However, this was not quite the end yet.

Although we had broken up, she was keen to try and keep me on a leash of sorts, with messages still pinging in. I was still receiving the odd message saying that she missed me, and that she could do with one of my massages again etc., and I was doing my best to turn a blind eye. There was the matter of me collecting my items from hers among other things, but I had another issue to deal with, which was my return to work. I'd had an email from the person that dealt with the HR side of things, asking me to give them a ring when I had the chance. I took this call to be one of admin purposes, making sure I brought in the second doctor's note, and to receive my new password etc. It turns out, this phone call was to tell me my contract had been terminated with immediate effect. The day before I was due to return. This hit me pretty hard. In the space of two days, both my relationship and job had come to an end. In retrospect both were well and truly for the best, but the mental whirlwind I was in at the time, I wasn't to know this. And I was only more fragile now.

Amy's messages continued in ambiguity, and when I broke the news that my job had been terminated, she rang me out of the blue. It was a call that reminded me of the first ones we had; she wanted to listen, and she wanted to know that I was alright. It was left that she would be in touch and again I wondered whether there was even the chance of things working out. I didn't know whether I wanted it or not.

The following day, I broached the subject, and was told there was categorically no chance of us ever getting back together. Somewhat conflicting with what she had implied the previous days, and I can only assume that after sleeping on the thought that I was no longer earning anything, she would cut ties and move on to someone else – which I believe she was already in the process of doing. I guess my face was no longer worth parading to anyone without the job behind it.

Talking of money, it's also important to say by this stage I had transferred her some for everything she had alluded to before. Not anything like what she had specified though – I arrived at what I believed to be a more sensible sum of £1300, which included everything for my clothes, and a heavily subsidised contribution to what she was asking for the mortgage and groceries, and also a bannister that had been broken when I had genuinely lost my footing down the stairs and used it for leverage. I had at least expected the bill for that one and I was ready and willing to pay it. (I won't bother with her reaction to that fall at the time, as you can see it yourself I'm sure). She was at least grateful of this payment.

Anyway, I had taken the above message relatively well, and I wished her all the best. That should have been the end, but there was still the matter of collecting my items from hers, which I had now paid for. A few days later, this hit home, and with it came the red mist that I was used to seeing over her head rather than mine.

Now I will always paint myself in the worst light when I believe I deserve it. My mood swings were now as uncontrollable as hers, and I was about to get nasty. Make of the rest of this chapter what you will.

It started after I had spent a night of drinking later in the week… my way of trying to come to terms with the fact I had been sacked essentially over illness, and that Amy had been a large perpetrator of this and then turned her back after the damage was done. I was of course now exacerbating the issue, though, without her influence, and it wasn't just drink either. One of the things with cocaine is that it will block your real emotions off, meaning that if you have been obsessing over something causing you pain, the doors are suddenly opened for you to pursue it without the upset, and learn perhaps what you need to for closure, then deal with it emotionally the following day. You are still obsessed, but without the emotional ramifications, for a while.

I had long since been blocked, but I don't mind saying I was digging to see whether I could unearth any evidence that she had moved on. I created a fake account, searched her name, saw her profile again, and at this stage there was nothing to indicate that she had yet. In fact, the same night I came across her old dating profile once more, and, although as I say emotions are largely blocked when under the influence of coke, I do recall howling with laughter when I saw a new profile comment describing herself as generally one of the happiest people you could ever meet. Christ almighty.

There was the matter of getting my items back, and when I remembered this around 05:30 – the time she would be waking up – I opened dialogue, and it wasn't pleasant. I was demanding them back that day, threatening to shatter her living room window and collect them myself if this wasn't agreed to, and although she apparently had a car service that day, she took my comments seriously and contacted my father to ask whether he could come himself. Something I was happy to hear. Later that day I had all my items back, including the TV, and surely that was the end of it.

Now that I had established what I believed was closure, I was starting to work much better through everything that happened with her and indeed the year. It was a lot to take in – especially for someone who typically struggled to process things like this, and, blaming myself, had been making it far worse by leaning on short-term and damaging solutions. It had been the first time a few days had passed between us without any contact, and to all intents and purposes it was now fully over, thank goodness.

The weekend came, a Bank Holiday at the beginning of

May, and I was invited on a family trip to an open day in the nearby woods. It was just the sort of atmosphere that appealed to the centenarian population of the town, with antiques and stalls alike, and the tranquillity of the woodlands made for something that should have been an enjoyable day for all. It was certainly enjoyable for the rest of the family, and should have been for me, but my mind was well out of the woods. This is exactly the sort of event where Amy and I would have actually had a good time, and the best of us would have been in show for the rest of the family as well.

Talking of best in show, not only would Amy and I have enjoyed this woodland day out, but her dog would have likely come with us, and she would have loved it too. Amy had joint-custody of a dog (Jenny) from a previous relationship which had been left amicably. She was the world to her, and I can understand why; she was a truly lovely soul. I had met her on four or five occasions over these four or five months, and towards the end we had a real connection.

I am not an expert on dogs. I have always grown up with cats in the family, but I have always been smitten with everyone else's dogs, and I've always seemed to connect with them. Jenny was a Dalmatian crossed with something I forget, and, in stark contrast to her owner, placid and affable in nature. Never once did I hear her bark, unlike her owner, and I hate the term obedience when it comes to a pet but the word does come to mind with her impeccable attitude. It was a miracle.

A couple of weekends before this, we had gone to a heritage site where my mum worked voluntarily, and the four of us had been in perfect harmony. Mum had a friend who we bumped into, and everyone was keen to remark just how much Jen and I got on and how much she appeared to love me.

I am not saying this to feel better about myself, I am saying it because it's true – and animals have an acute and intrinsic basic instinct to recognise a good spirit when they see one. Amy even said this herself on multiple occasions, that I *must* be a good soul because Jenny wouldn't make a bad decision like that.

It was fascinating to me to see how the relationship played out between them, too, as it was a telling one. Amy, of course, looked after her and loved her, but with what I had in terms of canine psychoanalytical skills, I saw a poor little thing that knew she was safe and sheltered, but didn't want to be there. She was curled up and asleep on me within minutes of me coming over, and overall it was a far more fruitful relationship than the one I'd ever had with the person sat to the right of us, glaring in jealousy. Anyway, enough about Jenny; she wasn't here, and neither was Amy.

Now, I mentioned I'd come back to the band This Will Destroy You. In writing the rest of this chapter, I realised that this band (and the song in particular that I alluded to earlier) is a very, very fitting accompaniment. As it was in the film *Room*.

If you wish, scan the code or search "The Mighty Rio Grande" on YouTube/Spotify etc, and listen alongside the rest of this chapter. I strongly recommend it.

Or read on as normal, the choice is yours.

So, this was the first family outing for some time without Amy, and it was the first time I was to really get depressed about the breakup. It would have been a happy day with her and it still should have been without her, but I made my excuses and drove home. Well I did drive home, but I didn't enter. I was straight down the pub, and this was to be the start of perhaps the most serious session of my life, in every sense of the word. I'll discuss my opinions on drugs in a later chapter, but for now let's say that it almost always followed the same trend. It would begin with the emotional turmoil and the desire to escape. This would lead to accelerated drinking and, after five or six pints, an immense craving for something else – something that even in the sleepy towns and villages of where I lived, was all too easy to get hold of, and of a high quality. Before I knew it, it was well after midnight, and goodness knows how much I had drank, but by this point I was wired back into obsession-mode again.

It's important to say that by this stage we were well and truly finished and Amy had every right to move on, but I wasn't ready to let go of all the suffering just yet. Perhaps I'm just a glutton for torment. Much like the previous time, I had convinced myself without good reason that she was seeing someone and, with it being a Sunday before a bank holiday, he was probably going to be over there with her right now.

This is where my behaviour went to a place that really can't be excused – perhaps explained – but without doubt inexcusable. As I was blocked through all channels except email (that would have required the effort of creating divert rules and such, and I doubt she would have bothered with that), the emails began. It started as I recall with a fairly lengthy one, that was relatively well-wishing believe it or not, but as dawn came and the cocaine wore off, the sheer amount of alcohol I had drank started to take full effect, and with it all the emotion came flooding back. And with that came a string of malicious messages.

"Malicious messaging" is something you may have started to hear about in the news, as a firmer stance is being taken on it now. It falls under the domestic abuse umbrella, and is undoubtedly one that can cause a lot of unseen pain. Not only was I sending nasty messages, but I was calling her, every other minute. My phone number itself apparently hadn't been blocked, as it was ringing each time. Amy answered on several occasions, asking what I wanted, but I had no intention of speaking – I just wanted to hear her end of the line. I didn't know whether someone was there, but something told me there was (quite possibly psychosis, I know. Plus, technically, it was none of my business). That didn't stop me ringing. By the time it got to 04:30, I must have rang some 70 times, with the occasional email in between saying I wished they were both dead, and similar sentiments. I knew these were veiled messages, but she didn't.

Another hour passed, and I was continuing to drink and was becoming more fragile by the second. Finally, again around 05:30, I snapped. And this time I *really* snapped. Although my head had gone like last time, I was thinking with a weird sense of clarity, and I knew exactly what I was going to do. I was going to go after one of her material items; the only one that existed without access to her house; her car. I rifled through the garden shed, looking for an item that could both smash a window and slash a tyre, and I eventually found a heavy duty garden weeder – a 4 foot or so wooden pole handle with a large metal corkscrew at the end. I had no intention of trying to hurt her, and I knew that an implement like this was not classed as a "bladed article" and likely wouldn't be construed as something that was to be used a "weapon". By this stage, my father had woken, Amy had screen-shotted and sent some of my messages to him, and he came down to check whether I was OK. Which, of course, I wasn't. Within minutes, the weeder was in the back of the car, and there were screech marks on the drive. Dad was powerless to stop me, and he did the only thing he could which was to ring her and tell her to *get out immediately*. I knew nothing of this, of course, until a few days later.

Forget Amy for a minute – I was now in the process of committing the other joint-worst crime from last year, which was to drive over the limit again. And although I arrived at hers perfectly safely, that does not excuse anything. Although I don't know you personally, I would like to take a moment to apologise. You could have found yourself in the crossfire that morning, through no fault of your own, and thank goodness you didn't.

I arrived around 06:30 and, as I pulled into the road, I immediately clocked the police car on her drive, next to hers, and the two officers that were stood facing me, who had clocked the description of my vehicle. I knew the game was up, and that whatever I did, they would follow and arrest me. In the emotional state I was in, I thought *"well why not, then"*. I screeched some 10 feet or so down the pavement, got out of the car, produced the garden weeder, and strode towards her car with it. This is where it became somewhat of a film scene. I was screamed at to *"DROP THE WEAPON"* and all of the usual spiel, red dotted with a taser, and, once I realised I was getting nowhere near her car, I complied.

I was knelt on and cuffed, as aggressively as I'd asked for, with several other police cars screaming onto the scene within seconds. I was sucking asphalt for at least 10 minutes as all duties were carried out and, just before I was carted into the van, I had time to look up at her bedroom window for the last time. I didn't know whether a silhouette or two would be there. But if they were, I wanted them to see me. Especially Amy. To witness first-hand the complete wreckage of the person that she had first seen so jubilant back in those Florida vlogs she watched the week before we met. And perhaps in this final moment, she'd finally understand. It turns out she wasn't there and had heeded the warnings to get out. At least the neighbours got an eyeful, and some heavy drama and gossip for an early Monday. Amy's car was still on the drive though, and as I obsessed over the following 24hrs, that all but confirmed to me that someone *had* been there and his car was the choice of transport.

I know I described the incident fairly succinctly, but it

did unfold in an incredibly short matter of time, in relation to everything that had preceded it. The next day felt like an eternity, but trust me I am not going to complain about that. It was justice and it gave me the time I needed to sober up and reflect. Although I remember the incident well, I don't remember much of the police custody, other than the phone call to my mother, knowing and saying that I was not going to be released under investigation this time, and that I was about to get my first taste of prison. I knew nothing of jail at the time except from shows like *Porridge*, and I was scared, as were my poor parents. I could certainly hear it in Mum down the phone line. She hadn't earned this.

The following day I was in front of the magistrates, and bail was predictably refused in favour of me being remanded in custody. I had pleaded not guilty to one of the charges, namely "Possession of an offensive weapon" – because I knew I had no intentions of harming anyone physically, and my defence agreed. However, the offence of "malicious messaging" can carry 8 weeks on its own, so I knew my fate, and before I knew it I was on the bus from Chapter 1.

Talking of chapters, I appreciate this has been a long one. I make no excuses for what I had done over the past week, and I will continue to paint myself in the worst light when I think I deserve it. It is also important for me though to get down some of the intricacies that led to this. Not *caused* it, but led to it. Hopefully, you are not a sufferer of anxiety and, if you are, hopefully it's not added to being a hopeless romantic, which can cause enough stress on its own. And if you are both of these, hopefully you don't cross close paths with someone that just isn't good for either of those afflictions, whether their fault or not. Because this is how it happened for me, and I'm sure similar things have happened to others out there.

I don't ask for sympathy. I accept what I did and I knew elements of it were hugely wrong, and I served my punishment for it. And eventually the lesson was learned. Not straight away though.

I spent 11 days on remand, before being put in front of the court again in a second request for bail, which this time was approved. The time in jail had been a significant event, but I still need to talk about Amy for a minute. And myself. These 11 days were not nearly sufficient to process everything that had happened and get my mind back into shape.

I was bailed and home hours later, which I had expected, but I hadn't banked on the mental anguish being worse than it even had been before. Amy would have known that I had been jailed, and also been informed that I was now bailed. I also knew that her email address was an open line of messaging and probably wouldn't have been cut off just in case I was stupid enough to try contact her again. Which I promptly did. After a few drinks, I no longer cared about any restraining order.

By this point my father and I were at breaking point, and with me sleeping on a pop-up bed in the dining room (as I had been throughout the last year), I was still not getting my own space which I sorely needed. This meant that my "safe place" was to be outside the house, two doors down…

It led to a continuation and indeed acceleration of the previous behaviour, and though I am not proud of the amount of coke consumed that week, some rock-stars certainly would have been. But once the alcohol came back in force, again I was fighting not to email her every step of the way. Eventually I buckled… and here's why.

Amy, due to her still quite recent separation from her ex, had always been reticent to even hint about me in any of her social media posts. This may seem in contrast with how she paraded me in person, but it's how it was. She had essentially allowed me one online post on one occasion, which included both of our faces, and I strictly wasn't to tag her in it. The whole thing felt overt one minute, illicit the next. But so it was, and I went along. The single photo that did exist of us, I'd had lasered into a glass crystal structure and this had sat upon her shelf in the lounge. Despite this supposed pride and the fact I had been shown off to her work crew, outside of this I was being kept a dark secret, and it was a strange thing to contend with.

I know it might seem suspicious, but trust me she wasn't cheating – she was spending every waking second on my neck – no one else would have had a look in. Like I said I was told that this was still because of ties to her previous relationship; there was all sorts of information pertaining to it on Facebook and her account hadn't really changed when they separated, let alone when we got together. It hadn't changed until now.

One night that week, I was a few lines deep and decided I'd use the fake profile I'd set up before and search for her again. She didn't appear. *How has this account been found out about and blocked, too?*

Well, it hadn't. I tried using her middle name instead of her surname and sure enough, there she was, and next to a new bloke. As my emotions were cut off at the time, it almost felt a strange relief that I'd found closure over this. And, as the coke wore off and the drink kicked back in, I realised I still didn't particularly care that she had a new boyfriend (she had every right to after all), but what bothered me, significantly, was how public she suddenly was about it. This could only mean one thing to my state of mind at the time, that this was a last laugh aimed at me. I later heard in court that she was flummoxed as to how I'd discovered this, but not only had she made it public to everyone, the face still appeared next to her name in my Messenger app, even when blocked. She'd asked for it to be seen, deliberately asked, and it was obvious. It appeared somewhat in desperation, too, as her face was screaming *"Look how happy I am"*, and his, well looked rather different. I didn't find it particularly funny at the time, and really I shouldn't have let it bother me like it did – but after all the secrecy of our relationship, it was a gut punch. Sure enough, the emails started again.

Not to excuse myself in any way – I knew I was breaking the law, I knew she didn't want to hear from me, and so nothing defends what I continued doing – but at least this time there was no malice. Sure enough the police were at my door a day or so later, and I spent a hell of a long time this time in their station, well over 3 days as I recall, waiting to be taken back to court. So long in fact, that it caused a significant blunder on their part – they hadn't brought me before the magistrates quickly enough, and, amazingly, had no choice but to let me walk free, right into her neighbouring town. Obviously, I realise how lucky I was – again I will be all too glad to point out whenever I got off lightly or was lucky throughout this year, and this was most definitely an occasion. I deserved to go back to prison and, but for an almighty cock-up from their constabulary, I would have done. Can you imagine the look on her face when they told her. It was all I could think about at the time.

Unfortunately, this wasn't the kick up the arse I needed – though it did allow an incredible opportunity to happen the following week. I'll get to that in another chapter though. In the meantime I was an emotional wreck, and starting to become somewhat of a physical wreck from all the binging. Dad had even deserted the house to let me get on with it and was recuperating himself in a hotel in Cheshire. That's how bad it got. I have very little recollection of that week, except for watching the new series of *Black Mirror* which had just landed. Not the best show to watch when you're already an emotional wreck. Especially a secondary plot-line in the episode 'Smithereens', which to this day, with a clearer head, is one of the most beautiful and touching things I have ever seen. I can't believe anyone can have a go at the recent series' of the show (4 and 5); they are superb. Charlie Brooker and Annabel Jones, how do you do what you do. Talent beyond my comprehension.

Anyway, whatever you make of all of the above, I do hope you continue reading. I found myself in some dark places and, yes, I fully admit I did some fairly despicable things back there. I cannot blame Amy for those; I can only say that she played an epic part in the build-up to it. In that respect, you can think what you will of her, too. I'd like to finish on the following and then get onto other parts of my journey that were every bit as significant.

Later that year, I found myself being contacted by Amy's new boyfriend, that I had seen in the photo. Turns out I wasn't the only person who'd had their mental health put to the sword, over and over. She had likely revelled in telling him at the start that *"I tried to kill her"*, something I am sure she has dined out on many occasions by now. But, as time went on between them, he had clearly suffered enough to question her side of events, and wanted to compare his experiences to mine. I both could and couldn't believe what I was reading.

My instinct should have been to laugh, but I'm not that kind of guy. I had no animosity towards this stranger at all – quite the opposite in fact. I felt a sense of virtue to do what I could to help, and also, with this being a direct message to him and in no way indirect to her, I knew I wasn't breaching any restraining order this time. And what followed felt like group therapy. Before then the poor bugger must have wondered *"What was* wrong *with him"* every bit as much as I had, and this at least gave us both some validation that these had been her issues all along and not ours. More on this later too.

Although it felt good to know I hadn't been alone, there was much sadness to this as I knew he was going through it all too, and I wouldn't wish it on anyone to be honest. I can also reveal that her ex-partner who had exited stage-left merely weeks before I entered stage-right, had apparently also done so from mental health issues. I can't speculate on those, but equally I can.

I was no angel with her towards the end – far from it. I accepted and took my punishment, and by the end of last year I had had more than enough time to process everything and learn any lessons I needed to better myself. I had certainly learned what I *didn't* want in a relationship, and the others in the year, thankfully, didn't provide much of this. Though they're a story in themselves. You'll learn of them.

As for Amy, well she is who she is, and I don't know whether she will ever learn her lessons or not. Without being bitter, I don't care. We crossed paths, what happened happened, and being behind bars felt liberating in comparison. We'll get back to jail in a moment. One final thing though.

Oddly, and perhaps irrelevantly – you'll be the judge – something happened today as I was finishing this chapter. I mentioned the game *Dark Souls* earlier, and its parallels at times with the relationship. As I also mentioned, I have recently bought another PS4 and returned to the game for 'downtime' whilst writing the book (I don't know why I chose *Dark Souls*, it was nothing to do with writing about Amy. Clearly I still haven't got bored of my own suffering).

Well, I finally just edged pass a boss fight and further than I ever managed to last time. It was a battle with myself more than anything; whether to put the controller down for good again or keep at it. It's not even that far into the game apparently; a pair of bastard gargoyles on a parish roof. But this game is a slog. Clearly though I learned from my past mistakes, I'm stronger this time, and hey, I've reached a new chapter.

3

Our new home

So, we covered the journey to prison (in every sense), we covered reception, and now we're on the wing. Let's lighten the mood again if we can.

Where to begin. Each wing is like a mini nucleus within the overall facility. Your neighbourhood, and citadel. Usually on 3 or 4 floors. On one particular induction wing I was up on the 5th, in a penthouse suite as they called it. Each level has a couple of phones at the ends, usually an office where the SO (Senior Officer) resides, and a big gap in the middle with netting, so you're essentially wandering around the perimeter looking up and down the core (yes *exactly* like the Guggenheim museum!)

You also have the showers (more on them later – let's face it, that's half the reason you're still reading, isn't it). Then of course you have the cells, better known as pads. I'll describe how a wing works in more detail once we're through and off the induction wing, but for now let's talk about the pads.

The doors aren't aesthetically the most inviting, but hey, you can understand why they've gone for practicality. They have a handle that looks like a cross between those you'd find on an aeroplane (that you're terrified to even stand near), and the overhead ones for stowing luggage. They usually lock automatically as soon as they are closed, but some do have a latch inside, although, as I said, you don't use that and walk off unless you're an idiot. There is a tall rectangular window, about the size of a relay baton, with a flap on the outside for the screws to open and check on you when they do the rounds. Sometimes they don't shut it again afterwards, which is still a first world problem I guess.

The dimensions of each cell are pretty much always the same, I'd say around 8 foot by 15. You *will* have a pad-mate, unless you are classed as vulnerable. Apparently, in private jails you have your own cell, with your own shower and phone, but this is HMP we're talking about, and the P doesn't stand for private. In one corner you'll have the bunk beds – hopefully with a wooden frame not metal, but either way your feet will know about it before long if you're on top, as the steps are not the most ideal in terms of size and comfort, and really better suited to your average squirrel. The beds do come with a mattress, which are essentially the same as the old crash mats from your school gym. Quite possibly exactly the same.

Usually in the other corner next to your bed you'll find the toilet, which, if you're lucky, will have a curtain that partially covers it. I'll never forget my very first night in jail, where I was paired up with an old boy who was also there for the first time. He was like a cuddly Clint Eastwood, except we didn't cuddle. I was mortified at the thought of using the toilet, but knew I would have to eventually. Luckily, he fell asleep relatively early. Let me tell you – if you've never taken a crap two feet away from a sleeping pensioner's head, then you haven't lived. The next time you visit the bathroom, you make sure you thank the door and the lock on it. Then thank them again. (And yes of course I let him have the bottom bunk, because chivalry still exists in such a place when I'm around).

There is a basin which is perfectly fine for its purpose – the hot running hot reasonably promptly, and the cold being seemingly good enough for drinking. Well I never got ill. And you might be disgusted at the idea of drinking this water, but put in that situation you will concede your pride to your thirst before long.

There's room left after this for a desk with a kettle, and hopefully two chairs. Again, the next time you use it, do thank your kettle, because no matter how slow you believe it to be, it ain't. I was just thankful that I even had one. There's also cupboard storage for your stuff, though there's an argument for just keeping it all in the sack to deter any opportunistic thieves, as you really can't turn your back for a second, and, remember, you could be sharing with a convicted shoplifter. The windows vary in size; you do have the classic steel bars in them but usually there is a metal gauze of sorts in front. Great for letting air in and keeping flies out.

And finally, we have our TV. Again, they're always the same, about 16" with a meagre selection of Free-view channels

(ITV2 and the like). If you're in England, you get a prison channel, which was amazingly handy for having a clock in the bottom corner – great if you were waiting for *Match of the Day* or the 9pm offering on Film4. If you're in England you also get E4, which is a mixed bag of emotions if – like me – you like *How I Met Your Mother,* and dislike *The Big Bang Theory.* If you're in Wales, then you get an additional Welsh channel instead. Amusingly, it was Channel 9 (*scorchio!*) and in many ways it reminded me of those sketches. As Steve Hughes once joked, it's like the Welsh language was invented when some dude tripped over carrying a box of Scrabble.

What made TV the weirdest in Wales, though, was the fact I was there over the festive period. The juxtaposition of watching adverts of unity and decadence whilst leant over a bowl of Ko-Lee curry flavour instant noodles. It was one part amusing two parts depressing, and a stark reminder of what I was missing in the outside world. I actually decided to keep a mini Christmas diary, which I'll enclose later on.

When you're locked up at 17:00 for the rest of the day and still waiting for library access, really the TV is all you have for recreation. My two separate stays coincided with two separate James Bond marathons and I've finally been converted. I also developed an interest in classic car restorations (nothing to do with James Bond, but rather a magazine left behind by a former resident). In my most recent stay, I was starved of library access due to it only being accessible to my wing on Wednesdays, which coincided with Christmas Day and New Years Day. I did manage to get in there on my first week, though, and so I made do with the excellent *The Directive* (Matthew Quirk), the also excellent

Frankie Boyle's *My Shit Life So Far*, and a book on the finer laws of rugby union. A confusing sport at times, this cleared up several things at the breakdown. More and more each day I realise it's a far superior sport to football. Thankfully the Six Nations 2020 will have finally been concluded by the time you read this.

As I had to make these three books last for the duration of my stay, I ended up watching more TV than I anticipated. Being a huge fan of both *The Simpsons* and *Frasier*, this helped both my morning and early evening routines. By far the best thing I watched though was *The World's Most Scenic Railway Journey* – from Fort William to Mallaig. I had been to Scotland as a child, but as I was barely a child at the time, suffice to say I do not remember any of it nor could I have truly appreciated its astonishing beauty in the moment. Thank you to Channel 5 for capturing this journey in full and for sharing it with me. I think I was probably the only grateful man under that particular roof at the time, but don't let that make you think it wasn't worth it. Cheers.

Moving on, your first night in prison should involve a visit from the chaplain, and also being delivered the initial paperwork pertaining to your sentence. This includes things like your conditional release date (you will typically serve half the overall sentence), and also your prospective curfew (tag) release date, which is 40% into the full sentence if eligible. More on tags later. You also get two blank letters (now they were something to write home about!) and a breakfast pack, which you will continue to receive every evening.

A breakfast pack usually includes 3 or 4 teabags, 5 sachets of sugar and whiteners, a small carton of Viva semi-skimmed (more on those later too), and your cereal will be either Cornflakes, Frosties, Cocoa Pops, Muesli, Rice Crispies, or Weetabix. No Eggs Florentine, I'm afraid... sorry old bean. You can take your Coco Pops on to the wing, though, al fresco. Lean on the balcony, close your eyes, and you're in Monaco.

4

Induction

Right, we've covered the fledgling steps and now it's time to get ourselves inducted. This is spread over two days, though it could really be covered in one, depending on your aptitude and eagerness to get through it. However, perhaps two days interspersed with downtime is for the best, as let me tell you it's a real banquet for the senses.

Joking aside for a second, it was quite interesting to be tested formally on my English and Maths for the first time in a decade. It will be no surprise for those who know me to learn that I bossed the English test, and buggered the Maths up something chronic. These tests were held on old Dell Optiplex PC's, which reminded me of my days in the NHS. They are accessed through an intranet portal, and this is the only time you will see a web browser during your stay. Strictly no smartphones or internet access of any kind, and that's fair enough.

There were 4 stages, increasing in complexity, and at the end you're essentially lumped into Level One or Two; two being the higher. Now, if you want me to correct the grammar in a paragraph, I'll gladly oblige. If you ask me to calculate a percentage, though, or the length of one side of a triangle based on the others, I'll gob in your face and run a mile. I was subsequently a floundering Level One in Maths, but could at least bask in the clouds of the English Level Two fraternity. In Wales there was an additional IT test, which I was intrigued by having worked in the IT sector for many a year. This one went to Level Three, and although I did get a few wrong, I was relieved to see that I was in there at the end. I'm not bragging in any way here, I'm not proud of any of this, but just letting you into the full experience. This concluded the computer tests for the day, and in the afternoon it was time for the gym induction.

This was an entertaining one, and wildly different in each prison. The equipment though was fundamentally the same; a generous cardio-vascular room with everything you'd expect to see, and then another standard room of free-weights and resistance machines. In the free weights area, testosterone reigns supreme. If this were a boys school, the weights room was the football pitch chalked into the playground, and the CV room was the arts and crafts workshop. A metropolis next to a ghost town. Vegas and the Mojave. The music being piped in was about as you'd expect, too. The things that have passed for music since the late 90s... I'm disgusted. Especially the last couple of years. Do you like Drake? If the answer's yes, then please get the fuck off my book. We'll get to proper music at an appropriate stage later, as it's a huge part of my life, and if you're still reading, maybe yours too.

What made the gym especially entertaining for me, was one of the instructors. We were all sat completing a health questionnaire for our induction, and in he strode. He was fairly big in stature, but I wouldn't call him strapping. Just tall-ish. I believe 5'9" to be the average height in men (I'm 5'10"), and I'd say he was around 6 foot. But in his head, he was much, much bigger than that. He had a routine of going round the room, asking us where we were all from, and then administering the best insult he could. I'm from Hammersmith in West London and his gambit was something along the lines of *"Oh yeah, the Odeon. Shithole"*. Firstly, it's been the Apollo for years you cretin, and, secondly, it's a fine establishment. I've seen Steven Wilson and also *The League of Gentlemen* live there and enjoyed the venue as much as the performances.

I smirked, avoided riposte, and let him move on. It's important to say that I don't think he was trying to be funny. None of it was delivered with a dry wit, but rather an air of genuine hatred. It was bizarre. He was so keen to impress upon us that we were pond-life to him, one couldn't help but fantasise about his home-life. I reckon two divorces and now his cat wore the trousers.

A whistle-stop tour around the machines followed in much the same style, and then we were dispersed back to the induction wing, with a timetable of when the facilities would be available depending on which wing we were to end up in.

*

If day one was about intrigue and amusement, day two is about mind-numbing monotony, which is more typical of how things are in jail. For the morning, you'll be parked back in front of a computer, back in the education district. For me – when in front of a PC/laptop, or smartphone, I'm at home (figuratively and usually literally). Whether I'm listening to music, watching comedy, gaming or learning, I always know what to go for and, rarely, am I just browsing aimlessly. My father likes to think all I do is watch videos of parrots playing harpsichords but the reality is if I'm on YouTube it's either to watch the *Extras* out-takes (a monthly ritual), cricket highlights, or theme park vlogs and construction updates. BABE-MAGNET.

So, yes, I'm usually happy with a screen in my face. But here I was sat at a computer ready to pour my mug of hot coffee over my testicles, just to check that I could still feel anything. Why? Because I was in the middle of a two-hour questionnaire, comprising of questions I had already been asked by various people (or questionnaires) over the previous three days. If I had known the purpose and indeed the outcome of this, then I may have been onside. Instead my question to boss-man was nonchalantly parried. Surely it was fair to ask one in return? And a pertinent one at that. I don't know why he had to be so coy about it. Still, to ask the same question twice is to piss someone off here, and so I kept shtum and powered past it. In the end, the only discernable result that I could see was that I had been profiled in some way on their system; the sole outcome I had expected it would be.

That wasn't the end, though, as the next task was to input my academic and employment history and build a CV. My academic history was several things really, but ultimately one of exciting promise shot to ribbons – a classic case of 'unfulfilled potential' that is certainly not exclusive to me, and has agonised many a good teacher down the years. And I'd had good teachers for the most part.

Allow me to offer a whistle-stop tour of my upbringing and ultimately my CV creation.

5

Education

I was born into a hurricane in October '87, in a flurry of sparks and flames reminiscent of the entrance in *The Terminator*, which had hit cinemas a few years earlier (the first and last bit of that sentence are true).

But let's fast forward a few years. My first ever school was in the village of Upton Snodsbury, in Worcestershire. Not the last amusingly-named village I'll talk about. As I was here between the ages of 3 and 5, I don't remember a great deal other than the usual playground tomfoolery. My first proper schoolfriend was a chap called Mike Pinfield (though he was still a Michael at this stage). We would play kiss-chase with the girls during break-times, and chase each other about during lessons. A great laugh was had, and it is also great to have recently reconnected with Mike again. He is an absolute tank these days, and you most definitely wouldn't want him chasing you, for any reason. Dude is hench. If this book angers anyone, Mike, just know you're the first I'm calling. (And remember you got this copy for free. That wasn't charity.)

The thing I seem to recall the most, though, from my time at Upton Snodsbury, was an incident that happened in class and, I suppose, my first dark memory. I have no idea what lesson it was, nor can I remember the teacher's name, but I will never forget the face as she suddenly stopped mid-sentence, swaying around and gazing at the ceiling as if being spoken to by God. This went on for 5 to 10 seconds before she collapsed into the bookshelf behind her, hitting the ground in a way I shall never forget. The books and crayons followed, and then the screams. None of us had any idea what had just taken place and it was terrifying and upsetting. It wasn't long before another teacher came rushing in, and after the paramedics were called and the chaos settled, we were sat down by the headteacher and had explained to us what epilepsy was. This was the end of our school day as there was no substitute teacher, and it was fair to say we were all sufficiently traumatised as to have lost our appetite and retention for learning for a good while. Plus we had just been given a first lesson on ill health. You may know someone who suffers with epilepsy – you may have even witnessed a fit yourself. You can never truly prepare yourself for the moment, though, when it happens; much like breaking a major bone, or hearing a Destiny's Child record.

The God analogy that I drew is apparently an apt one for what going through the experience can be like. There are fascinating articles online around this. My heart goes out to anyone who's life is impacted by epilepsy – rightly classed as a disability due to its unpredictable nature and subsequent inability to be considered for driving and in many cases working.

To end Upton Snodsbury school on a somewhat happier memory, by this stage my parents were recently divorced (bear with me), and I was into a routine of visiting my father in London on alternate weekends. Not that I can remember much of what we did over these particular weekends, but I can tell you that on one occasion it involved watching the film *Gremlins*. As I walked into school declaring this the following week, it was overheard in horror by a teacher due to it's 15 rating. Now in no way did this film scar me at all, especially compared to the above. It is largely a comedy, with slapstick violence rather than any true psychological terror, but it was apparently terror enough for my father to be summoned 100 miles north and given bollocking of the month.

I then moved on to Cherry Orchard School in the nearby town of Pershore. I was only here for a few years, but I have fond memories of it too. My first actual kiss, first goal scored in a competitive football match (it crashed in off the underside of the bar, too, which always makes it sweeter. See Tony Yeboah vs Liverpool, and Tony Yeboah vs Wimbledon for that matter). Good times. It was about this age that I realised I excelled in English, but that I was struggling to work with numbers in any shape or form. This trend continued up to last year.

It was then that my brother and I were whisked away to the Lancashire town of Garstang, and it was here that I would traverse the ripe old age of 7 to 9. We had a marvellous headmaster and an excellent network of teachers around us. I continued in the same vein and also began to realise and harness a whole new talent for getting into trouble. Nothing major and certainly nothing compared to recent events, but enough to find myself in and out of detentions. I also remember during a talent contest, standing in front of the class and singing Baddiel and Skinner's 'Three Lions', acapella, switching key and tempo like nobody's business. This was around the time of Euro 96 and, let me tell you, my rendition played no part in the song's success, or recent reprisals. It was all kinds of appalling.

I also remember submitting a short story to the school newspaper which was picked up on immediately and I was asked to continue the narrative for subsequent editions. I wish I had kept these, as they were some of the formative stages of my creative writing. Everything in this book is the truth though, I promise.

I was very much settled at this school, around great friends, and my first proper girlfriend. We were on and off throughout the three years, but very much more on than off, and she will always have a special place in my memory. No sooner than I had settled into this though, we were whisked away again, over to Yorkshire, this time to the village of Holme-Upon-Spalding-Moor. The village itself was nothing of great memory, as I wasn't really there long enough. I will never forget the neighbouring village however, which was legitimately called The Land of Nod. School life in Holme was short in existence, but I hit the ground running largely due to my football abilities, and I immediately embedded myself in the top tier of popularity. On my first day I was approached and asked out by the prettiest girl in the year, much to everyone's envy. Absurdly, though, I remember turning her down – not because I didn't fancy her, but something to do with trying to be cool, or an idiot, or both. Anyway, not a mistake that would go on to smear my name.

Although school life was great in Holme, home life was anything but. My stepfather, who had been part of the family for around 7 years by now, was well on the way to a mighty decline from alcoholism. I first knew him as a Marketing Director, and a most successful one. We had lived in nice houses over the years and had been driven in various cars to match. But, during this period, his fondness for alcohol had crossed into dangerous territory – for his career, his health, and ours. Only once had he ever been remotely threatening towards me, chasing me around the garden with an axe (I think it was meant to be for a laugh). But this was some time ago, and although I wasn't his child, he had still accepted me as much as I thought he could. I didn't feel troubled by his existence nor did he appear to be troubled by mine. But he had started turning on my mother at this point, and these incidents escalated in a very short space of time.

I remember my mum, brother and I went to the cinema (I even remember the film – *ANTZ*). We had left him in the living room with a bottle of vodka, and returned some two or thee hours later with no idea what we'd walk back into. He hadn't moved rooms, but had taken up new position on the floor, fast asleep, with his head virtually in an open fire. We were asked by Mum to leave the room and within minutes the shouting started, followed by the smash of something against the wall (presumably an empty bottle), and then a most piercing scream that I will never forget. I don't know what happened in there – I've never asked – but minutes later we were packing our bags to leave Holme-on-Spalding-Moor forever.

This actually meant moving back to Pershore in Worcestershire, this time to Abbey Park Middle School. (Yes, middle... I know most schools just have primary and secondary, but this is the Midlands). It was an amazing experience joining a completely new school but with many people there I already knew. A great pal of mine, Chris Finch (not the twat from *The Office*), had done a sterling job in talking up my name when he had realised I was coming back, and I practically had the red carpet rolled out for me. I was only there for the remainder of the year, though, before we were all to ascend to Pershore High across town.

I'm sure you remember your first day at high school – if not for school itself then your family's sudden exuberance for photography when you were trying to set off. I enclose one for good measure. (Far right; the only face with what appears to be masked concern).

The school was walkable from the estate where several mates and I lived, and so we convened beforehand and walked among the elders en route. Of course, we were immediately split up once we got there. Besides our middle school of Abbey Park, there were also two others in the catchment area for joining the High School, and at the age of 12, it was like Coke and Mentos at first (sadly omitted from GCSE Chemistry). Testosterone fogged the air, up to a two-mile radius for those that walked to and from school. I can't imagine what the buses were like.

You see, all schools and their classes have their factions and subsets of troublemakers. And it's not always lads lads lads. Many girls of that age love nothing more than to stir up trouble, but they will adopt a more indirect approach which usually absolves them of any blame. In the first month, I would say more issues were caused by rumours whispered around than fists thrown around. Many relationships, if you could call them that, had been carried over from middle school. Some had quickly bitten the dust, and many new ones formed.

The same went for friendships. The difference there, though, was that most people would remain connected with those they still lived near or were especially close to from their previous school. And making new friends was largely governed by the classes you were put together in. In lessons like English and Maths, there was an algorithm of sorts based on ability, whereas the tutor group (morning and afternoon registers) was seemingly arbitrary. I would say more friendships were based on the tutor class, as they were a congregation point and a check-in for what had happened elsewhere. My tutor group largely consisted of people I already knew from the estate I lived in. This was initially comforting, but perhaps not ultimately for the best, as, being the impressionable sprog that I was, I fell into a crowd perhaps not best suited for me.

Don't get me wrong, these were good people in the grand scheme of things – I still know many of them – but they didn't necessarily have an appetite for making the best of themselves while they were there, or, should I say, when they were there. And when they were, you were far more likely to find them in one of the many "designated" smoking areas rather than the classroom they were supposed to be in. Much like you would condition yourself to like a lot of the music you were supposed to at that age, you would do much the same thing with smoking. All the while ignoring how ridiculous it was, and not just detrimental to health, but warranting serious trouble if caught. Therefore we would huddle like penguins, with a delegate to *"keep a cock-eye"* for anyone coming. No one appeared to particularly enjoy the act of smoking itself – I didn't – but there was a sense of community, and I suppose fun, holistically in what we were doing. A secret society. No joining fee, as long as your +1 and 2 were Lambert & Butler. Or Benson & Hedges in the upper echelon.

By this point, I was discovering just how impressionable I was, and my desperation to ingratiate with all circles rather than just bed into one. I don't know whether this was my social anxiety first taking hold, or just wanting to be popular. I know they sound mutually exclusive, but I believe both were at play. In my English lessons, I had a great connection with the majority of the class. We were all of a good ability and were there to learn. We were friends with our teachers, as much as can be possible, and achieving good results.

Occasionally though, I would be inexplicably missing from these lessons, as I had another plate to spin with the L&B massive. This double-life went on for the remainder of that year and beyond. It was emotionally quite draining as I recall. I was juggling learning and my friendships in those classes, with learning how to stay tight with the others. I remember even buying Hubbabubba chewing gum just because I thought it was cool, all the while loathing the synthetic taste and consistency of the stuff. Probably no better for you than nicotine either.

Going back to conditioning one's self into music at that age, I was very much leading a double-life here too. Many of my more intellectual friends were embracing the nu-metal craze, with bands like Slipknot and KoRn. I wouldn't say I was necessarily a fan of either, but I listened at length, desperately seeking the moment that would finally resonate. When Linkin Park's debut *Hybrid Theory* came out though, it all changed. Metal is a wonderful genre – I have a keen interest in all parts of the musical spectrum, but there are certain metal bands in particular that are among those I listen to the most. The genre to this day is still largely niche and frowned upon, but has perhaps the most peaceful of fan-bases, believe it or not. And the music itself has a high level of passion, artistry, melody and complexity behind it that many people will not realise they could fall in love with if they could just desensitize themselves slightly.

Hybrid Theory struck a chord with not just me, but half the year as I recall. It wasn't a case of being uncool if you didn't like it, but that there might actually be something wrong with you. The same can be said for Limp Bizkit's *Chocolate Starfish and the Hot-Dog flavoured Water*, another belter of a record in places. These two albums tapped into the angst of the time, and brought us together. Every generation has those one or two albums that unified them all and, I believe, these were those. They're certainly the two I think of when I look back at High School as I do now.

With middle school, amusingly it had been Britney Spears who entered the scene and took over from Yo-yos as the new craze. It was the first time I remember music being popular and the topic of discussion. All the girls wanted to be Britney, and all the boys wanted to be in her (sorry, *with* her). I certainly got the album on the basis of infatuation rather than a liking of the musical content. I even named a cat after her, would you believe it, although, less than a year later when we learned of its actual gender, the name was changed from Britney to Shady. And that brings me nicely back to high school where we were – as on the estate where I lived and in the designated school smoking areas, no one was into metal. It was pretty much Ministry of Sound or hip hop, and in particular a new name on the scene: Eminem or better known at the time as "Slim Shady", hence my poor cat. I even started wearing hip hop clothing, which gave me the nickname of Ecko. On school trips I was switching between Linkin Park hoodies, and Ecko Unltd ones, thinking I was it. I'm not sure.

In terms of high school relationships, I'll omit those as they're not as relevant to my story as any recent ones, and frankly none of them were that memorable either. You don't need to know about my first time, or second or third. There's only one relationship from these times that truly means something to me.

Towards the end of Year 9 (our second in high school), I was to make a friend that would change my life. He had been here since the start, but always in different classes, so I had never got to meet him. One of my best friends who I had known in middle school (pictured in that photo), knew this fellow rather well by now, and told me a few times that he was legendary and I was not to mess with him (I don't know why he thought I would). One day, in Maths, the person next to me had been promoted to another class, and so the seat was suddenly available. The narcissist that I was at the time, I viewed this seat as rather like the number 7 shirt used to be at Manchester United – and so it was not to go to any old chump. The door knocked and was suddenly opened by a teacher from another class, and with her the fellow mentioned above, who was now to join us. I instinctively shouted "Loz!", and seconds later we shared a desk.

Now Loz is one of the most wonderful and complex human beings that you could ever hope to cross paths with. I knew he wasn't one to be messed with – he was a huge chap – but I very quickly found that he was a gentle giant, and we clicked immediately. I don't know exactly at what stage we discovered we had the same sense of humour, but it must have been in that very first class, and what a revelation.

I have always been one for silliness. This was around the time *Jackass* first aired, and that was an equal revelation to me and the year. It was also around the same time that *Shooting Stars* was on primetime TV, though it only was in later years that I would truly discover Vic and Bob. They too, are my absolute heroes. What I love so much about Reeves and Mortimer is that they are naturally silly; there's no brand of humour being pushed – they are just doing what entertains themselves, and that for me is entertainment. I never cared for anything that could be described as *zany* – and there are several shows that are pigeon-holed into the same category as Vic and Bob without a shred of the brilliance.

Loz and I, within a matter of months, had very much a Vic and Bob relationship ourselves. We were inseparable, and brought out the best in each other. Everyone has a silliness deep down inside, whether it's a desire to pull a face or let out a stupid noise from time to time. Whatever it is, it exists in us all. And if we don't get to open the valve on these occasions, it's not healthy. We need to embrace the craziness within ourselves, without fear of the reaction, and in Loz I had a confidant for this, as much as I was for him. Every minute was a celebration.

I sadly don't have many photos of us during High School, but this is from around then, circa 2002, and sums us up rather well. Apparently I was ahead of the times with selfies.

When we moved into Year 10, and all the classes were shaken up, I was over the moon to discover that Loz and I were in probably 80% of our classes together now. At this same age of 14/15, I had been to Florida many times with my Dad, and with us we had always taken a Mini DV camcorder. Mini DV cassettes were the format for filming back then, as indeed minidiscs were for storing music. The concept of celluloid might seem alien to you depending on your age, but it's how things were then. No hard drives, memory sticks or clouds. There was definitely a tactile magic of working with these things, though, which you won't find in typing your Google password.

"Why has he just gone on a riff about Mini-DV cassettes?" My Dad and I had accumulated a drawer full of them from the holidays and had many unused ones left over, which fell into the hands of Loz and I. We would go over to one or the other's after school, and just film ourselves in improvised discussion and sketches. It was a high that couldn't ever be beaten by anything else. We would film for maybe half an hour, completely forget what we had talked about, and then plug the camera into the TV and remind ourselves. I still have many of the cassettes.

We then learned, eureka, that the medium of filming could be used to turn in certain school projects. We had both signed up to Drama, and naturally this was an area in which we could use the camcorder. This then crept into other lessons, like English, and even history. Our first question to more or less any assignment would be *"can we **please** do this as a video project?"* and if the answer was yes, then you can imagine the reaction.

The things we got away with… good lord. In one particular English project, in which we were supposed to demonstrate an understanding of Shakespearean language, I was running across the tables playing a character named "Sarcastic Raul" (I remember nothing of the relevance of the name), and after an awkward landing propelled myself into a wall and broke my finger. That wasn't the only injury I would endure in the name of our own entertainment. It wasn't even the only injury for that project. Upon being told we could film for it, we had celebrated by recreating the *Dumb & Dumber* missing high-five, my elbow hit the table, and I caused permanent nerve damage to my right arm. Seventeen years later and I'm still deciding whether it was worth it.

Not only were Loz and I utilising and maximising this medium, but another very good friend of mine, Tom Clegg, also got in on the act for a history project. I had known Tom since the age of 5, and we had been close friends throughout high school, too. Again, he is a truly wonderful, genuine human being, and a talented actor. Not the great actor Tom Clegg born in 1927… I don't think he would have fitted in. No, this is the great Tom Clegg of 1987. If you've seen *The Trip* with Rob Brydon and Steve Coogan, then you may well have seen him acting alongside them in Series 3, as a wandering musician and ambassador of the local cuisine. He deserves every bit of success that he gets, and although I rarely see him these days due to his work, I am sure we will both always remember the project we submitted for history, in which we were newsreaders.

Needless to say I remember next to nothing of the purpose of the assignment, but what I do recall are the countless out-takes sat in the dark to the sound of 'Bakerman' by Midnight Oil, waiting to switch the lights on at the moment the main tune kicked in. Listen to it, and you might see why we couldn't hold it together. Regardless of age, if you're ever having a bad day, put on that piece of music.

In fact here it is:

Just try and picture our 13 year old faces. I'm glad I still can.

To compound the amusement, back then I did not have any editing software as such, and rather than rewinding the tape, we just stopped and started the next take. This meant that we had to sit through every single one of these with the class, as we promised the teacher that this was was *"nearly the final one now"*. Tom has rightly achieved recognition for his acting prowess, but I will always remember him tipping a box of Shreddies over his head in a skit for *"Coming up after the News...* When Breakfast Goes Wrong."

Outside of these assignments, Loz and I still were shooting our own projects in the evenings. We had moved on from just chatter, and now were directing our own miniature movies, which I could now properly edit thanks to a copy of *Pinnacle*

Studio. Out came a series of short films known as '*The Chronicles*', one of which featured a man named Terrence who was terrified of meatballs (he had been pelted with them in the shower as a child (and, yes, of course we filmed this sequence). Mum came home to discover a pack of meatballs missing, barely a few weeks since a box of Shreddies had vanished. Special mention to my brother Jack who was cast as a young Terrence, and the recipient of the meatball avalanche.

There was also a horror we wrote called *The Phantom Spoon*, which starred myself, Loz, and Clegg. Again, poor mother's kitchen was ransacked, this time for a serving spoon, upon which I drew a demon's face in permanent marker. We filmed the bulk of this in my house with Clegg meeting his demise over a bowl of Carte D'or. Events then moved to the neighbouring village of Drakes Broughton, where we had even gone out at something like 1am to capture the final sequence in the perfect light. I had already got up in the middle of the night for this film once myself, to get some chilling shots of the outside of my house for the opening sequence. If I had shown this kind of dedication during the daytime, perhaps my GCSE results would have been different.

The Phantom Spoon though was a necessary experience and would have put the heebie-jeebies up anyone, trust me. It was a piece that would be troubled throughout its production, too, much like *The Exorcist* and *Apocalypse Now*. Tragically we lost the footage before I could capture it to my PC as the tape somehow became unwound and twisted inside the casing. It may well have been cursed, and that by shooting this film we had tampered with dark powers beyond our understanding and control. Also, no joke, the spoon disappeared and we never found out how or where. That was before we discovered the tape. And there was me extolling the virtues of celluloid.

Talking of GCSEs I'm getting towards those now, but I must talk about one other video project first, which was the bridge between us messing around off our own backs in our own time, and getting it in front of our teachers and classmates. School assemblies were always a strange affair; in first and middle school they usually involved hymns, and we would be instructed to sing these as if we would have no virtue without them. By the age of 12, though, assemblies moved on to current affairs, or an outside party to lecture us on something. Not only was the subject matter tepid, but they usually found the most monotone speakers as well. There was the occasional mix-up, like someone coming in to demonstrate some falconry (not a single school year has gone by without that one, but hey you can argue it's as necessary as erosion, or prisms). Also, most memorably, I remember the drummer from Status Quo just 'dropping by' to field questions from us on his career. At the end I plucked up the courage to ask him *"How do you eat* your *Cadbury's Creme Egg?"*, and well, he gave me the response I pretty much deserved.

In one assembly, though, someone in the year had made and brought in their own video, and it was shown to all 200 or so of us. I had no idea that with a little innovation and, as long as it was in some way pertinent, that we as students had the opportunity to spearhead an assembly ourselves. I felt Loz's head turn to mine, and so it began.

This time, we would push ourselves a little more out of our comfort zone, and set foot into the town of Pershore to shoot. I don't recall a huge amount of the premise other than it focused on our protagonist Nigel, a man with a curious dress sense, and no friends. From what I do remember of what we filmed, with a few minor tweaks it could have been quite a touching observation on autism. Nigel was a big-hearted man who just wanted to share the love he had with the rest of the world, but hit a forcefield with strangers, who'd been conditioned to treat him almost with scorn. I'm afraid to say I don't remember how the story ended, but I do remember that we left ourselves with enough time to include some irrelevant sketches at the end, one of which was a throwaway that practically made me famous for the year... *The Sellotape Getaway.*

I approached a random man who was tending to his car, with a roll of Sellotape, and asked him to *"hold this for us please"*. I assume he was expecting a shoddy magic trick of some kind, rather than for me to go *"Cheers. RUN!"*. What followed was blurred footage of the pavement and heavy breathing as Loz and I sprinted from the scene like our lives depended on it. I'll never know what that man's reaction was; we never looked back. It was totally random, as was our style, and we knew that it was funny, but when it was broadcast in front of the year I couldn't quite believe the fanfare it had. One of my fondest memories.

By this point we were in Year 12, our final year of High School, and our GCSE exams were fast approaching. I had excelled in my mock exams, and I am sure I am not the first to have got cocky and nearly suffered big-time from the consequences. I aced certain exams which I knew I would, but on the more peripheral subjects like Geography and History, it was pretty much all Ds, which jeopardised my chances of staying on for Sixth Form. In fact, I was below the threshold. I remember the day I went to collect the results; it was summer after the school year had finished and I was working at a local ironmongers. I should only have been gone an hour or so, but they must have known something was up more than two hours later when I still wasn't back. I hadn't slipped off for a celebratory joint. I had essentially had to grovel and express my desire to continue in education, which I did genuinely want to do. I knew what my preferences were for A-Level and it took the breath out of me to realise that suddenly I might be ineligible for them. Thankfully, I got in, but I would have to forget the idea of Psychology, without the requisite grades in Science (again all D's). And so I was to do English literature, Theatre Studies, General Studies, and Philosophy & Ethics.

Most of these involved Loz, but that was not why either of us chose them as far as I recall. We had established that we loved acting, on our own terms, and I had furthered my love for the English language (though I inexplicably chose literature and I can't remember why). English Lit was a curious subject, and really it was pot luck which pieces we were going to end up studying. I was neither here nor there about Shakespeare, but thankfully Othello was the chosen piece, which I love. Say what you like about myself or Amy, but Iago is the ultimate villain. We also studied war poetry at length, in particular the works of Wilfred Owen and Siegfried Sassoon. This led us to Belgium and the site of the Somme for a school trip, but again I remember nothing of that. Clegg, another friend and I had wandered left out of the hotel when we had been told the town was to the right, and if we hadn't done this on impulse, we wouldn't have stumbled upon a peace festival featuring Bob Geldof, and The Levellers, to name two.

Keeping with music, Sixth Form was where I first picked up a guitar. There was one lying around in the common room, and something made me reach for it one day. Guitar is an interesting one for me, as I don't mind saying to you that I am typically a man that puts a new hobby down at the first sign of difficulty. Thankfully, something made me persevere and break through the first wall with it. And I think I know what that something was.

Prior to Sixth Form, my musical taste was still at sixes and sevens, and I hadn't managed to shake off the sense that what I was into should be cool. I was still flickering between metal and hip hop. I still had a connection with the L&B massive due to the fact I still lived in the same estate, and I had even squandered my mother's savings for my first car on a motorbike instead, under the pretence that it would get me on the road and to be independent faster. Nope, I just wanted to be cool. It was quite a cool bike, though, a geared and de-restricted 50cc Derbi Sender, which went faster than it should have done. I was also moving faster than I should have done by buying it. It wasn't too long before my overzealousness caused damage to some of the parts, and I ended up trading it would you believe for £400 and a Nokia 3650. Still back in the days of Snake and polyphonic ringtones, but this one had a curved keypad, and that was enough for the muppet that was me. I would have to wait a few years to get back on the road after that.

Anyway, back to music and the guitar. It was around the age of 17 that I happened upon the band Pink Floyd, properly, for the first time. I had heard of *Dark Side of the Moon*, and was aware of its status, and I think I may have been on a flight somewhere that year when I saw it in the menu, and decided to open my horizons and give it a listen. Because of the album's reverence, I paid special attention to everything about it; the chord progressions, the production, and something I don't usually pay any attention to, lyrics. Whilst it didn't especially grab me immediately, I retained interest, and when I got back home, I checked out some of their other albums. And that's when this turned into something else.

This band was the musical epiphany that I had so sorely needed. They were touching upon deep and meaningful subjects, and whilst the music itself was relatively simple, that was half the point, and it just hit me. It wasn't about a single facet, such as catchiness or being cool. Neither of them. It was a multi-sensory experience. It was art. I quickly became obsessed, and as my birthday and Christmas are fairly close to each other, I remember utilising this going into HMV in Ealing Broadway with my father and getting their entire discography in one fell swoop. Every studio record, and even the film scores they had done in their early years.

Although I had just found arguably the greatest band of all time, I was about to learn the difference between objective and subjective, when I was to discover my *favourite* band of all time: Opeth. A band renowned for their diverse musical expression, and bringing it all together cohesively within songs upwards of ten minutes. It just struck me straight away. They do fall firmly in the 'metal' category, particularly the first half of their discography, but you will see many people in their 50s and even 60s at their gigs. Their vocalist, guitarist and songwriter Mikael Åkerfeldt is another hero to me. As far as I am concerned, he is possibly the greatest songwriter to have ever lived, and I know that's a bold comment. The albums

Still Life, Blackwater Park, and *Ghost Reveries* are three reasons why. The holy trinity. Check'em out.

So within a matter of weeks, I had just had my musical world turned upside down with two bands. This should have been a happy time for me, but other things would happen that year that turned my real world upside down.

I mentioned earlier that none of the flings or relationships in high school were all that memorable, and, to be honest, none of them in sixth form were either. But there was one from back in middle school that I want to talk about. Her name was Rosie.

I don't remember Rosie from Cherry Orchard, so she must have joined Abbey Park from another school while I had been up North, but I remember meeting her on the day I got back. There was something about her. There was probably something about me, too, as I was the mysterious new lad who everyone but her seemed to know about. Like I said, red carpet. Cheers Finchy. I asked her out before too long, done in much the awkward style that you would expect from an eleven-year-old, and we became boyfriend and girlfriend. We were on and off over the course of six months or so before we moved to high school, and although we never ended up in the same classes in high school, our eyes always met in the corridor, and we never forgot what we had had before the weight of everything else took over.

By the time we reached Sixth Form, the size of our year had whittled down significantly, and you immediately noticed each other more. I had seen Rosie at the start of the year and had meant to find a moment to catch up with her properly. I wanted to learn how she had found High School herself, to learn what she was continuing to study, to learn the person that she now was. A short while elapsed, and I hadn't seen her in the common room, and presumed she had left. Her closest friends were not close friends of mine: we had moved in different circles, and so I didn't initially know of the reason why she wasn't there. Then, one day a couple of months later, I walked into the common room to learn, along with most others, that she had died.

She'd had cancer that had spread aggressively to her brain, and that was it – she was gone, like that. I say *"like that"* – for her close friends and family this horrible journey would have felt like a lifetime in itself, and I can't begin to imagine what it must have been like. For me though it was sudden, I'd had no idea – I had anticipated on seeing her around sometime and being able to have a proper chat and reconcile on everything and hopefully become close friends again, but it wasn't to be.

The announcement stunned us all. Back in Upton Snodsbury, that epileptic seizure was the first time I had seen what ill health can be like and, although I had not been around what happened here, hearing it hit me in just the same way. I had no concept of how precious life really was; I don't believe it can be taught, so to speak. I would need to see it first-hand, like I think we all do. This was also the first time I truly learned that age does not equate to health – these things can strike at any time, without reason or prejudice. One of us was gone, and it was too late for me, and many others, to show them how valued they were to us.

Barely a month or so later, a closer friend of mine at the time, Dan, also fell ill. He was in the same circle of friends in the year as me, and we always had a good laugh at parties. He was someone who loved to have a good time and to be around the people he cared about and, suddenly, wasn't able to, as he had leukaemia. This was every bit as sudden as with Rosie, and every bit as difficult to comprehend. He was hanging on though in hospital, getting all the treatment he could. It was the Christmas break, and Sixth Form broke for a couple of weeks with us all getting the time off we needed with our families. It turns out that Dan had also been discharged and allowed to go home and spend Christmas time with his family, too, but he died while he was home. This hit us like a brick as well. Again, I can't begin to imagine what it felt like for the family.

Then, just a couple of months after that, our good friend Jim – also part of the same crew – died along with his brother in a car crash. This was even more out of the blue, and almost too much to handle by this point. This was three in the same school year, and in the *same* school year. The common room felt it together, though some would no doubt have been hurting more than others. I can't speak for everyone of course, but I hope I can properly speak for myself, and with a newfound interest in getting stoned, I wasn't dealing with any of the emotions properly. They were being conveniently suppressed, and all the music I was discovering at the time was helping to take the edge off as well. This was not the end of the year of death, though.

To backtrack a little, around the same time that Rosie died, my grandma, still down in London with my father, suffered a huge stroke. Again, I was not ready to hear this, nor did I truly realise the extent of what a stroke could do. It took no more than ten seconds in her company to see the severity of it.

She had completely lost use of the right side of her body, likely forever, and she was in a care home, also probably forever. I was only able to visit on alternate weekends, and the deterioration each time was clearly visible. Along with much of her body, her brain was dying out, too. This wasn't for a lack of emotional or mental strength, but perhaps the acute realisation that her life was suddenly over as she knew it. She'd had a busy and fruitful one: during the war she worked in a factory which produced and supplied critical parts for planes and other machinery. She had also worked incredibly hard to buy her house in Ealing, which suddenly she may never see again. She knew she'd had a great innings, and I knew she was proud of both her son and grandson, but with the effects the stroke had had on half of her face, this wasn't necessarily showing. That, in and of itself, must have been killing her inside. Thankfully for her, she had always made this known to us before the stroke happened. She was an incredibly loving person. Her resilience was not going to give up yet, but it would only be tested further.

Months later, she suffered a second, and third stroke. All this was coinciding with the sudden deaths of Dan and Jim, but she was hanging on. Sadly, though, more strokes followed. The flicker of recognition was always there, but this wasn't life any more. And eventually, after another and final stroke, Grandma lost the good fight, and the news was broken over the phone to me. Each time I had visited I was mentally preparing for each wave goodbye to be the final one, and if I hadn't done this, I would likely still be holding on to a sense of regret. For a brief period, it looked as though she could stay at home and be cared for, as she had started showing faint signs of recovery.

The ground floor of the house had even been adapted in a number of ways to support her. As if her spirit was not already felt in the house, it was doubly hard with the small details such as walking through each doorway that had been widened to accommodate her wheelchair, or using any of the plug sockets that had been lowered to meet disability requirements. This wasn't nearly as hard for me as it would have been for my dad. He had been living with, and supporting her for some time, and was now living alone in the house and experiencing all of the above 24/7. Admittedly, I wasn't getting a huge amount of respite when I returned home, with everything that was going on there, but there was at least a sense of escape. We attended her funeral shortly afterwards, and said our final goodbyes.

So, four deaths in the space of around 8 months. Then, less than a month later, I got news that my grandpa on my mum's side had cancer. This I got to see at closer quarters, as he lived roughly a mile away from us and we were always seeing each other. He had a fondness for rugby and cricket, two things that I would not inherit for a few years to come. Again, he was a wonderful soul and I have so many fond memories from the years. Upon learning that he had cancer, he had gone for the conventional method of treatment. At this stage in my life, I had a growing interest in, let's say, alternative ideas, and had a critical mind to everything. Without wanting to sidetrack too much here, 9/11 had occurred by this point (I was actually flying back from the USA when it happened, believe it or not), and I had a keen interest in what *really* happened on that day.

Another thing that interested me was cancer, after what had happened, and the idea that chemotherapy is the only sensible way of treating it. Note I use the words *idea*, and *treating*. My father had a device called the LifeForce 2000, which serves to realign certain frequencies within the body, and it has incredible effects on almost any ailment you can think of. Some of the testimonials were astonishing. We offered this gently to Grandpa. It didn't require any effort – it certainly didn't require being poisoned – and could be used in the comfort of his living room. And it could run alongside the chemotherapy, which of course would be his decision alone to accept or reject. Sadly, he outright rejected both the idea and use of this machine and opted for the traditional, conventional methods. And a couple of months later, I was at another funeral.

I'm not going to say whether this machine would have helped him, but read on.

This one was especially hard to take for me. It was all too much with everything else that had already happened, and I simply wasn't dealing with any of it properly. I was high virtually every minute of the day, and if one good thing came out of that, it's that I was channelling my energy into my guitar-playing, which was noticeably improving by the hour. It had taken over my life; I was going to gigs every other week and music was proving to be the friend and medicine that I needed; certainly more than the weed. When sixth form was over, I just didn't know where I wanted to go with my life. I just hadn't given it the thought. I was artificially happy in my bubble, or so I thought, and I wasn't having it popped by anyone. My A-Level results were decent enough (I had learned from last time and studied much harder), and there would have been the option to go to University and further one of these subjects. But I wasn't willing to take the plunge without a deep sense of allure to any of them. I just wanted to be distracted. I decided that I would take a gap year.

I had enough wherewithal to know that a year in the working world would probably inform me more on life than a year in further education, and also that it might afford me the free time I needed to reconcile and declutter everything from the previous year. Also, I just wanted to have some fun again. I took a part time job in a supermarket that was walkable from the house. A few friends of mine from school were also working here, and soon enough I would be getting the fun that I was craving. Our boss was also a friend of ours, and a total pussycat. He would come clubbing on the town with us at weekends, and because we knew him so well, he was less an authority figure at work and more a gaping opportunity for clowning about. We knew though that first and foremost we had to get the work done, so that any capering would be all the funnier (and surprising) for it having followed a period of exemplary work. It worked swimmingly. We would never do anything in front of the customers, of course, but in the backstock area we would often hide in and amongst the cardboard. We could hear him patrolling, knowing that we were likely there somewhere, but were never seen. At one point I am sure he made eye contact with me, as I lay in the foetal position behind a row of Pringles boxes. Yes, I was nineteen at the time, but moments like this were the best I had felt in a while. Wrestling matches would be held in the walk-in freezer, again only once the work was done. They were majestic times.

I mention clubbing; by this point it had become ingrained in our culture to go out every Saturday. Even while I worked at the ironmongers at the age of 16/17, I would go out in

Worcester every weekend with the older lads, and chance my arm. The thrill of queuing at the nightclub, being given the up and down, and then being let in, was incredible. I would always bump into people from my year in there as well and we would commend each other on looking older than we were. We certainly weren't acting older than we were. The drinking and pill-popping culture was all new to us and we found our feet just like everyone else did. There were some messy nights, and plenty of waking up in unknown rooms, sometimes with work in two hours.

After a year or so of all this, though, it was starting to stagnate. The supermarket shenanigans would always entertain, but my earnings weren't fantastic, especially as I was close to frittering £100 every single Saturday. Something had to change. By this point I had established that music was something I wanted more and more in my life, and I can't remember quite how I arrived at the idea, but before long I was being interviewed for a place on a Music Production HND course at Worcester Tech College.

The interview, as I recall, was fairly informal; a brief talk through my academic history, a discussion on music in general – what I knew, and my aspirations for this course and beyond – and a guitar audition comprising of a piece I had chosen from a pre-determined list a couple of weeks earlier. I wish I could remember the song, but I can tell you it wasn't Opeth. A couple of weeks or so passed, and I got the letter advising that I had been successful and that I was to start in September. Worcester was easily commutable for me and so I could remain at home and be there within 40 minutes or so by bus, or 20 by train. Although I had moved house and indeed cross-country several points by now in my life, this, for the first time, felt like a proper paradigm shift. Something new. We'd had music lessons during our GCSE's, but this largely comprised of yawning through the theory studies, and laughing over symphonies with the animal sound effects on the keyboard (before Ross Geller was doing it).

Come to think of it, Clegg and I had a game we would occasionally play in lessons a couple of years earlier. We would simply bounce the word "*boob*" back and forth sporadically, increasing the volume each time, until we were shouting it at the top of our lungs. Ringing any bells? Yes, Dick and Dom *In Da Bungalow* started doing this on television a few years later, in public libraries and the like, opting for the word "*bogies*" instead. That's twice I've been potentially plagiarised. It's almost as if my life is being secretly filmed, a la Truman Burbank. Would that save me the hassle of this book? No, I'm enjoying it.

Starting the music course wasn't nearly as daunting as starting a high school or switching counties, though, as I knew I was to be meeting like-minded people here. We all met for our induction, a loose tour of the premises and to be given our MacBooks and paperwork etc., before we were set free for the large remainder of the day. This, unfortunately, was quite typical. The amount of time spent learning could have been condensed into three full-time days quite easily, but instead there were at least two of the week where I would find myself paying £5 to hop into Worcester, only to be finished by 11. And it wasn't long before someone popped the question, "*So who smokes weed then?*", which was virtually everyone. We would either chill by the river or go back to the digs of someone who lived in the town. We would also quite often find ourselves at the nearest Wetherspoons, sampling the ample variety of cheap pitchers. It was all good fun, and the studying itself was, too, to begin with.

We had Logic Pro installed on our laptops, which meant we had industry-standard professional recording software. My twenty-year-old stoner brain was awash with inspiration for weird and hilarious compositions; some of these were even turned in as assignments when they were relevant. Others were just done in the name of fun in my spare time with the school friends I was still in touch with, most of whom were also musical. Although I do write the odd riff here and there these days, back then was my most fertile period. Oh, how I wish I still had these recordings. The MacBook would go on to meet a rather dim fate, later in this chapter.

Anyway, as I said, fun left right and centre. We went by coach to the NEC in Birmingham for a world record attempt, only to have to leave before the attempt even started (the largest ever ensemble of guitars, playing 'Smoke on the Water'. I don't know if they ever broke the record). It was also a huge guitar convention, and I did come back with a sweet new BC Rich Bich.

Just browsing there had been nothing but fun, given that my fellow students were all a laugh. One in particular, Rich Cakebread, was incident after incident. As if his name wasn't comedy enough. I don't think I've ever met anyone apart from Loz who could make me laugh as hard as he did. There are many moments I could recall, but for the sake of keeping this chapter somewhere on track I'll cherry-pick one for you. A particular music project had actually involved some filming, and we ventured no further than 30 seconds outside into the college car park for a stunt that would involve Rich running up and over the top of a parked car, head on. I should definitely mention that this car belonged to one of our colleagues, Sam. This was even Sam's project, not mine or Rich's, believe it or not. Boy I wish I could remember the context of this. Rich had a couple of rehearsals at it and pulled them off remarkably well. The camera wasn't on for these. As soon as Sam and Rich were happy for the main attempt, I watched almost in slow motion as Rich caught the tip of his shoe on the number plate and proceeded knee first into a shattered windscreen, and crumpled torso over the roof. A few seconds of silence, before a craned head appeared to utter the words *"well that could have ended in tears"*. Which it did. Ours were of laughter. Sam's weren't.

So, yes, all good fun. But that was about to change yet again, thanks to cancer, yet again. And this time it was Mum.

To be honest, much of this period was a blur. For the most part as I recall Mum was still able to be independent. But it certainly brought things crashing home again, literally. Suddenly, I didn't know whether to race home after my studies, to be back ready for when Mum arrived, or whether to stay on in town for a bit and at least continue to have a social life and then arrive back a little later on in the evening when Mum was already home. I would of course see her every day, and I was there for anything I could do to help. I didn't drive at this stage but I was still able to procure anything quite easily at the last minute from the city centre, and indeed do anything else I could to take the strain off as much as possible. Mum and I are very different people, but we pretty much always got on. The only times when we didn't were solely down to me being an arse, predominantly in my teenage years, and a bit further down the line.

What made this time different though, was the treatment. I can't speak for Rosie and Dan back in sixth form, but I can speak for Grandpa, who had politely but flatly refused the alternate (well, additional) method that was gently offered. I'm sure I don't need to say I am not a fan of chemo. I don't know if you've ever seen *Breaking Bad*, but, if not, it's far more than just 'that show about crystal meth', and sums up chemotherapy very well. It's a touching introspection on cancer and its effects in different directions, among other things. It deserves its pantheon status, for the cinematography and cancer narrative alone.

Although my parents had divorced back in about 1990, once my father had been made aware of Grandpa being ill he had offered the Lifeforce 2000 machine, and was about to offer it to Mum. She had initially had the lump removed, however it had spread and was now at stage 3. Further surgery was advised, and listened to, and then came the suggestion of chemo. Mum, thankfully, was much more open to the idea of trying the LifeForce machine, in line with a couple of other 'alternative' medicines, one of them being dried apricots, believe it or not. She declined the chemo and tried these other methods in line with the surgery.

The LifeForce machine could be used in the comfort of the lounge whilst watching TV and, of course, she could tuck into a bag of dried fruit anytime. I can't point to a single thing as evidence for what followed, but I can thankfully say that the cancer was quickly eradicated. The process from the very start to end must have been a few months or so and Mum emerged the other side as healthy as ever, and I am very lucky to still have her today.

In fact, Mum, I can safely say, always has been and remains a stronger person than me. Despite what had happened with her own father just a couple of years earlier, she got on with it. There was no reason why I couldn't do the same. Yes, I'd had a few other deaths in recent times to cope with and, yes, this experience did bring much of it back, but it's no excuse. I should have got on with it, too. Instead, I merely upped the escapology act. I was also starting to become disillusioned with some fundamental aspects of the music course, which of course was called 'Music Production'. The clue was there in the title (and the interview/audition), but I somehow had glossed over it. I never had any interest in being a producer. I didn't care about what gating was, or sine waves. I just wanted to create.

In concurrence with Mum's cancer, my attendance dropped. I was either lying that there were no seminars that day and just staying home, or I was going into Worcester but evading college. By this point I had a network of mates there who shared a keen passion for drinking and smoking. I would drift in and out of the course, and it was evident that my heart was no longer in it. I wasn't the only one with this kind of attendance by the way – the course had quite a high drop-out rate, though I do wonder how much it had to do with the course itself. At least with me I can say it was a factor.

I was nearing the end of my first of two years on the course (with the option for a third at university) and I, like everyone else, had a meeting with the heads of department, to discuss my performance etc. There were no issues with my performance for the assignments I had handed in. The glaring problem was the ones missing. This was the first time I actually explained what was going on at home, but the truth is that's no reason or excuse; this was because of issues with me, and within me, not with or within anyone else.

It was agreed by the end of the meeting that I could finish the year but finish the course at the same time. It felt for the best, and I wanted a new challenge. I almost felt like I was falling out of love with music, and that was a worry.

Oh, yes, the MacBook. By the time the college asked for it back, it had succumbed to water damage. A spilt glass of water? A spilt glass of anything else? Not quite. I had taken it camping with a few mates by the river, consumed magic mushrooms, and – no it didn't end up in the river – but what I did do was fail to attach a very small but pivotal piece of fabric to the apex of the tent when pitching it. Although when we went to sleep the sky was beautiful and clear, I awoke to find that the laptop (which had been left on overnight with music playing), had been rained on for several hours. That'll do it. My sleeping bag was nestled to the side and edge of the tent, in a dry zone, ergo I didn't wake in time to perhaps save the old girl.

So, I've entitled this chapter Education, and to get somewhere near a summary, there are different types, aren't there? You have the academic, something you can look to on paper for a general idea of someone's history, but what that piece of paper won't demonstrate are life lessons and the profound education that comes with those. The things you learn on the side; the things that you aren't necessarily told to learn, or that you necessarily choose to learn. But that you need to as much as anything else that you grow from.

This, as I mentioned before, means that knowledge does not equal intelligence. I think most of us know that. An IQ test might give a more holistic understanding, but to me a set of GCSE grades don't. What they do demonstrate is discipline and retention, two things that, yes, are key to securing a level of intelligence, but they are not intelligence alone.

Talking of academic qualifications on paper, let's get back to CVs and ultimately back to our prison induction. I'm learning the dark art of the segue as we go.

Work is prime education, and we need to flesh out my CV with this, too, so I'll frog-march you through my employment. I would love to go at a slower pace, but I want this book to fit in your bag. And hand.

After the music course, I decided I would seek full time work, and believe it or not it was my mum that found what could be an ideal vacancy for me, working on an IT help-desk in the NHS. She also worked in the NHS, you see. I applied, was successful, and proceeded to spend the next 4 years in a hospital, taking a barrage of angry phone calls about defective IT equipment, before being promoted into a tech role, visiting the same angry wards and defective equipment. Defective staff you could argue, too, at times. *"[User error]"*, as we used to say. I had many love-hate relationships during these years, not least with HP Laser-jet printers, but also with my colleagues and the management. There was one person in particular that I met during this job, on day one, that also changed my life. Don't worry, we will get to them in time.

After five years I left for pastures new, into a nearby and similar IT support role, no longer in the health sector. The start of this job coincided with a very turbulent period in my personal life, and frankly it's astonishing I got through my probation there. Again we'll save that for later (that's becoming quite a catchphrase isn't it). A year or so onwards, I moved into a more advanced support role for another 6 months or so, before having the opportunity to apply to work in a different department there: Product. I had been curious about this line of work ever since I started there. My particular role had always been one of a reactive nature, fixing or suggesting things as they came in. It was always with mixed emotions, as I was passionate and empathetic, perhaps too much so. The emails that flew in weren't just ticket numbers, they were people just like me; and I never forgot that for a second. Some of the customers or clients that we were dealing with were people in desperate situations, and it frustrated me that I didn't have the influence to help them further. The Product team did though.

Now, if there was one thing this company enjoyed, it was rotating the management. My boss had recently been jettisoned and not long later there was a switch-up in the Product department, too. Two new Product Managers arrived, and I took a shine to both immediately. A good sense of humour, drive, and just eminently likeable. They also seemed to have what appeared to be the coolest job in the world; sauntering in on a completely different time-zone to everyone else, and using MacBook Lite's to the vexation of the IT department. I later learned that both of these ways of working were quite necessary, but from an outsider's point of view there was a touch of renegade about it.

A vacancy opened up for a Product Executive role, which looked and sounded perfect as a stepping stone to being a Product Manager myself, and being able to do the things I was dreaming of doing. I had a couple of interviews in which I recall bringing John Wardley (you'd better remember him) into a presentation. Not literately, alas, but through PowerPoint. There was pertinence for showing his face and discussing his career, and that among other things sealed the deal and I was made an offer. Again, it felt like a paradigm shift.

I remember my new boss describing the role largely as ball-catching and I suppose it was, and it was not only fun but hitting a spot that application support hadn't. Now I was actually involved in the change, the permanent fixes if you like. I was also able to proactively suggest new features etc. and I am sure it was a combination of my passion and hunger – along with staff resource it must be said – that led to me becoming a Product Manager way before I had imagined. The product that I had spent all this time supporting, I was now in charge of development-wise, and where we went with it. It's certainly an empowering role, and several emotions come with that. Business tripping to Malaga and back was also a joy, for the right reasons. I loved being the conduit between departments, and also monitoring the effect any changes that I had implemented were having, as this gave me time with my old team again. But the difference between being a Product Exec and a Product Manager is that one is now wholly accountable for the return on investment for anything one does. It's a fundamental area of the job; reconciling customer need or cosmetic changes with actual commercial gain for the business (e.g. ad implementation or Ecommerce). I was game for it at first, learning as I went, until the carousel kicked in again.

One of my fellow Product Managers had already left, which I had been secretly gutted about as we had not only got on well, but he had been a great source of knowledge and laughter. He had a wickedly dry sense of humour and was also a huge fan of cricket. I don't think I've ever enjoyed sharing a desk with anyone more. Then came the true sucker-punch. My boss, the person who had given me the opportunity to enter the realm of Product, and had then given me the opportunity of managing the company's flagship product, was gone as well, just like that. Part of another management switcharoo, and probably the worst one yet. I did get to see her once in person afterwards for drinks organised by someone in the team, but it really took some adjusting after that. She had a brilliant mind, was empathetic like me, but with a commercial head firmly screwed on, and, honestly, was on a different plane of thinking to the higher management there, who were throwing their weight around almost arbitrarily. She was too good for them, and I don't mind saying I was in wonderment of her; she had very emotive eyes, almost cosmic, and was just totally enchanting. There was something that reminded me of Lucy Porter (or rather I think it was Lucy Porter that appeared on TV recently and reminded me of her). Either way, I was always charmed. Hang on, they're both below 5 feet tall I'm fairly sure. Is that my thing? Strewth maybe it is.

The latest change of philosophy especially resonated for all the wrong reasons. One of the co-founders and back-seat directors of the company suddenly was taking a sharper interest, and one day huddled us all to announce himself properly, and as *"a capitalist with a capital C"*. I remember sitting there thinking *"you're definitely something with a capital C, mate"*. If I'd said that and walked out there and then, it might have been my defining moment.

I stayed for a few more months, until I was so sick of how things had become I handed in my notice without even having secured a new job. It was liberating to say the least. Frankly, without wanting to be churlish, most of the management there by this stage were people I no longer wanted to be associated with in any shape or form. Being able to look elsewhere became the new full time occupation I had desperately needed, and I was so driven I can't tell you. It was less than a month before I visited a company, yet again in another county, and my new role was wrapped up in a single 3 hour interview.

I'll try and speed up from here; I said frog-march and this isn't even sloth. I started at short notice and moved house also at short notice, and it was nice to exercise my new-found product skills in an entirely different area. I won't mention the clients we worked with, but some of them were huge. It's important to say that this new job was advertised to me as a "Product Owner" role, not "Product Manager". There is a distinction which I won't bore you with. It was all good with me, as by this stage I was a certified Product Owner through a course I had attended thanks to my former boss, and when

I learned of what this company were doing, it sounded the perfect fit. Not to mention they seemed quite progressive in their nature. They occupied an entire building, and the ground floor solely existed of pool tables. This was in the process of a lavish upgrade of other recreations, being worked out by a democratic committee within the company. Charmed.

I liked how the job started. I was working with a much larger development team and visiting the salubrious HQs of our customers. Arguably the largest of our clients in terms of revenue, was one that was assigned to me. I was forewarned about their main contact, but upon meeting her realised that she was nothing to be fearful of. She seemed to take a liking to me, and it must have seemed like I did to her, largely out of relief that she wasn't the witch I had been briefed for. Maybe others rubbed her up the wrong way, I don't know. One thing to be fearful of, though, was the upcoming renewal of this client's contract, and the subsequent revenue loss if it didn't happen. They had been essentially paying in blocks for the development work and we were moving them towards a new 'SaaS' (Software as a Service) model whereby it was an annual contract. However, they wanted the entire year's pipeline and roadmap specced out well in advance for their approval. I can't blame them. What it meant though, was moving away from what's known as Scrum (incremental) methodology and into almost a different language, for which I only had a rudimentary grasp. The client and I were happy enough with a plan, but upstairs had different ideas over certain things, and there were disagreements. At this point I started struggling, and also started enjoying the pool tables too much, if I'm honest. There was an in-house tournament that had been devised and coded by the dev team, whereby a certain amount of points were accrued or lost depending on the margin of victory and your opponent's league standing in proximity to yours. It was so gripping I can't tell you.

I was lamenting through all the documentation and the meetings that accompanied them, and though as I say the client was onside, my manager was growing increasingly concerned. Though he and I always got on, I mentioned there were disagreements elsewhere, and most definitely one or two in the business that wanted me ousted and were in his ear. One day, after I had turned in a spec and preparation for a client meeting at our offices later in the week, I decided to play a game of pool with one of the top 3 players in the whole company. Again, someone I had been warned of. I could see his skills, but mine were on point on this particular day, too. Well, I would have beaten him if I hadn't watched my white ball follow the black into a pocket right at the end, rendering him the victor. I couldn't believe it. Straight after this, I went upstairs and saw my boss who asked whether I had a minute. When I entered the office and saw the head of HR along with one of the directors, I knew this wasn't good. I was told there and then that I was being let go, with immediate effect as I was still in my probation period, and then followed the awkward few minutes as I handed in my company iPhone and laptop, and collected my belongings in full of view of half the company. Though there had been strain, I genuinely somehow hadn't seen it coming. I assume they went on to replace me with someone more malleable in their image. No hard feelings though.

This also meant that I would have to move out of my house and back in briefly with my father, again another county move, almost a year to the day before I met Amy. This year would be another story in itself. I mentioned in the Amy chapter that I got to fulfil a lifelong dream in my career. Well this year was it.

I initially looked for Product work again, but this time in the theme park industry, and though I didn't find anything that quite fitted the product management bill, I did happen across a very interesting-looking role in which I would work as a manager for a theme park company and get to rotate between their different departments. The interview for this was like nothing else I have experienced; there was a typical interview of sorts, but it was followed by a Dragon's Den-style pitch where I was to present a new prospective attraction for one of the parks. I knew I would nail this, and even got to utilise my love of gaming in the process. I spent hours crafting an entire new themed area through a PC game called *Planet Coaster* (from the makers of RollerCoaster Tycoon). I built a castle from scratch, an epic wing coaster, a dining complex, various interactive themed areas, and then using my skills from 'The Chronicles' years, edited a two-or three-minute video showing it off in all its charm. And it did charm, if I may say so. Within an hour of leaving the interview, I was offered the role and I leapt at it, despite a £16k pay-cut.

Now, in terms of the job itself, it was overall a great experience and I learned many excellent life lessons again. It was frenetic, very front-line and active, and I enjoyed that. At one stage I was averaging 40,000 steps a day. I didn't particularly enjoy the hours though, nor the on-site accommodation. In one room I stayed in, there was a hole in the ceiling and a bucket below, which dripped all night long. It may have been a management role, but I didn't realise a key strand of that would be managing this bucket.

In the same room, I managed to set off the fire alarm, on two separate occasions, with anti-perspirant. Under normal circumstances, this would mean just disconnecting or resetting the alarm. But this accommodation was tucked inside the theme park itself and, on both occasions, it meant evacuation protocol of the entire entrance square. In retrospect, hilarious. But just try and imagine how it unfolded at the time, and how I must have looked and felt. (Still hilarious, yes I don't blame you).

Ultimately, despite some of the delights of the job, it got quite wearing for me quite quickly. Not physically wearing – I loved the spring in my step – but emotionally. I took a short and much needed break in Budapest in November, and returned for the Christmas preparations, where things really ramped up a gear. I have to say they did Christmas very well, but within a couple of weeks of being back I decided I'd had it. I don't want to go into detail; overall I have fond memories of being there, and I would hate to breach confidentiality of my contract or anything like that. Let's just say I realised that I needed to swiftly get back on the other side of the curtain as to not sour my love of the industry as a whole. Plus, much of their customer feedback says it better than I can.

I had always planned to leave at the end of the year and seek a return to Product, having realised a dream, and it was agreed that I could leave early and at short notice. And, well, you know the next part, because the next part was Chapter Two: Amy.

So that's my career. I can certainly say I've enjoyed some variation, that I've stuck to my principals at times and taken risks at others, which many can't. It all makes for an intriguing CV I suppose.

Ah yes, CVs.

6

Induction continued

So let's get this quickly finished, starting with the CV creation. Now I can understand the value of this to many who had come in fresh off the back of hard times employment-wise, but I had enjoyed a relatively decent career for my age, and liked to think I already had a rip-roaring white knuckle ride of a resume, and unfortunately this section wasn't optional. To make matters worse, the UI (user interface) was prehistoric, making for an appalling UX (user experience). As you know I've worked in website and app design and would have been happy to offer some free freelance consultancy, had the right person been there to hear it.

Once your CV is complete, it will be printed off, along with your profile, and handed to a peer worker to conduct an interview with you about the prospective jobs and education courses available during your sentence. Jobs include things such as: kitchens, cleaning, recycling, peer work, laundry, and the education will include (besides the obvious): art, family matters, car mechanics, music, IT, and more. My interview was fast and, dare I say it, enjoyable, as I could choose 5 options from either, in order of preference. I can't remember my second, third, fourth and fifth choices, but I can remember that first time round I found the allure of music too much to resist – and liked the idea of perhaps getting behind a drum kit for a change and being paid for it. Albeit £15 a week or so.

So, my choices were made, and I was put on a waiting list and discharged. What did you go for?

In Wales, this was induction complete, whereas in England – a much larger jail, the library was of sufficient size to warrant a slot in the process of its own. Not much to say on this one, though. Name, prison number and cell number taken, directions and a timetable offered in return. You may get given some newspapers to tide you over in the meantime. Perhaps not what you're thinking, though.

ConVerse: *"The award winning national monthly newspaper for prisoners"*. Not much to say on this either.

Inside Time: This was the favourite and more memorable of the two, as it was largely written into by prisoners across the UK, and for a newspaper refreshingly unbiased. It was fascinating to see how people were doing elsewhere and what was happening, or not happening, to them. Turns out no one's having a whimsical time, and I realised in many ways how lucky I was, even through I did go through hell in prison at times myself (be honest, you're looking forward to that, aren't you, you little sadist).

All in all I made the best of the newspapers and gleaned a lot, though neither of them were any good for the Brentford results. I relied upon BBC's *Final Score* for that. An enjoyable show, particularly for Garth Crooks, a most endearing clown.

So, induction is now complete, but before we move on to a proper wing I want to tell you about one of the experiences I had during induction, over the course of the few days I was there.

7

Windsor

The story begins in court, right after the events of chapter 2. I had breached my bail again over contacting Amy, so, again, totally my fault and I knew my fate, but I still had to go through the carousel and be told by the magistrates. I was brought in by the GEOAmey bus, which sounded busy this time. As this transit is handled by a private firm (GEOAmey would you believe) rather than the police, you lose any trust and respect you may have gained from after the arrest, and are back to being double-cuffed and pulled around like a suitcase. The court cells are similar to police station cells – devoid of anything whatsoever; even more so in fact. Not even an arrow on the ceiling here. If you've ever been arrested and spent some time in a police station cell, wondering what that arrow was, it was (and presumably still is) pointing to Mecca.

Now, court security in my experience are a cordial bunch, and all too happy to do more for you than you deserve. It can be a hell of a long wait in there each time, for your solicitor, then the summon to the dock, and then back for the verdict. And finally, if you're on the end of bad news, the wait again for the bus. They are therefore happy to take requests for tea, coffee and water, as many times as you like – but I'd advise you to consider this carefully, especially if you're going as far as Wales. A bit like in prison, it's a pallid teabag (not sure of the brand but it certainly ain't PG or Twinings, which we can all agree are in the pantheon). When the door opened, I was expecting a cup of tea, but instead what I got was another person awaiting sentence, as apparently the court was at full capacity. Suddenly the two of us were sharing space for one, neither in the best of spirits and unsure about this new development, although at least with someone to chat to now. Let's call him Nathan.

Nathan was Bristolian, with a West-Country twang thicker than a malt loaf. He was super-slim, about my age and height and, due to some dental issues, boasting a hill-billy grin to match the accent. He was a fairly seasoned convict and knew he was going down, but not yet where or for how long. It didn't take too much conversation to realise he had the capacity to be quite an unsavoury individual. He was the first to be summoned, and then again, returning in the most foul of moods having been given substantially longer than he had anticipated. It was hardly my fault, and of course he knew that, but it wasn't going to stop him being a live-wire towards me now. Not knowing the man, and what he could be capable of, I don't mind saying I was on edge now, too. There was about an hour of this before it was my turn to visit the dock. I knew exactly what was to happen to me – my remand was to be resumed for a period of 4 days, until my trial. This was confirmed, and we were banged up over lunchtime whilst transport was arranged.

Lunch was a microwaved box containing an all-day breakfast. The name was especially apt, as it could well take one all day to get through the cack that it was. I accepted it and set to work, but Nathan was somewhat less recipient, ringing the bell for security and declaring *"Oy wouldn't feed moy dog this shoyte"*, before launching it forcefully to the wall facing us. Can I just ask:

Have you ever had to dodge a monsoon of baked beans?

It unfurled in slow motion, and looking back at 2019, definitely one of the funnier moments in retrospect. At the time though I was in a state of total shock – slightly scared, and very juicy (first time as a combo). To make matters worse, security opened the latch to take a look inside, and just shut it again. That wasn't funny at the time either. I tried to laugh it off with Nathan, still nervous, and looked to steer the conversation back into safer ground, football. I had ascertained in earlier discussion that he was a Manchester United fan (as I said, he was an unsavoury individual). Cheap joke – I don't mean it.

Thankfully, the two security guys that opened and shut the window had actually gone off to organise another holding place for him, and were back before long to take him away, with a cleaner in tow. I was passed toilet paper to mop the bean juice from my brow, and apologised to profusely. I was just glad to see the back of Nathan.

It wasn't too long later I was informed the bus was ready, and frogmarched aboard. The journey was a quiet and solemn one, and this arrival was the occasion when we had been told there was an incident and had to wait for what felt like well over an hour. Once I did get through reception I was dumped into another paddock with around 12 others, waiting for an induction cell to be allocated. I didn't really scan the room as I was feeling particularly anxious this time, and better to avoid eye contact. There was, however, a conversation going on in the corner which had my interest, and most others'. It was concerning the different blocks and wings there; which were the best and most quiet, and which were the ones to avoid like the plague. Not that anyone had a say in the matter. I had been here recently for two weeks, and so I knew what to expect from Blocks 1 and 3 (apparently two of the more chilled ones), and they were anything but chilled. It was clear from this discussion that Block 6B was the bearer of the most horror stories. Stabbings aplenty, drugs flying around, both of which the screws were aware of, but too scared to do anything about. The tales went on and on. Thankfully, Block 3 was the induction wing, and 6 was reserved for either 'Enhanced' inmates in 6A (if you're in for over 12 weeks and keep your head down you can qualify for 'Enhanced', which allows higher privileges), or the fabled 6B, which is where the nasties are sent when they have shown themselves to be nasties.

Every 5 minutes or so, a screw would come in and call two of us out by surname to go to our respective digs, and two more inmates would move up the reception conveyor belt to wait with us. It was the single best piece of organisation I saw in that place.

Eventually… *"HUGHES! WINDSOR!"*

I had been so transfixed on the floor in front of me and the conversation to the right, that I hadn't noticed who was sat two seats left of me, nearest the door. Nathan. And as he stood up with me, I learned his full name, Nathan Windsor. *Shit.*

It hadn't occurred to me that we would be boarding the same bus from court, to the same destination, to complete reception at roughly the same time. With our bags over our shoulders we followed the screw down the corridors, past Blocks 1 and 2, towards 3. Nathan had calmed considerably by this stage, and I started to think *"OK I can get through this – at least we have football in common and that's a vast enough well of discussion on it's own".* Things were about to change, though, when we carried on walking past the entrance to Block 3. *"Where are we going guv?"* Nathan asked. *"We're at capacity lads so you'll be on another wing for a little while".*

Yeah… you guessed it.

In 5 minutes, I had gone from mild trepidation to out-and-out unbridled fear. So had Nathan. This was going to be a trying few days. They really must had been at capacity to resort putting us there – especially me, as I was still on remand at this stage, which elevates you a slim privilege above the others. Eventually we got to Block 6, got inside, and as it was around 8pm at this point everyone was banged up and things were eerily quiet. I would have preferred the usual noises to this. I didn't like it at all. If you remember *The Lion King*, you'll remember The Elephant Graveyard. Nathan and I knew that the hyenas were there; we just couldn't see or hear them. It felt like they knew we were here, too; little lost cubs in a place we shouldn't be.

The block comprised of three 'spurs' – with A being the immediate on the left, then B up ahead, and an unused third to the right, which looked under renovation. Cruelly we could see down into the depths of the enhanced 6A wing, with brand new pool and ping pong tables at the bottom. It was not unlike walking through Business Class to Economy, and then further. I *could see* a pool table at the bottom of 6B as I looked down, but it appeared as though they had been playing rugby on it instead.

Nathan was getting twitchier as they took us to our pad, which I took to be nerves from where we are. I soon learnt what the problem was. But first, the cell.

JESUS. I can only assume this had become immediately available, as it was completely trashed from top to bottom. And I mean trashed. There were paper and magazine cuttings ripped from the wall and strewn across the floor, which was also soaking wet. I think it was just water (my senses were also trashed at the time), and thankfully the screws recognised even this was below the hospitable line, and cleared the debris and gave it a basic mop. Both mattresses had been ripped to shreds too, and we had no choice but to flip them over and make do for the duration of our stay. There were remnants of the magazine cuttings on the wall, along with a smorgasbord of scribbles and stains. It was as if Regan from *The Exorcist* had been in there. (When it comes to room-mates, she really did draw the short one didn't she.)

As we unpacked our bags, two further problems became clear. No kettle, no TV... jubbly. And this was about to become far greater an issue than I could have ever imagined. Nathan was straight on to the bell – I assumed about the TV situation, and although it was partly for that, he had a much more urgent matter to deal with. *"You said you'd get me a nurse – WHERE ARE MY FUCKING MEDS – I want a doctor NOW."* I then discovered that he was a heroin addict, and in pretty desperate need of methadone. Now I don't know how much you know about heroin addiction, but it is no laughing matter. Although I had my share of experimentation in my twenties, I had never gone anywhere near crack and especially not heroin. Insufflates were more my thing. I knew enough about opiates to know that the dependence and repercussions can be more or less immediate and can last your lifetime (although alcohol withdrawal is the only one that can actually kill you). You may be reading this as someone without an addictive personality, someone who can abstain for months – even years, have a bump or two on a special occasion and be done with it again, but this stuff is a different kettle. Please, stay away. Any junkie will tell you that. This was the first time though that I had witnessed what it can do first hand.

As with alcohol, heroin's withdrawal symptoms are physical, and deeply unpleasant. They include, in no particular order, mood swings, hot and cold sweats, fidgeting and restlessness, vomiting, itchiness and crawling under the skin, headaches, psychosis, and more vomiting. The term for all of this is 'rattling', and due to the severity of the symptoms, the medical team have a duty to act promptly. I believe it's commonplace to have to wait the first night until your script is sorted, but it became increasingly clear that Nathan was in a bad way and wasn't going to take this for an answer.

Another major withdrawal symptom is insomnia, so you can see why the lack of television was going to be a problem here. Immediately his only options were to stare at the walls or climb up them. Although 90% of this was self-inflicted and I struggled for sympathy, I feigned compassion and paid lip service to keep him from turning on me. Luckily, I did have a book I'd brought in with me: The excellent *Calm the F*ck Down* by Sarah Knight – a recent present from Amy. Irony on many levels.

I had taken the top bunk and was huddled against the wall, trying to read in the hope that he may at least slightly settle down, or at least keep his attention off me. It was the only course of action I had to keep myself calm and, hopefully, it would work with him, too.

Well, the plan backfired, as Nathan took issue with the fact that I was occupied with something and he wasn't. Apparently, it was only fair we suffered this together. Although I was drained and in need of sleep, I was very much fraught with nerves about what could happen any minute and still very much aware of the wing we were on and what we could be in for the following day. Even more reason to try and sleep. But such was the need for methadone that Nathan had now disregarded this and started banging on the walls… certainly not my idea of introducing ourselves to the neighbours.

I was now legitimately terrified and for the first time I had no choice but to assert myself with him, saying that if he didn't cool down or at least keep away from the walls, we were probably going to have the shit kicked out of us in the morning. He did see reason for a few minutes, but then picked up where he left off. Maybe I should add amnesia to the symptom list. In all seriousness though, this *was* serious. He was getting worse by the second, and had taken to ringing the bell for assistance – forgetting that minutes earlier he had rung the same bell, spoken to the same person, and received next to no assistance.

Let me pose you another question. If you ask a waiter to bring you the bill, how long would you leave it before asking again, 5/10 minutes? I'd say that's about par. Now, if you were asking for something that was certain to be actioned the next working day, like updating certain utility details, or cashing a cheque, or getting a refund on those bowling shoes you drunkenly bought your nan for a laugh, again wouldn't you wait for it to take longer than they had told you it would before politely chasing it up?

The only answer Nathan was getting was *"I've told you, there won't be anything until tomorrow, but I'll see what else I can do"*. Most of us would leave it there, trust them to do their job, and hope to hear something. All Nathan was doing was piss another person off. This bell was to be used for emergencies only, not things like asking for a deodorant or the same question for the 5th time that hour. He couldn't understand the futility and potential damage, and persisted for at least another two hours. It's one thing being unpopular with the inmates, but another to have the staff turn on you and make getting anything done even more complicated. And making veiled threats wasn't going to help. Remember The Boy Who Cried Wolf – a cautionary tale passed down the aeons. (Mind you, as Ricky Gervais once pointed out, the moral of that story wasn't *"Never tell a lie"*… it's *"Don't tell the same lie twice…"*). **Touché.**

This is relevant though, as Nathan had resorted to making continued claims that he would harm himself – or me – if this was not swiftly resolved. Eventually, I'd say around 1am, a doctor did appear, but refused to enter. All he did was repeat what the warden had said, that there would be nothing at this time of night – as per protocol – and that he would have to be processed just like everybody else. This did nothing to stop his threats, which I still just about took to be veiled. This doctor didn't suffer fools gladly, and with more or less an exclusive clientele of fools, he had seen and heard this too often before. He effectively said, *"Go on then, we still won't do anything until tomorrow"*. Hearing this got my heart rate back up (remember I was waiting on my medication too, which was for anxiety). This comment silenced Nathan, and the doctor left. Ships in the night. (Yes I've used that phrase before and probably will again, as I love it. Ever since *Extras*).

I knew the doctor meant it though. On my first visit, in Block 1, I had seen a poor fellow sat waiting to be transferred to another wing, with deep slashes all the way up both arms, which he was picking at obsessively. In here, you simply can't show a weakness like that and not be at mercy to the hyenas. He was being mocked heavily by a pack across the hall and he was very much aware of it too. I have never seen someone look so totally broken, inside and out, and it broke me to see it. I wanted to go over and try in some way to console him, but I didn't know how it would be received, by him and also by them, rendering me as a sympathiser. I had to look after myself first and foremost.

Back to Nathan. For the first time, he actually appeared to have listened. Gone was the rage, and now a vacant dejection, knowing the night he had in store. He got into bed, and though I could hear him tossing and turning incessantly, it was such an upgrade that it didn't bother me, and I must have drifted off around 02:00.

I don't know what time it was when I woke, and I forget whether it was light or dark outside, but I remember the rest like it was last night. Nathan was being violently sick. Believe me, it was chaos.

We've all been there over something, with that "*Urrrrrrrrrrrrrrrrrr*" when it's finally at an end. But none of these noises were human. He was burping as he did it too, the sounds blending together in the most vile way imaginable. If you're gagging reading this, good – I've gone just some way to conveying how bad it was. I'll never hear a burp again and not be whisked right back there. He's ruined *Rick and Morty* and *Professor Burp's Bubbleworks* for me now. That should go on his criminal record.

It was about to get worse, too, as in the spontaneity of the moment he had chosen his receptacle poorly. It went in, on, and all around the basin, which was literally right next to the toilet. Regan would have been proud. I know the initial stage of a chunder is one of desperation, but there's no excuse not to crane your head slightly to the left for the remainder of the job... no excuse. What little sympathy I still had was now completely gone, and I threw my head under the pillow without trying to alert him that I was awake, praying that he would have dealt with it to the best of his abilities by the time I needed to use it. The exact same thing happened an hour or so later, but believe it or not once was enough to be sufficiently desensitized and I was more or less straight back to sleep.

Shattered. We all know how it feels to be woken up after an hour or two of sleep (especially when the full eight or so are desperately needed), and not even this situation was enough to keep me conscious for long.

Next thing I knew it was morning, with Nathan perched on the end of the bed below, and a deep, deep smell of vomit. This had already penetrated all of my clothes on the shelf, which couldn't be replaced for 5 days (when laundry swap happens). He had already ploughed through his 3 vape oils in the night and was already asking for some of mine. We each had our breakfast pack (ornamental teabags of course), but I could at least have a bowl of cornflakes. All I really wanted though was a cup of water. I turned to look at the sink, which he had completely blocked. It was full of it, virtually to the top but not overflowing. His dinner must not have touched the sides on the way down, or on the way back up, as there were huge pieces chilling in there. I don't know how I didn't add to it to be honest. I'm on the verge right now just thinking about it. It certainly took every bit of my mental strength to ignore it at the time, particularly with no TV, and to think about exactly what we were going to do next. Yes, it would have to be *we*. Well, *me*.

To make matters worse (I know I keep saying that), it was a Sunday, which meant there would be no induction, and our door could be unlocked any minute, allowing anyone to drop by and confront us about the previous night's activities. And as soon as I was thinking this, the door did indeed swing open and we were exposed to the entire wing. I remember the fear, but adrenaline was carrying me too, and rather than hide away in our little hellhole, I stepped out for air and leaned on the balcony to take a visual sweep of the surroundings, or to coin a phrase from *It's Always Sunny in Philadelphia*, an "ocular patdown". It was still eerily quiet, and either the majority of 6B were enjoying their Sunday lie-in, or cowering. There were a few people out and about, but no one really took any notice of me, and really no one looked any different to any other block I had been in here. This was reassuring, but not enough to drop my guard just yet.

I decided my first port of call would be to drop into the office, apologise from the heart of my bottom about Nathan's disturbances, and to neutralize what I could of the situation. I like to think I have a way of conducting myself with people on a professional footing. Although I have a nervous disposition, in an interview situation I am cool as a cucumber. Always have been. I'm one of the few people who actually looks forward to them, I think. It didn't occur to me though that this would be a different set of staff to the night before, and Nathan would be but a name in the log book. I asked about the sink and when we were likely to receive our medication. Firstly, I was informed the meds would be available for both of us in the afternoon, which was a relief. I was then told the sink would get looked at some point, but frankly the lack of sincerity worried me. I thanked them anyway and returned to the pad. Nathan was nowhere to be found, and so I needed to get it unlocked. As soon as I did, the stench thwacked me again. I knew I would have to take care of this here and now.

At this juncture, I would like you to visit your kitchen, open the cupboard under the sink, and thank your marigolds (individually), as well as your plunger, Dettol wipes, and anything else I didn't have access to. Go on.

Nathan was a convicted shoplifter, but there was only one way I was willing to do this; play him at his own game. I opened his bag, and rifled through it until I found his plastic cup. I held my breath and stomach, opened the toilet seat lid, and started scooping and transferring. Scoop and repeat. Scoop, and repeat (*sing it with me now!*). Thank goodness the toilet was right next to the basin, and so this process didn't take too long, with an occasional retirement to the wing for air. Heaven only knows what I must have looked like, but I was beyond caring – I just wanted to get through it and get this sorted. This was also a good opportunity to switch clothes with him, as he had kept all his inside the bag, odour-free. I'm a man who tends to unpack on the first night.

Although the basin was now clear with the plughole visible again, this was barely a modest triumph, as the moment I ran water it just refilled immediately. Nathan's plastic knife wouldn't go down far enough to get any purchase, and so this is how it would have to remain for now. In fact, this is the way it remained for the entire stay, as no one ever came to fix it. The only solution was to use it minimally, and scoop what was left each time. At least it did breathe some character into that dreadful blue cup. He wouldn't thank me for it. Any of it.

As time went by and I ingratiated slightly with the others on the wing, I came to realise that they were all OK enough, though I still held on to a profound sense of dread at all times. Nothing worse than Amy's though. Perhaps, I thought, there had been a recent high turnover of inmates and most of the monsters had been replaced with exemplars like myself, who just wanted to get their head down and serve their time. Truth be told, the only real problems continued to come from inside the cell.

Nathan had wasted no time in getting to know people, and during association times it was not uncommon to have 3 or 4 people in the pad, cracking wise. This didn't bother me all that much, as it meant I could just sit on my bed up top and read without much disturbance. They could do their thing, and I could do mine. I never really paid attention to what was being said, but one thing did eventually occur to me. Every time I glanced over at Nathan, his vape was surgically attached to his mouth. When he had supposedly run out of caps. Presumably he had been wheeling and/or dealing out on the wing; either that or ticking them (borrowing), which usually means repaying with 100% interest. Either way, that was his problem.

That night, I took my own vape to my mouth and tasted burning plastic (even better than it sounds). My first cap was finished and needed replacing. I went under my duvet, reached into a rogue sock where I was keeping them among other items, and pulled out the box. One left. One of three. I didn't need a deerstalker and pipe for this – he had taken one. I don't know how he did it, but he had done it. I had been about as vigilant as one could be; always guarding them on my bed, and always taking them with me or locking the door when we were both away. And at night, when asleep, the sock had stayed pretty much exactly where it was, cosy with me between the sheets. But this is the only way he could have done it …waiting until I was asleep, creeping up the steps (like a squirrel), and rummaging around quite literally under my face until he found them. I was astonished, and also mildly impressed by the sheer audacity and execution of it. He was a known thief, but I thought I had done enough. The last thing on Earth I was going to do though was confront him about it. It was better in my mind to cut my losses, not fall out with him – as his moods were still unpredictable even with the methadone – and learn from it. Plus, another day was almost over.

By the time I did run out of oil a day or so later, he was still puffing around the clock and I couldn't understand how. One thing was clear though, he hadn't got it from me this time. I only had the one, which never left my vape, which never left me. I had even taken to keeping the vape inside my boxers when I slept, and I like to think even he would draw the line. Plus you don't want to disturb the beast that lives in there.

Back to reality. While queuing for lunch the next day after induction, something else caught the corner of my eye. The wing had many people on remand like myself, and so there was a smattering of colour in and around the greys. One person, who I had seen before, was now wearing a burgundy shirt with a 'Tokyo Laundry' logo on it. It was a TK Maxx special. It was also my shirt.

As I had been in police custody for a couple of days, then court, then here for a further day without being able to shower, I had changed shirts at the first opportunity, not only to feel fresher but also not to advertise it to anyone. Only one person had seen me wearing it, coincidentally the only one with access to it. It was an insult to the shirt, too, which was way too small for this guy. It was tight enough on me, but he was an absolute whale. Even more reason to not say anything. I certainly wasn't going to confront Nathan whilst we were eating, with baked beans being fresh in the memory (and still fresh on the shirt for that matter). I had stored it in my bag thinking he wouldn't possibly go there as it was so obvious, but it transpires he couldn't care less. And he had sold it presumably for oils. Anything and everything that I had, that he could have possibly cashed in on, he had done so in the space of 48 hours.

The thing is, yes I may have found myself in trouble a lot in the last year, but I have always been somewhat of a pussycat myself and I didn't have the courage to raise the issue. I like to think I had sense instead. He presumably knew that I would find out sooner or later, and that I wouldn't challenge. It's fair to say that everyone I met during my time in jail had a honed ability of judging a character. If you associate yourself enough with people who can hurt you, then you will eventually develop the techniques to see it coming and to circumvent it. As I overheard a wise sage utter once: *"Trust a snake, but never a scouser... a snake will hiss or rattle so at least you know it's gonna strike."* (Yes this was also in jail, not the queue at Sainsbury's).

I suppose seasoned criminals will know to recognise the traits, or indeed lack of, and perhaps this is how Nathan realised that I didn't pose any kind of threat, or indeed any opposition whatsoever to being robbed in broad daylight. As I said I am not the confrontational type and I just wanted some sort of harmony. Also, I must say, without interference from any lawyer or editor, that my experience of the Liverpudlian community is nothing but a great one.

Things settled after this, as I had run out of collateral, and we completed our induction the day before I was due in court for my trial, knowing there was a reasonable chance I wouldn't be returning. Two other things of note happened on this day, with my luck set to pleasantly change.

First of all, the door was unlocked by a screw that we had both got relatively chummy with, as he had been the only member of staff who genuinely seemed to be endeavouring to get us a TV. I had long since finished my book and Nathan still had no entertainment of his own, especially now theft had gone out of the window. Remember we were locked up together in close proximity for around 18 hours of the 24, so the TV was still as much an issue at it was on the first night. You can imagine the elation then, as a working TV – oh, purveyor of sweet delights – was delivered, plugged in, and switched on. It was a magical moment. It didn't even matter what was on, it was just a relief to have the attention on it.

Then, no sooner had we got an episode or two of The Simpsons under our belts, the door opened again. *"Windsor, get your stuff; you're moving. 5 minutes."* They had a space for him on the detox wing, and he needed barely 60 seconds to collect his belongings and off he went, with barely a goodbye and *"Thanks for everything"*. Really I should have been on the detox wing, too, for alcohol, but I had bluffed my way through the medical so I could stay on a 'normal' one. That panned out.

Still, it almost all felt worth it at this point. What a turnaround. I had expected neither of these developments, and I now found myself in sole ownership of the cell, knowing there would be no replacement organised at this time of day. I had the place to myself for the night, with a TV, and would be off in the morning hopefully to never return.

With this newfound freedom, I decided to watch TV in bursts, pausing to re-read the supporting paperwork for my trial in the morning, for the incident at Amy's. I had pleaded not guilty to the most serious of all the charges; I knew that I wasn't guilty, but I did have several things that could potentially go against me, and my solicitor had it at 50/50. It had therefore been playing my mind like a banjo, and every time I successfully banished the thought of it, it was at best 10 minutes before it wormed its way back in. I was hoping the 9pm offering on Film 4 would help me out, and it turned out to be *X-Men: Apocalypse*. For fuck's sake.

Regardless, this was the first time I slept like a log, and I was woken abruptly at around 06:00 with twenty or so minutes to breakfast and have my things ready. Although I was off, I was obviously nervous not knowing whether I would be coming straight back, and if so, for how long. The process took what felt like an eternity, walking back to reception, waiting in line to go through search, then inventory, then front desk for paperwork etc. As you'd expect, a fair chunk of the initial process in reverse. *"I do hope you enjoyed your stay; have a mint imperial for the road. Don't forget us on TripAdvisor!"*

Back to the bus, and a wait for others to join, and off we went. I had my paperwork clutched for the ride, and was clear in my head on the points I needed to make etc. I knew there would be two police officers called from that fateful morning at Amy's, ready to talk up the danger they thought they had been in. It wasn't too long at all before we arrived back at the magistrates' court. The staff remembered me. It had only been 4 days, of course. Their faces when I told them who I had been paired with again…

I accepted another all-day breakfast (I preferred this for energy than coffee – I didn't want to be wired. You would think cocaine abuse would immunise you to caffeine, but it doesn't work like that). Before long, my solicitor arrived and was ready to see me, and had some unexpected news. The charge for which I had pleaded not guilty had been downgraded in agreement with the prosecution. This, amazingly, meant there was no longer a trial – provided that I pleaded guilty to the new charge, which I was all too ready to do as it was now a fair conviction. *'Possession of an item with intent to cause criminal damage'* I believe it was. I pleaded guilty straight away, however, they could not pass sentence yet as they didn't have a senior probation officer available. This presented the magistrates with two options. The first was to 'return to sender', and I would have to wait up to three further weeks in jail while they prepared a senior assessment for a potential community order. Option two was to grant bail again, on the strict condition that I checked into rehab with a tag fitted for good measure.

So, let's talk briefly about tags. There are currently two types in the UK: a curfew tag and an exclusion tag. If you're familiar with one of these, then it's likely the curfew one. I had been bailed with it a few weeks earlier and it's the classic type that restricts you to your own home, between the usual hours of 19:00 and 07:00. Again, this is handled by an external private firm, who will visit you on the day and install a box in your bedroom or wherever you are going to spend most of your time. The box is akin to a Sky or BT one with a telephone attached. Your curfew tag is calibrated and paired with the box and you are asked to walk around the perimeter of every room in your home to establish the boundaries. They watch you like a hawk as you do it, and you no doubt look a berk as you thrust your leg into each corner of the room like a drunken rendition of the Hokey Cokey. If you're a smoker, then you'll have to request that the court grants you a mini extension to an outside patio space, where you can do your business. The tag itself is quite a bulky piece of gear with an infrared sensor that detects your proximity to the box at all times. You can fit the tag inside your socks, and I suppose it looks like a broken ankle would, except the conventional walking is a giveaway.

My previous experience of this tag was one of dismay, as it registered an apparent tampering for no reason at all, which triggered the phone ringing every 5 minutes. And when you try and contact them about it, good luck kid. Likewise, if like me they ring you for no good reason, that still doesn't mean you'll get an organism on the other end… ohohohhhh no. You'll be cast into a queue, for which I can only assume there is one poor shmuck manning the calls. No issues with them. Eventually, someone came out to visit and my defective tag was replaced.

The exclusion tag on the other hand, is the new generation, with a GPS chip. These ones know *exactly* where you are and are only enforced when you have a specific area you are not supposed to travel to. In future they may well be rolled out to all as, ultimately, they fulfil the same purpose. You would think this next generation of tag might be a bit smaller, following suit with iPhones and Fitbits and the like. Not only are they bigger, but they come in a most unnatural shape that makes them almost impossible to adjust to. I know you're thinking *"Tough luck, you're in this predicament and still wouldn't you take this over your incarceration?"*. Well the answer is yes, but that doesn't stop them being a bastard.

Further to the fact they are larger, they are also rechargeable, which presents two new options – plug it into a socket in the wall for two hours every single day, or use the charge pack. Option one, as above, is to schedule two hours of your evening for sitting with your leg suspended near a socket. If you want to recreate Hitchcock's *Rear Window* and your housing appliances are situated sufficiently, then this could be the option for you. The second choice is to use the chargeable battery pack, which was mine. Now as I mentioned, storing a curfew tag in your socks is incognito enough. But this one is going to be different. If the curfew tag gave the impression of a broken ankle, the exclusion tag with the charger attached gives the impression of a bona fide mutant. It will be noticed. I took to using it overnight, but trust me, your sub-conscience will detect this augmentation and do everything in its power to shift it – and will often succeed. This then means waking up to a red flashing light and the realisation that you are going to continue to be wearing that thing well into your day as well.

*

Anyway, rehab. I had actually visited one a week or so earlier with my father while I was on bail. This was entirely voluntary. It's safe to say I had been at my most ill over this period: I was a husk after the relationship with Amy, and my first prison ordeal had gobbled what was left. There was enough of me though to realise that I would be dead within a month if I settled back into where I was before. Rehab was quite possibly the only answer, and I am very lucky that I had a father who hadn't quite given up on me and was willing to instigate and finance this. A morning phone assessment was conducted (I was drunk for this but apparently conducted myself succinctly and admirably, which says a lot really), and a visit was booked for the following day with the possibility of checking in and staying on immediately.

My father came home that next morning, and despite the horror state of the house, was pleased to at least find me ready to set off. I won't give you the name or location, but it was an idyllic setting in the country and deliberately hard to find. At this stage it wasn't confirmed that I would be going, but I was given a tour of the open parts of the premises, and a lengthy medical and questionnaire. At the end I was recommended a month's stay, involving a detox process and intensive therapy, which were equally important facets of what they did. Of course I was apprehensive, but I knew I was almost at rock-bottom and I would accept any help to turn myself around.

I didn't have any of my belongings with me, and so I couldn't immediately check in, but it was left that I would go back and collect clothes etc. and return in the coming days. On the way out, I asked whether it would be possible to get confirmation of their recommendation in writing, which was emailed over to my father and myself. This simple request, it transpires, was more important than I could have ever imagined.

We stopped for lunch on the way home, and it was at this point I could feel alcohol withdrawal kicking in for the first time in my life. I had never before drank to the extent that it had become a physical dependency and I'd had no idea that I was physically dependent until now, as I just hadn't stopped drinking over the past week. I was shaking most of the way home and couldn't escape the sense that something else was wrong. Eventually we got back to the village, and immediately we saw a police van parked to the right on the pavement. My mind ran wild. *"They must be waiting for us to get back; they've clocked Dad's number plate and now they're going to follow us to the house".* I was correct.

We parked up, and as I got out to open the front door, I pirouetted to see said van heading towards us – with a dog unit, would you believe, in a second car behind. They drove past initially, but I made eye contact with the driver and I saw the look of recognition that I matched their description, and 10 seconds later I was being told I was under arrest.

Why? Take a punt. Three or four days ago, mid-binge, was when I'd emailed Amy again. It was still only a few weeks after the relationship had come to an end, and I really hadn't got any closer to moving on. I don't recall what I had said to be honest, and I'm not going through my sent items for the sake of this. Knowing my luck, a finger would slip and re-send it. I had a glimmer of recognition of having done this and when it was confirmed, my heart virtually stopped. Each previous time when I had been arrested, I accepted why and got on with it. This time though, with the physical state I was in, I went into full-blown panic attack and thankfully they gave me a good twenty minutes to calm myself down before they took me away.

It was mid-June by the point this happened, and my trial was less than a week away, so I knew it would only be a short stay in prison. But you know what that stay was like, as that stay was Chapter 7: Windsor.

Thankfully, the magistrates went with option two:

8

Rehab

So you know all about my relationship with Amy and you will come to learn of the relationships that followed, but before we get there – and before I check back into rehab for you – I should probably explain my relationship with drugs.

First of all, and I might be stating the obvious, they're everywhere. You might not see them, but you would be amazed how many exist right under your very nose. Of course there are the standard pharmaceuticals, which we probably all use when necessary. No issues with paracetamol and company; I'll continue with these, as well as fast food now and then. I enjoy a Meatball Marinara or a Boneless Banquet as much as the next, but I am acutely aware that I am taking drugs whenever I chomp into one of them. It's not just fast food; instant/ready meals are often pumped full of E-numbers and chemicals, and some of these are most certainly addictive too. In moderation, they aren't particularly harmful though. And that's the key word: moderation. I am not advocating anything, but simply stating that, in moderation, the vast majority of drugs, in particular illegal ones, are not nearly as harmful as some would have you believe. A few of them even have amazing medicinal potential.

Moderation comes more easily to some than it does others. That's why addicts exist and that's why certain eating disorders etc. also exist. I really hope I don't sound like I'm lecturing here; I just think it's vital to grasp all of this in order to have a more rational and reasoned understanding of drugs of all kinds, and to see their true place. I have a curious blend of addictive personality and both sense and moderation in other cases. I can't tell you why and how that works, but it's my own experience over some 15 years now.

By the time I was exposed to harder drugs, I was already interested in the culture, to some degree. Again, I doubt I'm alone here. I grew up with movies like *Human Traffic, South West 9*, and *Fear and Loathing in Las Vegas*, and I wager a healthy chunk of viewers during one of these thought *"Christ that looks fun"*. If only I'd watched *Blow* instead. Again, I am not excusing anything by telling you any of this, I'm simply offering an insight into what perked my interest. GCSE chemistry surprisingly did not include a term on narcotics. Also, to go back before I was born, I'm sure one or two watched a film like *Withnail and I* or even *Apocalypse Now* and went on to dip their toes in the water, with some correlation.

Originally here, I listed what I had tried down the years and gave them a fair hearing as I did, with a prosecution, a defence, and ultimately a verdict. I have since removed this for the sake of space, and also not to detract too much from the narrative at hand. Most of them just don't matter. I have tried most things at some point in my life, and for the most part, only once or twice. I had my fun and left it there – and it's been years and years since I've touched them. My two personal favourites were psilocybin (mushrooms), and ketamine. Both very different psychedelics and hallucinogens, and I suppose one good one bad, all things considered. The former has the power to remove oneself from one's ego and to truly better oneself in life, the other has the power to remove oneself from everything. Having said that I believe ketamine in very small doses is being studied for depression treatment. Anyway – it was of course a different two that played a part in recent times… two of the absolute worst. And though cocaine had most definitely been an issue for me, it never took place without the alcohol.

How often do you hear the term *"drink and drugs"*, or *"drugs and alcohol"*? I can understand how it's become commonplace, but it makes about as much sense as a lettuce leaf in a cheesecake. I have long enjoyed a quiet social pint and left it there, but my personal problem was that when emotional issues were proving overbearing, I used alcohol as a crutch. That's when there was a very different and distinctive pattern of behaviour. I was drinking to change my mood and I was doing it at pace. This in turn informed the coke cravings. And, as we know with the Amy situation, for me at least, it can become quite the vicious circle. You see, my problem with drink was never 'knowing when to stop', it was **knowing when not to start**. This is why the particular rehab I had visited looked to be so pivotal: it focused not just on the detox process, but on psychological and emotional therapy which would go after the catalyst rather than the by-product. And after the experience I'd just had with Windsor, I think I needed therapy more than ever.

So, as we know, bail was granted so that I could stay for a month. And this may not have happened had my solicitor not been able to provide the letter that I had requested back when I visited a week or so ago. Thank goodness that despite me being at my lowest ebb, there was still enough brain kicking around in there.

The court agreed bail with a few caveats, including having an exclusion tag fitted. This would remain on after I had finished rehab, as there were an additional two weeks until my sentencing, whereby I would have a chance to demonstrate my worthiness to serve the punishment in the community. That wasn't the reason for the extension, but rather it being the first available court date. The first of the caveats was as important as any other: I had to go straight home from court, collect my essential items, and check in by the end of the day. This wasn't guaranteed, as it was mid-afternoon by this point, and this sort of late notice wasn't the typical way of doing things. Thankfully, they still had a place, and after my solicitor left a voicemail and we played the waiting game in the courtroom, the green light came back.

Because of how rushed this all was, and the conversation during the ride, I didn't have much opportunity to take reflection on how mad this all was. I had woken up in the notorious Block 6B of one of the most notorious jails in the country, and was to be going back to sleep in one of the most tranquil retreats in the country, that actually wasn't all that far away. And I had forgotten the sheer extent of the contrast until we pulled up into the gorgeous manor drive, and I saw the same faces that I had seen last week. My face would have looked rather different this time I think. Although by now I'd had a few days off the booze, this had been quite dangerous in terms of self-detoxing and, though I had gotten through the worst of it, I was taken immediately upstairs to see the GP, who would advise on a personal detox programme. I was given diazepam, initially four times a day which would taper down to three a day, two a day, then one, over the course of about two weeks. The diazepam was largely to help with the shakes and to relax the body so that the mind could in turn start to relax as well. Diazepam falls into the 'Benzo' category and is a controlled and Class-C drug itself. I can understand why it has its place, and how it could be addictive like morphine. I would also be given vitamin tablets twice a day, and thymine, which was to help my brain cells sort themselves out. I hadn't been kind to them over the years, but God bless those little buggers, they haven't held a grudge. These days we're inseparable chums.

After the consultation, and a diazepam under my belt, I was starting to come to terms with the new world I was in, and it particularly hit home when I was shown to my room, and could start unpacking my items. This might sound pathetic, but frankly I could have wept at any of the following:

- A room to myself
- A carpet
- The ability to lock the door

- A proper mattress and bedding
- The ability to open the window
- The view outside
- The ability to go outside
- My own clothes
- A private shower
- Actual shower gel
- A private toilet
- Actual toilet paper

And last, but certainly not least,

- Peace and quiet.

If you asked me to sum up jail in one word, I suppose it would be "*loud*". During social times, it's a mass of testosterone harking back to school days, whether you want it or not. People jostling for status, seemingly getting a kick from being noticed. You cannot simply shut yourself off from it by closing the door. Then, when you're locked up, even throughout the night, there is the incessant banging on doors, and shouting from one pad to another across the wing (sometimes even across the courtyard to another wing). Trust me, there isn't a moment's respite.

You would be surprised just how much that takes adjusting to and adjusting back from. I knew there were other male clients lodging with me, but there were no sign of them at present, and this was the first time in what felt like an eternity that I'd had a second to myself. I would go on to meet the guys an hour or so later when I was welcomed over to the large separate communal lounge for an evening meal. I could have shed another tear:

- Food

A large steak and mushroom pie, with swede and potato mash, leeks and broccoli. Heaven on Earth. Although there was an on-site chef, I was mistaken in thinking I had met him when I first saw the man who was serving this up. I soon realised it was actually another client, who had cooked it himself rather beautifully. Here I felt my first reinforcement that by being in this predicament and by being here, I was not a lesser human being. This was a lovely gentleman, warm in spirit and with a lilting Yorkshire accent, who had gone through difficult times just like me. He was in his element putting this meal together and serving not just for himself and myself, but for the other two male clients, who were in the adjacent lounge watching a movie.

Rather than being *"the new guy who's just interrupted our film, and curtailed my dinner portion"*, I was welcomed again with open arms. These were lovely, *lovely* people. They had all come in at roughly the same time and were two weeks into their journey, with another two before they ventured back into the world. They knew they would get the opportunity to know me better in the coming days rather than peppering me with questions now, so there was a relaxed ambience as we ate and watched the film. Really the only thing they were concerned with was that I got a meal under my belt, was made to feel welcome, and would get a good night's sleep in the knowledge that I was going to be in good hands all-round while I was here. I can't tell you how much this worked, perhaps more so than the diazepam. After a hearty meal and a brief chat, I made my excuses so that I could wrap myself up and get some actual sleep, ready for the chapter ahead.

On my way back, though, I saw the silhouette of someone on a bench under the night lights, cutting somewhat of a forlorn shadow against the wall of the ladies' accommodation next door to ours. She was the only female client there at the time, and it turned out she had checked in merely minutes before I had. Her name was Tracy, and by having moved in an hour apart, we were about to share this journey.

Now I'm all too candid when it comes to discussing my own demons, but when it comes to Tracy and indeed any other client, you'll be unsurprised to read that I will be keeping quiet, out of more than just respect. What I can and will say, though, is that after a two-minute discussion, it was apparent that Tracy and I had things in common and that we would get on. Having only just arrived herself, she was not in a good way and so I did my best to be succinctly friendly and left her in peace.

I had what might just have been the most enjoyable shower in 31 years, and got my head down. There was no TV in the bedroom, and I welcomed this as much as the room welcomed me. It allowed reflection without distraction at the start and end of the day. My phone was still with the prison cashier, and it wouldn't have been permitted here anyway, as this was not just a detox from the obvious, but also from contact with the outside world (save for a visit once a week), and so no internet either. No qualms though, plus I'd already been weaned off that over the past week.

The next thing I knew, it was 08:00 and medication time. This meant a quick walk to 'HQ' where the nurse's office was. I then drifted back to my quarters, and the next thing I knew it was 13:00. I must have needed it. It meant I had missed the first therapy session in the morning, however there was no pressure on me to attend straight away, and it was apparently common to not dive into the first morning. None of us would see Tracy for a few days, except for the occasional cigarette outside the accommodation. Yes, tobacco was still allowed – somehow I don't think their success rate would be quite as high if not.

It was time for meds again and a quick lunch, before I jumped into the early afternoon therapy session. Now, for obvious reasons, I cannot divulge too much about what went on in most of the sessions either, but I can certainly explain to you the structure. Although I was ready for it all, there was one detail that had caused some apprehension, and I daresay it would have done with many. It was pretty much to be entirely group therapy. This meant that I would not just be bearing my soul to a counsellor, but to four other perfect strangers. I didn't know how to feel until I set foot inside, and then quickly realised that I wouldn't have it any other way.

The therapy room was at the back of the large communal quarters, beyond the kitchen and the lounge. It was the perfect size for up to 8 clients to sit in a circle of armchairs, with enough from the windows to let in natural light and a fleeting glimpse of the surrounding fields without being a distraction. There was a stand with a large paper pad and selection of sharpies – as you'd find in any conference room – and behind it a nice feature wall with a faux-bookshelf design. A large clock loomed on the wall behind us in view of the therapist, but beyond this the walls and rest of the room were nicely minimal to keep our heads from wandering. Overall, formal but friendly in perfect balance.

Regarding the sessions, a timetable was given out each fortnight so we would know to some degree the nature of each session in advance. Most of these were led by the therapist with group input and discussion, however I had already noticed during this week's timetable that some had initials against them. Two minutes into the first session and it became clear what this was; the initials were that of one of the other clients, the gentleman master-chef who had welcomed me the previous evening, and that he would be leading the next 90 minutes. Not only this, but he had come prepared with what was essentially homework.

This meant that after a quick hello and introduction at the start, there was no requirement from me to add anything, but rather sit back and soak up who this person was and the journey he was on in life. I immediately realised that group therapy could go either way with some people, but for me it was definitely the way forward. This did not mean I wasn't nervous about my first session, though, and I wouldn't have to wait long to learn what it was, as at the end fresh timetables were handed out, and two days from now I saw the words: **'13:30 to 15:00 – SH: Life Story'.**

This gave another burst of excitement and trepidation. I knew that there would be the inevitable intro to myself with full and frank detail on the issues that had brought me there, but I wasn't sure whether there would be any chance to talk through all the preceding years. What was so principal about this, though, and it may seem obvious, is that it allowed an early chance to reflect lovingly on the better times. I took the new timetable away with a blank pad to start on the notes later that evening. First though it was time for a smoke break and dinner.

I mentioned the on-site chef; I met him this time on the way out as he dropped in to take stock on what we had in the kitchen and to take requests for meals the following week. He would cook for us three nights each week, with the alternate nights being handled between ourselves. This meant a little pre-planning on our part as to who would be cooking on these evenings and what. This again might have been daunting to some, but was something I relished the thought of. I would not cook anything myself that week as the goods had already been ordered in and the rota was planned. I did at least pitch in for the following week, though, ordering the ingredients in for my signature salad.

Although my diet had been predominantly awful over the past couple of months, and I had put on weight both at home and in jail, I had not lost my passion for healthy food. A packaged salad from a supermarket bores the heck out of me, but when I make my own, I like to think I do it well. I at least do it my way. I'll spend half an hour or so on a large batch, mixing two types of cous-cous (normally a sweet Mediterranean and a smoky chargrilled), a whole cucumber, 3 or 4 mixed peppers (you'll be pleased to know I hadn't been put off them for life), sweetcorn, kidney beans, plum tomatoes, some form of tandoori or barbecue chicken, and mixed leaves. The piece de resistance: Nando's Perinaise. I could happily eat this mix every day; it's bursting at the seams with flavour, and

I was genuinely excited about getting back into the habit of it. This batch would comfortably last three or four days, and as I learned in discussion with the chef whilst ordering it, the life could be extended days further by simply washing the beans before adding them, and only introducing the leaves when serving.

Again, a paragraph on salad could seem a little off-piste, but this was representative of my desire even from day one to get back into all elements of good health as quickly as possible, and also to chip in for the group. It took around the same time as cooking a meal, and could accompany the other meals over the course of the week or suffice as a lunch on its own. After requesting the items, and an all-round agreeable chatter, there was roughly an hour's wait for the dinner to be brought over and, rather than making a start on my life story, I thought I'd give my brain a rest and take a walk around the grounds to familiarise myself, in a pleasant summer eve's drizzle.

If serenity didn't exist within these gardens, then I don't know where it does. They were well hidden from view of the driveway and indeed more or less anywhere, but I had been told there was a garden and, as I walked the perimeter of the communal quarters, I suddenly saw a sanctuary of different flora and benches, and what appeared to be a badminton net over in the corner. Another welcome sight. The weather wasn't looking clement enough for this anytime soon, though – it had already been raining heavily on and off for days – and the forecast was even more miserable; there were even concerns for flooding within the grounds. Plus my mind was on work not play. This wasn't a holiday as much like it might have felt like one in contrast to the week before. As we ate, my mind was still on the life story and how best to tackle it. The plan was to finish the meal and set to work, looking to instil some self-discipline right away and to attain the sense of reward of knowing it was done and ready in good time. However, in conversation during dinner, another option was presented for the evening, an interesting and equally important opportunity, if not again fraught with dread.

Now, in terms of alcohol and my relationship with it, I was in two minds when I checked in about whether I ever wanted it back in my life. I knew that the ability to control it could be sustained, as long as I wasn't in a prior wrong frame of mind. Like I said, knowing when not to start. The therapists were reasonably relaxed about this; they had heard it before and were sensibly holding judgement while they got to know what made me tick. For some others in the group, alcohol was a different story, and a very necessary part of the rehabilitation and recovery process was to attend AA meetings which the staff ferried us to three times a week, again on alternate evenings.

Although, as far as I'm aware, these were optional, there was an unspoken expectancy to attend, perhaps not so much with me yet as it was still my first day, but I decided I would go for many reasons. I wanted to make a good first impression with my fellow clients and the staff, but more importantly I wanted to push myself into another new frontier, and learn what I could, not just about myself.

Though I didn't have an acute understanding yet of how they worked, I at least knew the premise and a smidgeon of the 12-step program that was central to these meetings. I assumed I would get to hear horror stories of others' experiences, which

I also assumed would offer me better perspective on my own. Forgetting the alcohol for a second and focusing on what I always felt was the true crux of my problems, I was keen to take on my social anxiety and other insecurities as early as possible, and this seemed like a tremendous early opportunity. Sitting in a room with up to 30 other strangers, perhaps speaking myself if I could drum up the courage.

In terms of 'public' speaking, I was used to leading meetings through my time in product management, but it didn't mean I ever adapted to it. Meetings that I weren't chairing were even worse. I had a tendency to hyper-overthink anything I was potentially about to say, and what that creates is the feeling of it being a performance when I'm saying it, rather than it coming out naturally. And afterwards, rather than keeping my head in the moment, I'd agonise over whether it came out properly and the perception and reception of it. I don't know how visible it ever was to others, but it was certainly something that dined on me. I had learned through my Fitbit that my resting heart-rate was significantly above the average, and it's easy to understand why when I think of how my brain worked in these scenarios. Although here I was still tired from the past week, I felt a sense of duty to myself to have a go at this and see how I fared. The life story could wait for now; I still had the following day, which wouldn't involve any evening excursion.

One of the support workers took us in a minibus to a town some 5 or so miles away from where we were staying. On arrival we were met and greeted by two friendly faces, one of whom was the host and the other a guest speaker. The host recognised everyone but me, and so the two of us exchanged pleasantries before a tea or coffee was offered. This believe it or not, had been a talking point amongst the others on the journey. Back at the ranch, there was strictly no caffeine, or sugar. They are both drugs of their own and we were under a detox from them, too. Interestingly in a recent study, albeit on mice, sugar was found to be more addictive than cocaine. Some of the clients had been looking forward to getting a proper coffee under their belt, whereas I felt an aversion to it, not least because it was 8pm by this point, but also because I had already grown to like both decaffeinated tea and coffee, and wanted to stick exclusively with it while I was there. I had thought ahead and swiped some decaf teabags from the kitchen. Another thing absent from our kitchen were biscuits and confectionery of any kind, but my resolve wasn't quite strong enough at this stage to turn down a Jaffa Cake when I saw one. This – like many other AA meetings – was held inside a Methodist church and a long table had been arranged with I'd say around 15 to 20 chairs. A banquet scene if you like. It certainly looked like one to me... I could take or leave the Jammy Dodgers and the Custard Creams, but the Jaffas, devilish little sirens that they are, were always going to be too much for my novice will at that point.

I noticed on the walls there were two banners; one consisting of the 12 steps of the recovery program, and the other holding the 12 traditions, which are essentially the rules of engagement. I didn't have time to register them, though, before a bell was rung and the meeting opened. This started, as I learned pretty much all AA meetings do, with a minute's silence for the still-suffering alcoholic, in and outside the rooms. As you'd expect, impeccably observed, and with a powerful energy that genuinely really hit me. Although I have never been a religious person so-to-speak, and I disagree on the whole with most of their institutions, I can understand how they must create an immense feeling of unity during a communal worship. This felt exactly that.

Talking of religion, I must admit I felt a tad flummoxed when the host opened the meeting with words to the effect of *"Alcoholics Anonymous is not aligned with any institution"*, which seemed in stark disagreement with the banners on the wall that must have said *"God"* twenty times between them. I quickly learned, though, that the AA's understanding of God is essentially what you want it to be, but fundamentally a higher power. I think there may be a misconception (certainly for me for a while) that AA is a heavily religious programme, but that just is not the case. It is a heavily *spiritual* programme, and it ties in the idea of God very effectively. It certainly chimed, and once it did, I hung on every word that followed.

Now again out of respect I wouldn't divulge anything specifically from any of these meetings, but what I can and will say is that typically the first half of the agenda involves the guest speaker, who will share their experience in detail. More often than not, incredibly harrowing, but carried by strength and hope, and about as inspirational a story as you could hope to hear in any room. After this the room is opened to sharing from others, which will occupy more or less the remainder of the two hours or so. This is when I felt my heart rate go up, even though I knew that I was in a safe place. I knew that I wasn't going to speak just yet, but the silences between shares at least felt painfully awkward to me, as I adjusted to the experience. I kept feeling the urge to disrupt what felt like a more prolonged gap than it probably was and, had I done so, it would have come out naturally, rather than a performance. That's the strange thing with me, there appear to be the forces of supreme confidence and extreme anxiety doing battle at all times. Possibly with lightsabers, I don't know. I resisted and stuck with sitting back and absorbing it all. Then at the very end, something happened, which I later learned wasn't typical of these meetings at all. I had heard many others, but not everyone, speak, and some of the other clients had done, which was fascinating for me to see how they dealt with the social situation themselves. Not at any point did I feel anyone look towards me; there felt no pressure whatsoever. And as I assumed things were about to be wrapped up: I heard *"Scott, do you want to say anything?"*.

This caught me off-guard and I'm grateful that it did, because what followed was one of the most well-conveyed monologues that I have ever given. I didn't rush, nor did I blabber, I just spoke comfortably from within the heart about circumstances that had brought me there; small but significant details, and spoke about the love in the room and my first experience of the AA community. I knew exactly when to wrap it up and with it came a most exhilarating rush of liberation and a powerful response from everyone. A very different love to which I had ever felt from friends or family, not to discredit or de-value those in any shape. This was just different. It was a feeling of true understanding, for once, of my problems. A sense of connection. It has long been said that the opposite of addiction is connection, and this is so true I can't tell you.

There is another nice phrase, which is *"The best thing about recovery is that you get your feelings back. The worst thing about recovery, is that you get your feelings back."* I'd heard it earlier that evening and little was I to know that I would start to experience it first hand just minutes later, even at such an early stage in my own recovery. I shall hopefully never forget that evening.

The meeting ended, as tradition, with everyone linking arms or holding hands in the serenity prayer. Nothing *Wicker Man* about it, it felt a very suitable way to bring proceedings to an end, on an excellent mantra not just for alcoholism but for life in general:

"God, grant me the serenity to accept the things I cannot change, the courage to change the things I can, and the wisdom to know the difference."

If we all lived by that, imagine where we could be.

The drive back as you can imagine had none of the tension that the drive there did. I was commended all-round for my input, even though I'd had it sprung upon me rather than instigating it myself. This had still only been day one, but it already felt like a real break in the weather, inside and out. It was around 10 when we got back, there was medication to be had, and a definite yearning for bed. And for day two.

It started with the same routine of meds at 08:00, but this time rather than stumbling back into unconsciousness, I skirted round the puddles to the communal lounge for breakfast. As I approached, the sound of drizzling gave way to the sound of sizzling... bacon sandwiches. As much as I enjoyed it, I was looking forward to something else which I had ordered in for the following week... smoothies. I had a NutriBullet at home, and would have had it delivered by my father during the weekend's visit had I not already managed to swindle one for us through the chef. It wouldn't be used until the ingredients arrived through; chiefly spinach, cucumber, banana, pineapple, blueberries, raspberries, kiwi fruit, chia seeds, and oat milk. Not all in one; a different fruit each time. For me, a smoothie like this bolsters my readiness for the day more than a coffee normally would, and remember this was decaf. I was very glad of a bacon sarnie on the day, though, and twenty minutes later it was time for the first session of day two.

Having slept through yesterday's, I didn't know what to expect of these, especially as it always said *"Readings and Group Process"* on the timetable. There was still no sign of Tracy, but by this point I felt tight with the others, and we entered the therapy room buoyant for the day ahead. It was the same therapist as yesterday. Although there was a rotation of sorts, we would predominantly have the same therapist for the month and this made perfect sense, especially for these morning sessions as it was very much an informal case of *"How did you feel about yesterday?"*

For the first time I really got the chance to talk, and I had plenty to talk about. I didn't hold back when I spoke of how welcome I had been made to feel, not just at the ranch but also the previous evening. I was getting more and more comfortable by the minute and knew that I would have the confidence to go through my life story the following day in as much transparency as I have given to you in these pages and will continue to do so. In fact, I would not have been able to type so openly here about all of this, had I not already gone through the life story with them. But we haven't quite got to that yet.

The readings suggested in the timetable came from a litter of books upon the coffee table, which I had noticed the previous afternoon without giving much thought to. They could have been ornamental for all I knew. We were all about to pick one up though and read the page associated with the day's date, which I believe was June 17th. Each book held a different reflection of sorts, to kick-start the day in a certain frame of mind. None of them conflicted in any way with each other, and they all gravitated I would say mainly towards gratitude. After this, we were to pick from a splay of cards called 'Today I will', from the therapist:

"Pick a card; any card". What do we associate with that? Well every time I would pick one of these over the course of the month, as if by magic, it could not have been more perfect for my own position on that particular day. The cards weren't suitably ambiguous either like, say, a horoscope. They were all fundamentally different, with a different consideration, based on different past experience, and it became somewhat of a running joke that I always picked a different one out each time, even on day 28, that could not have been more fitting for me and how I was feeling at the time.

The session concluded with a decent break before the next one later that morning. This allowed me a good chance to have a peek around the communal lounge, beyond just the dining table and the television. There was a large plastic container which held various arts and craft materials, which would soon come in handy for certain assignments. In a cupboard unit next to them, I found a nice little selection of board games. This brought a smile. Despite my introverted nature and hyper self-awareness, I bloody love a board game. Perhaps the most popular in the UK is perhaps the one I enjoy the least, which I prefer to call *Monotonous*. There were others here though which evoked some great memories, such as *Who's in the Bag?* – essentially a cross between *Charades* and *Articulate*, pertaining to a known figure dead or alive. My personal family favourite had always been *'Absolute Balderdash!'*, which appealed to my skill-set of constructing outlandish yet plausible stories, something which I hope to exercise in fiction in the future.

I also had a penchant for creating parlour games of my own, which had been on form just a few years earlier when I cohabited a house with a very good friend, in the village where I currently lived with my father, some 200 yards down the road. At the time I owned a felt dart board, with magnetic darts that stuck firm and true with a satisfying popping noise. You may have seen the same style board in Mark and Jez's flat on *Peep Show*. Rather than the traditional 501, we always opted for a *"who can score higher"* approach, with a series of ridiculous spins on the proceedings, for example sprinting or dancing sideways across the room and throwing the darts underarm, or bending over and releasing the dart between the legs from behind, or better still playing co-op, with one teeing up the dart for the other who would bounce it to the board with their t-shirt or a tennis racket.

My personal favourite, though, was *Hide the Ginger*. Marvellous in its simplicity. For between two and, I'd say, eight players. We would form a Kitchen Team and a Lounge Team, with the door closed between for the simple objective of, you guessed it, hiding the ginger. When one team had decided on an adequate location, the door would be opened and the other would be timed on how long it took them to find it. If you wanted, you could also place written clues to be deciphered. This could only work with a fresh piece of ginger, and with my housemate having easy access to organic produce through his work, we were never in short supply. Being the inventor, I was also equally proud one time to come up with a most ingenious idea I thought, which was rather than balancing or concealing it somewhere within the furnishings of the room, to simply stand innocently with it in the open palm of my hand. It took the kitchen team something like 10 minutes to see it, to great animation, and the lounge team were comfortably the victors. I tell you something, if *Hide the Ginger* goes on to be a family favourite up and down the UK, then I will consider this book the most roaring triumph, and die a contented man.

Seeing these games in the cupboard restored in some way the sense of playfulness that I have always had. Whether childish or not at times, I have always harboured a desire to piss around and make light if I can of the mundane things in the everyday world. I remember many many years ago I had been given a book of stickers of facial features, where you could pick and combine to make up a comical cartoon face. This was one of the best things I have ever been randomly gifted, and I spent the next days finding locations for these faces around the house, again measuring my success on how long they took to be discovered. One was kept in a drawer underneath the cutlery, another was stuck to the inside of the hatch to the loft, so that whenever it was next opened the face would swing down and present itself in spectacular fashion. Another went on the bin of the vacuum cleaner, and another on the dining room table beneath the mat that held the salt and pepper shakers, and as I recall this was one of the more satisfying as by time it revealed itself even I had forgotten about it. Imagine the laughter. Call me an under-achiever, or a child, but these little moments in life have yielded as much personal pride as pretty much anything else.

One final thing whilst we're on the subject of games; I thought you might like a quick *Dark Souls* update. Back at the end of Chapter 2 (Amy), I talked about conquering a fight I had previously got stuck with years ago and given up on. As I said, whilst trivial on the surface, this was actually rather a poignant marker of where my mental resolve is today compared to before all of this happened. And I've been pushing further through the game whilst I continue this book. After dispatching the gargoyles and ringing the bell in the bell-tower, the next objective was to ring the second bell, which was way down in the depths, involving a trip through a place that will send shudders through many that have played this game before... Blighttown. Overall, not the friendliest of settlements. Snake-headed gentlemen and flaming dogs lay in wait around every turn and at the bottom of every ladder, of which there are *many*. Little by little I made it to the bottom, and was rewarded with a poisonous swamp of mosquitoes and blob-monsters. The crescendo if you like was getting through said swamp and into a cave of webs, which hinted in some way at what was ahead. However, this could only partially prepare me for my first meeting with Chaos Witch Quelaag, the boss and guardian of the second bell. Yes, a giant spider, but not any. Atop the fiery arachnid-wasp-thing was a pale buxom woman, fused like a centaur. Google "Quelaag" to see just what I mean. It's an enduring image, as Ron Manager would say.

Dark Souls isn't particularly kind when it comes to checkpoints either (bonfires, which you rejoice and light upon finding), and so this meant each failed attempt required negotiating the entire swamp again. And this fight was tougher than the gargoyles. But I persevered, and persevered again, and eventually ding dong the bitch was dead, and I rang the second bell in pride. Ding dong again. This pride would have been swiftly checked, though, had I realised the new house of horrors that I had just unlocked. Not only that, I had to fight my way back up through the whole of Blighttown to get there, with all the enemies back to life. But your man went and did it… and another bonfire was lit.

Back to rehab for now, though, and let's see if I can get any further with *DS* in my off-time.

Day two continued in a heartbeat. There were three sessions each day, with the exception of Saturdays when I seem to remember there were only two. At weekends the support worker staff would be more involved with the sessions, as the therapists had their time off. Most if not all of the support workers were former addicts themselves, and this gave Saturdays an entirely different dynamic. But we still had Friday before I would get to experience that – and Friday was the day of my life story.

On Thursday eve after the sessions were complete, I did as promised to myself which was to have a nice bath and finish the homework, ready to present the following day. If I hadn't accomplished it that evening, then I would have set a precedent of indolence that I just didn't want. I'd had enough of that in school. There's no way I was going to wing it; I wanted everyone to properly know who I was and why I was, and I knew this required structured notations to go off. The only question was whether I could make it last 90 minutes. I looked at the notes I had made, but didn't know quite how far they would stretch. When it came round to it, and I got half-way through the session, it was clear this was going to need at least another one. I don't put it down to narcissism, or even getting carried away, it was just how it was. I may have only been 31 at the time, but I had much to tell that I thought was important. It was the feedback and questions from others that largely pushed the time on, and I was happy to field them. All in all, it took over three hours to do, and hopefully (like I hope with this), it was done in an engaging manner. It was a quite exhausting exercise, but one that never felt too much.

Because I'd eaten through two sessions, this was it for the day and I could now relax and wait for fish and chips, with it being Friday. A good tradition that. We in Britain can be fiercely defendant of our poor culinary reputation, and rightly so, as I believe it to be a little unjust. Yes, Greggs is popular, and I've no reasoning for that, but when it comes to staple British meals, what on Earth I ask is wrong with a full cooked breakfast, or a carvery, or fish and chips? Or an honest steak and kidney pudding and mash? And talking of pudding, I maintain we have always been the world's vanguard when it comes to desserts. Jam roly-poly and custard. Sticky toffee pudding, and custard. I mean, come on. The only thing that might pip these to the proverbial throne for me is a good tiramisu.

Chef arrived, and it was about as classic a fish and chips as you could get. A good cod with a good batter, the chips weren't too thick (I hate it when they're wedges or pseudo-roasties) and there was a healthy serving of minted mushy peas and tartare sauce. Sticky toffee pudding to follow. It was perhaps the best moment of the year so far. We then went to another AA meeting, a much bigger one this time (I even shared again, this time of my own accord), and watched a film upon our return before taking to bed. Another big day and step towards well-being.

Over the weekend I would have two visits. The first was from my father, who had been permitted to travel even though this usually wasn't allowed in week one. An exception had been made because of the rushed circumstances in which I had checked in (you'll no doubt be shocked to learn the magistrates would not grant me extra time to go through my DVD collection). More clothes were brought, an MP3 player which Dad had very kindly loaded with some of my favourite albums that were in the house, and a selection of some of my favourite films and TV series that I owned. I was pleased to see *Ex Machina* in there and knew that would be one of the first to go in the player whether the other clients wanted it or not. I also had the entire *Black Mirror* collection, again perhaps not the best choice when you are already emotionally crippled, but here they were.

Dad and I had around an hour to chat in the men's digs which we conveniently had to ourselves. Although I'd technically only had three days of therapy so far, I remember him noting how strongly I appeared to be coming back to myself. I had put not just myself through it in recent times but him, too, and seeing me shimmering made him shimmer. My new favourite moment of the year.

And the second visit was from EMS, to fit my exclusion tag. **Jubbly**. This proved to be quite a saga, with them failing to get any signal from the box they installed in my room. With this rehab being out in the sticks, they could only get my tag to talk to the box and couldn't get the box talking to their HQ. This meant that in the night I could have run to Basingstoke and back and they would never know. Don't know why I chose Basingstoke there. This was frustrating not just for them but for me, as they departed saying they'd figure something out and, in the meantime, I was wearing this chunk on my ankle that wasn't doing anything. As I grew used to it over the Sunday, the other gents were taken to a salubrious hotel and golf course nearby in the country, where the clients had access to the gym and sauna. This was also optional on Thursday evenings I learned. I would have to complete my detox before I would be eligible for these visits, but I couldn't wait to add it to the health drive.

I did worry somewhat about wearing my tag there. Although it was called waterproof it would not withstand being submerged, which would render me unable to use the pool or jacuzzi. And there would be no way of hiding it in the gym either. I thought of it as another good test though; a chance to overcome the self-consciousness and vanity of the situation.

One other person that I would get to have a good chat with over the weekend was Tracy. She had got through the worst of the withdrawal by this point and was starting to show herself a little more around the communal areas. Although she wouldn't mind me saying she was an emotional and physical mess (as we all were when we first arrived), I must say she did not look her age at all. She had multicoloured hair usually tied back, glasses, and a nice selection of kooky jumpers and dresses. We found we had more things in common (I too have a wicked kooky dress collection), and we continued to hit it off. She said that she would be present for therapy from the next day onwards, and it would be nice to have another face in there. By this point I had really become accustomed to group counselling and couldn't see how I could ever get enough of it. I also had more assignments the following week with my initials against them and had already begun planning for these. As I said, I won't go into most of them, but in terms of my own assignments I am at a bit more liberty to talk, and I'm looking forward to sharing a couple with you.

With the weekend over, I decided on an early night and lay in bed reflecting on the past seven days. I'm not sure how much at the time I really could comprehend how remarkable the transition was. Earlier that week I was inhaling a junkie's vomit as I scooped it from a prison basin, seeing my personal items stolen, and just days later here I was inhaling the country air and seeing some much more treasured personal items returned to me.

When I look back on all of 2019, and my life in general, it's difficult to pick out certain days that were crazier than any other. There are some obvious examples many of which you're yet to know about, but, really, I don't know which would make the podium. It's easier to look back on weeks rather than days that stood out, and this was one of them. I was still only in week one technically, and I had a long way to go, but I went to sleep in the sound consideration that this might just be the most important month of my life.

On Monday there were more new experiences to be had. The usual morning session was especially pleasant as I had the whole weekend to talk over with the therapist. The other clients had been with their families, too, so there was an all-round sense of cheer. Tracy was welcomed in and it didn't take long for her to laugh with us. It felt much like a family already. We all knew intimate details about each other that perhaps no one outside the room did, even family. Tracy would get to do her life story later in the week, but for now there was no pressure or expectation to settle in quickly. It was the same welcome that I was given, and it was lovely to see someone else getting it, plus it was nice to no longer be the only newbie.

In terms of my next big assignment, I had to complete what was known as Step One. In Alcoholics Anonymous, this reads: *"We admitted we were powerless over alcohol and that our lives had become unmanageable"*. In rehab we treated Step One in the same way, but for whatever was more fitting to our own predicament, and mine didn't need a great deal of conversion. It may not have been the case for everyone, but my first assignment, the life story, was one predominantly of happiness. Yes I had some grim memories; the alcoholic breakdown and combustion of my stepfather, the year in which five friends and family members died, Mum having cancer, and more recently the Amy ordeal. But we've all had our shit to deal with. Mine had consisted primarily of joyous moments, the things I was passionate about... think back to Chessington or Florida in Chapter 2, or meeting Loz in Chapter 5, and then the discovery of bands like Opeth and Pink Floyd. My life story, on the whole, was about as uplifting to do as Step One was about to be horrendous to do.

The purpose was to revisit past moments in which my actions had caused harm, not just to myself but others, even tenuously. And I would have to revisit these in granular, unflinching detail. Each one had a different pretence, for example to recall an occasion when the urge to drink was too powerful to handle, or to describe a time when I had tried to stop and ended up resuming it all too quickly. Etc.

Ultimately, I had to give, I'd say, 15 instances. As I echoed before, the best thing about recovery is you get your feelings back and the worst thing about recovery is you get your feelings back. And this is where it started really hitting home. I was suddenly comprehending the true gravity of some of the things I had done in the recent past… fabricating reasons for needing money so I could shove a gram up my nose and then the repercussions of what happened afterwards. Many examples could be tied to the Amy relationship. It was the first time I'd looked back on those in detail, too, and it was still all too fresh in the memory to have gotten over. Another relationship in particular had been the bearing of a huge amount of my emotional problems, which I was to write about in great detail there, but won't here, just yet. Overall, it was a powerful exercise, and although I was in a great deal of pain working through it, this was hardly undeserved let's face it, and the long-term value was always clear.

As if recalling and writing it all down wasn't fun enough, I then had to regale it to everyone for two hours. Though three of the other clients had done this assignment themselves, I hadn't been there to hear it, so this was my first experience of anyone bearing their soul quite to this extent, and it happened to be me. Rehab was never going to be sunshine all the way, and this was the first time I found things truly hard. And it must have shown, from the hug Tracy gave me afterwards.

That was quite enough for one day. After dinner, Tracy stayed behind to spend a first proper evening with the other clients, while I plugged my MP3 in and sang myself to sleep. I believe Simon & Garfunkel's *Bookends* was the record. Another few days passed, and before I knew it I was approaching half way. That next weekend, both parents visited and we were allowed the time and the trust to go out for a meal. I say trust, I would be breathalysed on my return, not that it mattered. I had some real clarity back by now and I was loving every minute. After you've traversed the depths of alcoholism and other afflictions – the nine circles of hell as is *Dante's Inferno* – then a new-found and almost unsurpassable high comes from the sobriety. I couldn't wait to show this to the two family members that had seen me at my worst and suffered it with me. I knew that they would share this high with me too. Everything that was good and celebratory about me was coming back, in a better way than ever, perhaps for the relief that it was back at all.

We had a most enjoyable meal – a mountain of nachos and all the accoutrements – salsa, guacamole, sour cream, dollops of red and green jalapenos. Despite my passion about some of our cuisine here in the UK, I do bow in inferiority to Mexico.

Not only was it great to spend time with my parents again, they had brought with them more clothes, and two very special items. One I will save for the end of the chapter and the other is something you're already familiar with. Another of my prized possessions, something that has always represented the best of me, contrary to what Amy might tell you, my Ibanez. Oh lord it was good to see it again. Like I said, I had always been one for mainly learning and jamming to music rather than writing my own (at the time of writing I am in the process of learning the entirety of Tool's recent album *Fear Inoculum*, a god damn masterpiece). But with my mind as fertile as it was again, I started working on some musical ideas of my own, back in the communal lounge where I would keep it. It was nice to play for the other clients, too. This is something that in the past would have got my nerves up, but I felt strangely comfortable. During my stay I wrote most of a song called 'Within Without', which was to be a symbol of everything that I struggled with that year. I thought about including it here, but, hey, I haven't recorded it professionally, yet.

Should I?

The rest of the second week wasn't without its moments. After the frustration of the first visit from EMS, little did I know behind the scenes my solicitor had been on the case and managed to negotiate the removal of the tag altogether. When I saw their faces arrive, I was overjoyed to learn the nature of their visit. Although I had started looking forward to the test of wearing it to the gym, and seeing whether it discombobulated anyone including myself, I was much happier with the notion of having the fucker removed. As I have said before, one would be surprised how quickly they can adapt to certain things and, as I went to bed that night, I was incredibly aware of having two normal ankles again.

As week two was about to creep into three, the half-way point in my stay, I was handed a personal assignment that felt closer to the bone than anything that had preceded it, and one that I will gladly share with you now.

This month was not just a rehabilitation from drugs, it was an introspection on the pre-cursing factors, and for me, this had been chiefly anxiety in all its shapes and colours. In the most recent timetable that had been handed out, the first thing I took real note of was **"SH: Letter to my Anxiety"**, and here it is.

Ann Xiety,
The Mad House,
Never-ending Road,
Darkshire.

Dear Ann,

I remember 2006/2007. I'd reached the end of my teens and it was around the time Facebook launched. Not that they're responsible, but you've been sending me friend requests ever since. Harassment is an understatement. I had met you, in fact you were there throughout my high school years, but must not have got the memo that

I didn't care for you very much. Yet to this day you've persisted. The audacity.

I can't remember your first appearance exactly, but I can remember the feeling, and it has followed me. Or you have, rather. In social situations you've tagged along uninvited. In shopping centres and supermarkets you're never more than an aisle behind. You've even managed to break into our family homes.

I suppose on the flip-side I have sent you some invitations. I have made a total mess of my finances, again and again. I've not exactly looked after myself either. My behaviour, especially recently, towards my own health and others, has led to court for the first time, and prison for the first time. Of course, these are areas where you thrive, and faithfully you were by my side. So I understand why you're confused. But you're not as confused as me. Have I deserved you? I've done some regrettable things in my time, but my friends and family know my soul and that I haven't done enough to warrant this much of you. Most bad choices that I made felt passive to your influence, and, all in all, I don't know who's to blame. So let's try and address this once and for all. I know what I can do at my end, and I'm starting to do it. I don't know if you've noticed actually, as I haven't seen you for a couple of weeks now… pleasant holiday?

That gets me thinking actually, you never followed me abroad. Especially around theme parks, even in this country for that matter. You're not banned from them are you? No, you can't be… I've seen some people's faces in the queue for Nemesis and The Smiler. How many 'clients' do you have exactly? You're certainly irrational; at least I haven't figured you out yet.

Anyway, let's get back on point. In fact, let's jump straight ahead to this year, 2019. There are two key areas in which you've involved yourself. Let's start with work. I've had it before with you, but boy you really ramped it up this time. In my interviews, I was calm, cool as a cucumber. I was confident, assertive, impressive. This led to an offer, and I joined a small team there of eleven. Nothing but good vibes from good people. And I couldn't have asked for more tranquil surroundings; a farm in the heights of the country. It was an hour's drive from home, in the middle of nowhere, and yet it didn't take long for you to find me, did it? Suddenly, everything I showed in my interviews was bled. Any confidence long-forgotten, and I was scared to open my mouth. When I most needed to.

Incidentally, the day of my second interview was the day that Amy and I matched and started talking. You were nowhere to be seen yet here either. It's almost as if you already knew her, though; as soon as I set foot in her house, I noticed you. She even noticed that I noticed you, but nothing changed. Was I being conspired against? Talking of Facebook, I should have checked her friends list first as clearly you were on it. Her house was big enough for three, yet it felt cold and oppressive. You followed us everywhere, and even when I couldn't hear your presence I knew you simply waiting in her kitchen... your favourite room it seemed.

The point is, sometimes you're rational and explainable, sometimes not. Put simply, you just never buggered off. So I'm taking action.

I'm stopping my silly invitations. I've been friends with cocaine long enough to know it doesn't have my best interests at heart, so I'm unfriending and blocking them. I'm going to take control of my finances, and freeze you out. I'm starting to spend time with others who have suffered at the hands of you as well. Opening up to them, and listening to them, learning as much as I can that will help me. And trying to help them if I can.

I'm also recognising that I can't escape you altogether, and as a result I will simply change my relationship with you instead. I will put myself in uncomfortable situations, as I recently have in therapy and AA. And I will emerge stronger and less alone. You are ultimately an opportunity for me to face my fears each day, which we are told is healthy, and for me to grow with them.

I have therefore finally decided Ann to accept your friend request, however please be aware I have muted your status updates so they won't appear in my timeline and interfere with my real friends.

Yours sincerely,
Scott.

When I look back on all of my assignments, this is probably the one that sums me and everything up the best, and it was quite fitting that it was introduced and somewhere around the mid-way point, as it is here.

By this stage, even outside of the assignments, everyone now had a sense of who I was, including my sense of humour, which I guess you'll be the judge of. Humour was creeping back into all facets of my daily activities, but never at the expense of earnestness. Banter was flowing with Tracy and co, and I was even starting to test the waters with the therapist. I always recognised the values of each assignment, though, taking those very seriously, and was willing to forgo films I hadn't seen in and cigarettes I didn't need in order to spend extra time on them. Another milestone had just been achieved too; I had completed my detox, and was no longer on diazepam. I didn't see much in this, but I can't tell you the amount of times I heard *"Well done"* with a sincerity. It was apparently common that clients would get through the detox and promptly discharge themselves to start all over again, not in a good way. This was polarizing to hear; I had got so much out of this I failed to see how anyone else could be different, but ultimately it reminded me that everyone *is* different.

That weekend, Tracy and I visited a farm up the road with a support worker, and for the first time had a caffeinated coffee. There was an arts and crafts exhibition inside a large barn, and it was most tranquil hearing the pattering of rain against the corrugated roof as we perused everyone's handiwork. It's quite remarkable what people can do when they harness their love and creativity. Although I never considered myself into this sort of affair, I must admit I felt a newfound appreciation for it as we meandered. Ironically, the only thing I would take back with me that day was a Brentford FC mug, which I had custom-made from a shop next door. I'm using it right now.

As we progressed into week three, I was about to have

two more new experiences for the year on the same day, both at polar opposites of the Hughes Enjoyment Scale. The first was something I'd never heard of before… ear acupuncture. This took place in the therapy room and lasted around thirty minutes. I suppose you could say this experience alone was at both ends of the scale, as the relaxation part couldn't take place without having five needles driven into each ear, and the ears are not exactly as fleshy as one's back where one typically associates acupuncture needles with going. This was no more than a pricking pain, though, and apart from a couple falling out on occasions, I was never particularly aware of them once they were in. We could choose to recline in an armchair, or lay out across a mat on the floor. For my first time, I opted to stay in the chair and put my feet up on another one. We were forewarned, rather bizarrely, to expect stomach rumbling as part of the process. Sure enough, about five minutes in, it started. This was most amusing given we were supposed to be in total silence. It's always funnier when you're not supposed to laugh, isn't it. Tracy and I in particular were giggling just like Mike Pinfield and I used to back on the primary school playground, especially between rumblings, as it was impossible not to fixate on when the next one might be coming, and from whom. At the end, I couldn't pinpoint what it was that made me feel better, the acupuncture itself, or the comedy of the experience. Either way, I'd recommend it.

The serenity was about to be cut short, though, as I made my way back to the men's accommodation, opened the door, and heard the buzzing of a winged intruder. It sounded like it was in the living room, but as I got into the living room and heard it again, I realised it was coming from upstairs, and was now much louder. Worryingly loud in fact. *"What is this thing?"*. And as I edged up the stairs, I saw it. For the first time in my life, I was face to face with a hornet. And I genuinely thought I was going to have a heart attack. I can safely tell you my friend, that if you're not sure whether it's a hornet or a large wasp, it's definitely a large wasp. This thing was colossal, and there was no mistaking it for anything else. I am not joking when I say I think it was over three inches long. I've seen the images of these murder hornets in the news lately and, whilst perhaps not as dangerous, this thing was undoubtedly much larger than those. Worse still than the size of it, my god, was the noise. I will forever hear it in my nightmares. So loud and deep in frequency it could penetrate a Gringotts vault. I was not about to mess with it and so retreated to the safety of the exterior of the building, and as I went into HQ to consult the staff, I was chortled at somewhat. *"Definitely a large wasp"*.

As one of the support workers flexed his muscles and grabbed a can of Raid. I couldn't wait for his reaction. We edged into the lounge, and up the stairs, and then it took off. I have never heard someone go *"Oh"* like he did, and I bent double both in laughter and fear. We (he) sprayed it, and it circled the landing with its piercing hum for some thirty seconds, before a 180 and nosedive into the bathroom floor. I'm afraid I don't feel any pang of remorse over the matter; it was clearly going to be a performance trying to usher the thing out of the house. The support worker stamped on it to put it out of its misery, except the beast was somehow *still* alive. Apparently these things are terrifyingly hard too. This was also the first time the support worker had seen one, and he scooped it up on a CD case to take back and show the others. When I went back for my medication later, they were still marvelling at it on the kitchen worktop, taking snaps of it next to various items to display its might. The thing made a pound seem like a penny (a bit like Brexit *wheeeeeeeeey!*). A few days later there was another hornet incident, this time in the ladies' quarters, which Tracy still had to herself. It wouldn't surprise me if it was the same brute from beyond the grave.

In fact, that same night, I had a third new experience for the day and year. It was time to visit an NA meeting rather than an AA. Narcotics Anonymous is essentially the same and with the same traditions, but a very different crowd and with it a different feel as well. The main sharer had a quite incredible yarn, and was celebrating their three-year anniversary, which was wonderful to be a part of. If you're uncomfortable with hugging strangers, this wouldn't be your gig. Given the current situation in the world, I wonder when strangers will ever hug again.

Week three would continue in poignant fashion, as the three male clients that I had met my first night, good friends who had made me feel as welcome as they did, were all about to have their final day and then leave the bubble to return to their lives. They had all had their own voyage of self-discovery and it was mixed emotions for all of us as they departed. The staff were used to these situations, but for the rest it was a big deal. And in a flash, five were down to two. Tracy and I for the foreseeable moment. Because we were close friends by this point, it didn't require much time to adapt; we'd already become our own little bubble anyway, and it was nice to now have a little more time with the therapist, too. I failed to mention that we did all get a 1:1 session every week on top of the group ones, and this meant we could now have potentially two each.

During one of these I asked for feedback on how they thought I was getting on at this stage, and I remember being asked why I needed to know – not in any cut-throat way, but it did stun me slightly. And they were right; I didn't require any validation, the most important thing – the only thing in fact – was how did I feel about it? Overall, I couldn't have felt much better. I had given everything to each session, listened, properly listened for one of the first times in my life, and was putting things into practice that I could before even leaving the bubble. No, I was not the finished article, nor would I be at the end, but I felt the sense that I, and everything, was going to be alright.

I mentioned the arts and crafts container in the lounge for certain assignments, and I'd just been handed another of these which was the novel idea of tracing the shape of our hands on A3 paper; one for past, one for future. The hands should be decorated with the factors and triggers of everyday life, how we had dealt with them before, and what would be different next time. I was really pleased with my output for this, despite the cheesy title of *"It's in my hands"*, and it was another overwhelmingly positive project to undertake. This perhaps lulled me into a false sense of security before the next one, which was simply titled 'Shame and Guilt'.

Step One had been difficult to do. Tracy had found hers equally difficult. It was, after all, the point. But 'Shame and Guilt' was going to be far worse; traumatic even. I don't know about you, but I had never really delineated much between the two words, but one of the purposes of this assignment was to recognise those differences. And again, I would have to list many examples from my past, in grizzly detail. In terms of homework, this took by far the longest and, though it hurt, I'm glad it took the longest and hurt as much as it did because it meant I was probably getting to the nub of things.

Without wanting to go into too much detail, the examples I gave were largely family-related, as you might imagine. My parents had never raised me to do some of the things that I had done and, with the haze I was in at the time, I never really stopped to properly consider how it might have affected them, both in the moment and beyond. Not just my parents, but my brother, and one remaining grandparent. My brother, though technically a half-brother, is with no doubt in my mind my brother, my bro, and always will be. He is three years younger, and though as I learned with Amy money does not equate to success, he has done well for himself in that aspect, and earned it. I have great respect for him and always will. Though we did have a short phase of being at each others' throats, this is what true brothers are supposed to do, isn't it? It's a rite of passage. We've been tight ever since, even without necessarily seeing each other often. Amusingly, he did join one of the companies I worked for once – technically the same team as well – and although that sort of thing could have gone either way, it was definitely the most enjoyable time I had working there.

My one grandparent still alive, whom I also love very much, again had never deserved to be on the periphery of the madness that I was in at times. I never thought that it would have really affected her in any way, but *of course* it would have. For the first time I was truly realising all of this now. Realisation: to *make it real.*

I suddenly felt something like how they must have, or could at least see it now for what it was, from their perspective. I can't tell you how much that finally hit me. I would later get to present this assignment again to both parents, and it was an emotionally-charged experience, for they now saw that I did have both guilt and shame over everything after all. Or rather, that I *do*.

Another person that I would write about here was Loz, who again was not unaffected by any of this. Our friendship would thrive when we were both totally sober and, ironically, at our craziest together. We just went like Pimms and lemonade. Then in recent years I set about ruining it. I would get coked up and the general mood just wasn't quite the same. I quite rightly lost the respect of Loz over the last year too.

Curiously enough, or maybe not, Amy didn't get a mention in this assignment. Although I had totally lost control of myself towards the end, I didn't at the time and still don't feel much guilt, shame, or regret about what happened with her. The drink driving, absolutely yes, and that was mentioned, but in terms of my treatment of her, that and the consequences were a much needed event for me, and so even though it must have very much affected her at the time, all things considered, I'm OK with that.

There was another ex, though, that did feature heavily in this assignment, and who's name was more familiar to the therapist and Tracy than Amy. You will know her name soon.

Like with Step One, the rumination and writing down of these times was only the first part of it. Having to deliver this, again over two hours, to both Tracy and the therapist, was gruelling, and was the first time I cried while I was there. Poor

Tracy had a horrible time with this assignment, too, a few days later. Again, though, that meant it was working. If we weren't close friends at this point, we definitely were after that.

It could have been easy to have had a meal and then gone our separate ways in the evenings, as we were both introverts in nature, however, I don't recall an evening where we actually did that. Even while one of us was cooking the other would drift in and out of the kitchen for a chatter. I don't remember everything I cooked, but I did on one occasion make a huge (and I mean huge) batch of vegetable chilli, that went down a storm with the staff, too. Even more so, I had asked for one of my mum's greatest recipes, which was a slow-cooked salmon and cucumber risotto. *"Cooked cucumber, you say?"*. Trust me, it's a delight.

After meals we were working our way through my *Black Mirror* DVD collection, and by the end of our stay we had got through series 1-4. Due to the anthology nature of the show, we could watch them in any order, and I would let Tracy pick as she had never seen any of them. Amusingly, the infamous first episode was one of the very last ones she chose, and the reaction was priceless.

That weekend, which was just before our final week there, I had another visit from the parents which this time included my brother, and another two I haven't really mentioned before this chapter, his lovely fiancée and my wonderful little nephew. We went to the same farm up the road which was the perfect spot to relax and catch up over a wedge of carrot cake, and by this point I must have looked notably a different man. Not just in my face, but my shape. I'd had three weeks of healthy eating, plus a couple of visits to the gym which was now available, plus a few hilarious games of badminton. I mentioned how the weather broke for me and, thankfully, it had properly broken now, too, and all flooding had subsided.

Tracy had a visit from her husband on the same day, and it was lovely to meet him, too. They were both keen bikers (although I did own a scrambler at 16 as you know, this was not something we particularly had in common), and it was nice after hearing his name to see the man in flesh (he was every bit as tall as she had comically warned me about), and to get to see her in her element. Likewise, she got to meet my parents, and it was the happiest visiting day yet.

The weekend also meant another gym visit. The hotel was even nicer than the clients had described. Upon pulling in and past the entrance sign, there was another sign warning us of deer that may cross the road and to be alert. Having been born in West London, and with my father continuing to live there for many years, I was well used to deer. That might sound strange, but West London is where you'll find Richmond Park. An odd blend of free-roaming fauna, and self-righteous cyclist wankers. I have no problems with cycling itself (who would?) but there is a certain sanctimonious breed of cyclist, lycra and spandex n' all, most holier-than-thou, and Richmond Park can be a wretched hive. For this particular hotel, replace "cyclist" with "golfer", and keep the rest. Are deer attracted to wankers? Are wankers attracted to deer? That's for another book.

Also, as my tag was long-gone, I could make full use of the swanky facilities. We typically had 90 minutes each visit, and I'd hit the gym as hard as I could in 45 so that I could unwind for the other in the jacuzzi, pool and sauna. After we got back, we heard there would be a new client joining us the following day for our final week. Sure enough, the following day, there he was and I had a housemate again. His name was Andy, and he was a most soft-spoken fellow, with a keen shared interest in music. We had a very long chat that day in the men's lounge, and I got to learn quite quickly about his life.

Week four, then. The final frontier. Tracy and I were given our final assignments, Andy was given his life story. Forgetting the assignments for a moment, I want to talk about the vibe outside of these in the communal lounge. It was mid-summer, and though there was plenty going on inside our bubble, there was, of course, plenty more going on in the outside world. Two sporting events were in full swing, the Women's World Cup, and Wimbledon. We had a blast watching these. In the tennis, Coco Gauff was making a name for herself, and we were all passionately behind Joanna Konta who had a great campaign herself. And in the football, England did us proud. I'll never forget the debacle that was the Cameroon game; quite one of the most astonishing things in sport that I have ever seen. I know these players ultimately do not represent the nation of Cameroon in general, but their behaviour was about as low and pathetic as mine had ever been. Thankfully I was never on national television.

Racket sports in the living room were inspiring racket sports in the garden, and Tracy and I had our badminton game tight. It was fun to now have Andy involved, and one of the support workers who was also a personal trainer often joined us. After the match ended, we had a plank-off, and I impressed myself by taking him all the way and collapsing after 100 seconds. Not bad that, when I'd only started working out again a couple of weeks ago.

Back to the assignments though. I had two distinct final ones to do. One was the inevitable exit strategy, which I will save for now, and the other was the final visual assignment, something which again I was simultaneously looking forward to and dreading. '**SH: Self-portrait**'.

The brief was to gather art materials and find a comfortable place to sit, with a mirror in front of me, and to start outlining my head on paper with a pencil and go from there. I didn't have to be exact; this wasn't an inspection of my drawing abilities. I could be abstract if I wanted. The purpose was to spend time with myself, learning the curves of my face, the colour of my eyes, and crucially, to not judge the work too much. Fighting my inner critic was an essential point of the assignment.

I would then write down how the experience was for me, before presenting to the group.

Now, not to have missed the point already, but I do just want to say, I'm not much of an artist. Yes, I do write music, and have always enjoyed creative writing, but when it came to drawing it always frustrated me that I never had the talent to render my ideas properly to the page. I had always indulged in silly little caricatures – back when I worked at the supermarket I had a character I drew called RoboBean, which took under 30 seconds to execute. As was my style, I would always leave one concealed somewhere within the checkout so that the person taking over from me would find it at some point later, perhaps whilst checking pricing on nectarines, presumably leaving the customer wondering what was so amusing about the price of nectarines.

Not a show-piece; I don't need to be told. But I really took my time with the self-portrait, and I got it first go. It's the first time I had ever drawn myself, and it was an odd feeling holding it aloft. The assignment as you read was not only to draw the portrait itself, but to write about the experience and how it felt. As by this point I was pretty much fully back to myself, I decided I would go to town on this, and narrate the actual process of drawing it, in a film-noir style.

*

A glass of orange juice. A desk two feet inwards from the wall, cleared of deodorant and other detritus. A chair in the corner that once housed the box for his exclusion tag, perched to the table and facing the mirror of his wardrobe. The scene was set.

He looked up and shared a stare-out with himself, taking time to observe the shape and intricacies of his reflection. He had looked into a mirror at length before, but this was different. This wasn't a soul search, but to capture his face, ready to sketch his first ever self portrait. He looked to his pencil, and a splay of other crayons ready to work on the complexion later. These colours were largely acquainted with him already, having been credited in other projects. They were more than acquaintances at this stage; they were his friends. But could he trust them here? And could he count on himself? This wasn't another RoboBean, this was to be a still-life, or as close as he could get.

He looked up again to take in the outline of his head, a quite difficult practice to keep visualised when looking back down. He reached for his pencil, and rather instinctively jotted six dots on the page: the tip of his hair above the cranium, the bottom of his chin, and the top and bottom of his ears. A cursory glance back up told him he had fluked it rather well. A steady hand joined the dots, taking pause to convey the curvature. Something told him this was one of the most important steps and he didn't want to set himself up to fail already. He then mused upon the purpose of the assignment and realised that this in itself did not constitute failure, but that missing the point of the project would. "Chillax" he though to himself… "this is not about perfection". The work gathered pace.

He made further dots outlining the height and position of the mouth, followed by his nose, then eyes. He wondered if he had left enough room for his gargantuan forehead, but would worry about that later. He outlined his ears in relation to the eyes, then finished the outline of the eyes themselves. Another cursory glance up. He was relatively happy with the start, knowing in some ways the hardest work was already done if this was to look anything like him. He soon realised the hardest was yet to come though… his nose.

Although he never had any confidence issues around his nose, he spent minutes with it here, analysing, frustrated. "How on earth do I get this down?" The lighting wasn't helping either, with the lightbulb to his left being blocked by the door, meaning the light was skewed naturally by the window to his right. He looked out and noticed a pigeon on the power-lines, pointing nonchalantly in his direction. If it's a stare-out he wants, he will have to wait his turn...

He began the outline of the nose, starting with the bottom tip between the nostrils and working his way lightly to the bridge until he reached between his eyes. Not fantastic he thought, but this'll do. He was more concerned with acknowledging and including the mole that for 31 years had stood proud and central on it. He was always aware of the moles on his skin, but never bothered by them.

The nose was complete for now, and out came the coloured pencils to start on his eyes. His eyes had been the subject of discussion down the years – were they green or blue? Most people had said blue, but he always maintained they were closer to green. "It doesn't matter right now" he thought, "This is about my perception". Regardless, the conundrum was quickly solved by a crayon that appeared to be perfectly equidistant anyway. Huzzah!

The eyebrows followed, and the same colour continued up and around his hair. He hadn't had it this short for years, and it was nice to have it frozen in time like this. Short downward strokes outlined the fringe, not before ruffling it to face where it should. Now this was complete, he outlined his mouth, keeping as deadpan an expression as possible. He noticed, perhaps for the first time, that it sort of lopped down on one side.

He quite liked it, observing the subtle curl into cheeky smile. Heartbreaker.

Next up: facial hair. This was as simple as dotting around with a brown pencil, taking care to acknowledge the small scar above his top lip where it doesn't grow as fruitfully, and his feeble attempt at a soul patch below the bottom lip where he once had a stud piercing. He pondered the idea of getting it again, and still ponders. He also noticed that the facial hair became more sparse around the chin area. His chin had always been a see-saw of emotion, resembling something of Peter Griffin's whenever he was feeling self-conscious. On a good day, though, he would reflect back to the Disney films of the 90's, when all the princes had one. Although it was a bum-chin and no mistake, he had grown not to mind it, and currently had it at stubble-length with the crack on full show.

Time for more colour. An array of pinks were tested on a separate page, before settling on one with an orange hue. He began with a light shade across the whole face, and then deepened around the cheeks and forehead to match his current tan. One thing that had always bothered him was the fact that it never seemed to tan as well under his eyes, accentuating the "bag" look. He then considered he hadn't exactly taken care of himself down the years, and felt blessed to apparently still look in his twenties.

The colour was complete; now it was time to outline his shoulders and the top of his shirt. How convenient he had been wearing white that day. A cursory glance up, a few lines of blue and the top of a pineapple. Shirt complete. Another cursory look up – he had finished.

He reclined, regarding his work. A flicker of pride adorned his face and it's reflection. He was pleased.

*

The instructions for the assignment had been for me to get comfortable looking at my own reflection, which had been achieved. It was the final creative project during my time there, and arguably the most fun to do, not to mention being the most fun to reveal at the end. Tracy had done hers, and Andy did his at the same time, and it made for a happy hour.

A couple of days later, Tracy and I returned to the room with our exit strategies in hand, for our final session. I couldn't believe we had got here already. We had both grown and learned so much, and there was no question of our renewed vigour for life.

This permeated throughout our exit plans, which we presented to each other, Andy, and the therapist. Although I had taken it most seriously, it may not have seemed that way to others when I announced that top of the list when I got home was listen to the new Plaid album. But there was good reason; music is one of the biggest things in my life, they are one of my favourite artists, and the new record had dropped whilst I was in hell with Windsor, so I had been looking forward to it for some 5 weeks by now.

The rest of the plan was as resolute but more serious; coping strategies for my anxiety and other triggers that I had identified along the way, such as boredom. Making peace and rekindling with people such as family and Loz. No plan to revisit alcohol any time soon, I was enjoying my time without it too much. To continue with the gym, at least three times a week. Also, to continue with healthy eating. By this point I'd lost a stone or so and I had no intention of slowing up. There were certain strap-lines and acronyms that I had learned in rehab which I wanted to find a prominent place for. One would go in my wallet, in the way of the debit card. I had it fairly well mapped out.

We'd also done a recent assignment called Hopes and Dreams, and I could tie most of these into the exit plan, as they were aspirations for within 12 months or so. Whenever the therapy had been tailored to me, it had predominantly been around relationships, and as much as Amy had taught me what I didn't want, my progress over the past month had told me very much what I *was* looking for in the future. Someone warm and open, someone who seemed to genuinely appreciate who I was, and who wasn't governed by vanity when with me around other people. Someone with a creative flair… the dream scenario would be a fellow guitarist, and singer. Like it said, "hopes and dreams". But I wasn't thinking ahead too much in terms of that; it would hopefully happen naturally in the not too distant. What was much more pivotal were the relationships with my family and friends, and it was these that were built into the exit plan.

I delivered mine, Tracy delivered hers, and within the hour we were both to be collected and taken home. A last game of badminton, a huge hug, and "*they're here*".

Before I move onwards with the year, there's two more things concerning rehab that I want to talk about. Back in the second weekend when my parents visited, they had brought me some more clothes, and also in tow a very random item, one which I must admit I took one look at and thought "*Nah*". It was a thousand-piece jigsaw of the London Underground map. I've never really been one for jigsaws, so I did wonder what on Earth their cognitive process was to bring it here. I was busy enough with the sessions in the day, the homework and AA meetings in the evening, and this just looked like an awkward conversation in advance.

A few days later, I decided I would at least make a start on it so that when I inevitably said at the end, "*I did begin it, but ran out of time*", there would actually be some truth in the statement. Though I had never attempted a jigsaw myself, I was on nodding terms with the general approach; corners first, then edges, and work in from there. Slight problem with that though… all the corners and edges were totally white. In fact half the bloody jigsaw was. I had no idea just how tough that was going to make it, until I really I got stuck into the thing.

"*Different change of approach*" he mused. Rather than doing the edges, I would just focus on a particular tube line – each easily distinguishable by colour – and see what progress could be made. With Ealing being close to my heart, it made sense to start on the central line, especially as Ealing Broadway is one of the ends. I went through every individual piece in the box and segmented them by colour. This was the only methodical way of doing it, and finally I gained some traction. Then it dawned on me.

This jigsaw, was perfectly symbolic of the position *I* was in. I myself had arrived in pieces, and to make any progress I would have to spread myself out further, leaving no piece unturned, and slowly try and put myself back together. As my time went on in rehab over the month, I was struggling more and more for time. I didn't turn down a single AA visit, and outside of these I was prioritising homework above anything else. However, I always found a little time here and there to make some progress on the jigsaw. Another line was done, then another (the right kind this time…), then I completed the Thames, then the little matrix in the corner, and before I knew it, I was left with just the blank white pieces. At this point I thought I had it in the bag. I had no idea, though, just how hard it was going to be to try and arrange these and find where they were to go. I tried various techniques, I was thinking systemically, but, in the end, I truly did run out of time and, if I'm honest, patience.

But that's when it *really* dawned on me. If this jigsaw was going to be a metaphor of my recovery, then surely it made sense that it *was* left unfinished? Eureka.

I ordered a large perspex frame through the support workers which arrived the next day, gingerly got it inside, and much like my self portrait, holding it for the first time was an unexpected proud moment. The importance of this jigsaw to me cannot be overstated, and it has been my favourite thing by far that I have ever put up on a wall.

The final thing I want to talk about was just as central during my time in rehab, something also visited on a daily basis, this time in the therapy room. I mentioned a past relationship that caused significantly more pain than any other, and I was never going to not tell you.

9

Kerry

February 2011. I'd just been offered an IT Support job in the NHS, to be based on the top floor of a hospital. Upon accepting the role I decided to get a new car on finance (the very same from Chapter 2 (decent innings)). This was less than a year after I had bowed out of the music course, around six months after Mum had beaten cancer, and so on the drive to my new workplace in my new motor, and just about to move into a new house in a new town, it really felt like a fresh start again.

My first visit here had been for the interview, and this was my second, for a quick induction and to sign the contract etc. in readiness for starting the following Monday. The place was a labyrinth, and I was starting to think that, as Theseus did with the Minotaur, I should have carried a ball of string last time and left it unravelled. Eventually I fluked it to my new office and saw my new boss for only the second time. She was a most peculiar woman, about 4 feet tall (no crush this time), and whilst ostensibly bubbly, dangerously easy to piss off. Straight away she wanted to introduce me to the team. It was a small office of four, and being a busy team, everyone was on the phone which meant staggering the introductions when each person became available. One colleague was actually the mother of someone I had been to school with (I hate the term "*small world*" but I probably did use it). There was a chap named Mark, and he would go on to be my best mate and partner in crime while I was there. He was one of those fellows who was just naturally funny without even doing anything. Endearing mannerisms and, I'm sure he wouldn't mind me saying, a comical face. I mentioned our boss was all-too-easy to get on the wrong side of, and well, he was chief perpetrator. I never really got beyond apprenticeship.

The final person to get off the phone and become available, was the person leaving at the end of the week and whose job I was inheriting. Though she was the last to be introduced to, she was one of the first I had noticed when I entered the room, largely due to the garish way in which her desk was decorated; pink glitter and the like. I was taken over to say hello and familiarise with the workstation, but no sooner had we been formally introduced there was a knock at the door, and another flash of pink, which this time caught my eye in a much more pleasant manner.

I'd passed this particular flash of pink hair in the hospital entrance, and in a weird quirk of fate she had indirectly followed me all the way up to the very same office. And as she entered, I saw her face for the first time. It turns out she didn't work here but was actually a close friend of the person next to me; was visiting the hospital on other business, and as it was this person's last day she had been permitted upstairs to say a brief hello. What a coincidence that we both happened to be here for the very first time, at the very same time. Ships in the night… you could say.

She apologised for interrupting but was beckoned over, and only in close proximity did I realise just how gorgeous she actually was. Rather like Fearne Cotton, with big starry blue eyes. She jokingly apologised again on behalf of her friend for all the tinsel, and my retort was something like *"on the contrary, saves me putting it up myself"*, which got a laugh. A sprinkle of Hughes charm… sowing the seeds of love, as Tears for Fears would say.

The pink hair, and also her makeup, told me that she was both a girly girl and a bit of a rock chick. *[tick ✓]*. And to go back to her eyes, it may have been because I was besotted at the time, but I didn't know if their sparkle was because there was an immediate connection between us. Yes, her name was Kerry (well, again, no it wasn't).

I made sure to remember her name – and I knew that as she was a mutual friend of someone here it wouldn't be too difficult to track her down and drop her a line if I could find an excuse in the future. I struggled to take my eyes off her the entire time she was there, which was perhaps 20 minutes but felt like 2, then off she went so I could finish my induction and sign the paperwork without distraction.

"Was there a connection there? Is it fate we were brought together like this? How do I find a plausible way to contact her?"

These were swirling through my mind as I left the office some 30 minutes after she did, and made my way back through the entrance to the visitor car park. *"I wonder if I'll bump into her again here."*

Anyway. Fast forward a month, to when I'd bedded in (at *work!*). Mark and I had established a budding friendship by now, built on a robust foundation of being mutual fans of The Fast Show. The team shifts were staggered (two would do 8-4 and the others 9-5), and it didn't take long for Mark and I to be kept on opposite shifts so that we were never together on our own for an hour. By now I had become connected on Facebook with our mutual friend, and when Kerry's profile was suggested to me without even searching for it, I decided it was time to bite the bullet, throw caution to the wind and drop her a line. And just minutes later, her name appeared in my inbox. Although it was nine years ago now, I still remember the way my heart fluttered.

It got the ball rolling and we chatted throughout the morning, although, to coin another Greek myth, my fluttering heart was about to burn and plummet like Icarus when I learned to my dismay that she was actually in a relationship, and had been for some time.

Let's fast forward again then… three years… 2014. Kerry had suddenly split with her boyfriend and was newly available, though of course I had more tact and sensitivity than to jump straight in. She did have a strong social media presence, though, and more or less every time I had opened Facebook over the years she had posted something. And from now on, as you can imagine, each time I saw her face the temptation was increasingly there. A recurring theme in particular were her cats, and I was almost as besotted with them as I still was with her. Both were very long-haired; one was Siamese with large blue eyes like hers, and the other was rather more Gremlin-like but equally adorable. Eventually, I buckled, and messaged asking whether I could get to meet them sometime. This wasn't 100% false pretence, I did genuinely want to meet them, but certainly not as much as I wanted to meet her again. I had only ever seen her once in the flesh, but going by the photos of herself that she was continually uploading, she hadn't changed much. A few experiments with the hair, but always her.

The wait was agonising, but after a while she replied and agreed to let me meet them, and also that it would be nice to catch up in person again after all this time. It was arranged for some time the following week, but sadly this didn't materialise as she dropped me a message out of the blue to say she had decided to give things another go with her ex. This knocked me straight over the pavilion. I was already having a bad day at work and now reading this was too much. Not that I did or said anything to her whatsoever, I was respectful and amicable in my reply and wished her all the best, but I did post something later on Facebook about it being a day to forget, and the next thing I knew I was blocked… She must have seen it and thought I was having a go at her, but it was nothing of the sort, I was just opening the valve and venting some frustration. Nothing directed at her, nothing that even hinted at her, but just like that, after three years, it looked as though I would never see or speak with her ever again.

Next week, though, equally out of the blue, I got a friend request and message apologising for being an idiot, asking me there and then quite bluntly whether I had a thing for her.

Imagine the rush. I thought long and hard before confirming that indeed I did, and always had done, and that I was mildly broken by the previous week's events, not to mention confused by the subsequent blocking which didn't quite seem deserved. She acknowledged that she'd had a bit of a brain freeze, and that she also felt things could have happened between us. I can't remember why she had decided to get back with her ex, but it had clearly not worked out, and here she was inviting me over again, and this time with the uncertainty removed as to whether she was attracted to me.

I love a good romance story and, though I mentioned the Nora Ephron films before, there is no better one for me than *The Office*. Tim and Dawn in the UK, Jim and Pam in the US, take your pick. Although Kerry and I never worked together, we had first met in an office, and, well, this was starting to feel like it might just be another successful spin-off.

She lived in Malvern, which was closer to the hospital than my new house at the time, so it made sense then to stick around and swing by hers after work once she'd had a little time to get back and organise herself and the cats. I don't know how I would have coped with the situation had I not already been informed that there was a mutual attraction; I'm not sure my nerves would have handled it. That being said, I still didn't know how she truly felt yet. After all, the breakup was still so fresh and, trust me, I am not one for ever trying to capitalise on something like that. I had no intention of making any kind of move when I went over, in fact I promised myself I wouldn't, and my mind was clear. Plus, I was still thinking about the cats, and almost as excited to meet them too.

This meant that when she did open the door and I finally

saw her again, I wasn't overwhelmed by the moment. It felt just as it had those three years ago, and we immediately clicked again as mates first and foremost. Thankfully all the correspondence in between hadn't made things awkward in the slightest, and conversation bloomed. Of course, having the pets as a centre of attention was a convenient way of deflecting any discussion about us and, as she took me upstairs to meet them, my heart fluttered again. Quite marvellous little buggers.

I'd grown up with many different cats over the years and have developed somewhat of a modus operandi, especially for a first encounter: yes the classic kiss sound seems to register as an affable greeting, but always let them come to you, no matter how long it takes. Don't accidentally block a doorway, this way they can exit any time and don't feel cornered. Don't go straight for the top or back of their head (imagine a giant doing that to you), oh and here's a goodun: slowly squinting your eyes is a big display of affection that they recognise, and may indeed reciprocate. I'm sure I'm stating the obvious by saying it's all about trust, and must be on their terms, and if you heed the aforementioned you should strike a bond. If you want them to really like you, cardboard or Dreamies. Christ I feel like Moses now.

Anyway, Kerry was obviously smitten with them herself, and it was pretty much all we talked about over the hour or so that I was there. Although we'd discussed many other things down the years, for some reason I don't ever recall taste in films and TV really coming up. Music definitely had, and as I had suspected on day one, she was indeed a rock chick and very much into her metal, too. And when I browsed her DVD collection it felt almost a quirk of fate when I saw *The Office* in there. Further to this, the entire box-set of *Frasier* – a show I knew I liked and had always wanted to watch properly in order. More on that later.

After playtime with the cats and discussing the DVD's, an hour had easily elapsed and we needed to think about wrapping it up. Then, on complete impulse – as unexpected to me as it was to her – I kissed her. I remember back to my first kiss in school and others down the years in other relationships, but this was the first time it had felt like this. The ice hadn't needed breaking, and there might have been even more magic in it had I had the mystique and discipline to have waited for at least our second meeting, but I couldn't help myself in the moment. And in that moment, the stars and planets aligned, and I felt quite possibly the best I had ever felt before in my life. In some ways, I consider it my true first kiss, the first time I fell unconditionally in love, and, thankfully, I wasn't pushed away at the time.

It was still time to leave though. We simply left it that I would be in touch, perhaps to meet again at the weekend. Imagine the drive home. The grin would not leave my face until I was asleep. Even then I'm not convinced it did.

That weekend, we would have our first actual date. It remains to this day the best one I have had. I'll paint the scene. A music festival on a boat. Not a bad start. I can't remember if it was Friday or Saturday night, but drinks were flowing with a raucous yet controlled atmosphere, perfect for a gig. Neither of us would drink that night though, as I was driving and Kerry did not drink at all. In another quirk of fate, we got back onto the topic of music, and one band in particular of whom we were mutual fans; Radiohead. I asked her what her favourite song of theirs was, which was also one of mine, and I kid you not, minutes later the band started playing it, as if they had heard us. We looked at each other in disbelief. Fireworks.

Although, as it did later with Amy, things moved at pace, it did not mean staying at hers that night. Neither of us wanted to mess this up; it was too perfect, too fragile. The following weekend she would visit me in Upton-upon-Severn, and the second date was almost as perfect as the first. We went out for a meal and then sat by the river for hours, before returning to mine to cuddle up and watch Alan Partridge's *Mid Morning Matters*.

And a few days later, we were officially in a relationship. I still couldn't quite believe what was happening. She was the love of my life; I had felt it years before, and boy did I know it now.

OK then. Unlike with Amy, it just doesn't feel right to me to tell you too much about the details of the relationship itself. Largely because – unlike Amy – it was for the most part a joy, doesn't pertain to the overall story I am telling here, and out of respect deserves to stay mainly between us. I can give you the whistle-stop tour though.

It didn't take long for me to meet her mum and stepfather, and I knew we would get on. I've always had a way with parents (ironically not so much my own), and when it came to meeting her family, the Hughes charm was on full show. Her stepfather was especially easy to click with. He was a Walsall fan, and at the time we (Brentford) were battling it out with them in league one. At that stage we hadn't started pinching their manager and best players, which helped.

As I ingratiated with the family, this continued to include

the cats. I had some amusing nicknames particularly for one of them, but I'm quite happy for those to remain a private joke. I was spending more and more time over there and, as my birthday was just around the corner, I was about to be gifted (and most touchingly in the way it was presented), the spare key to her place. I hadn't moved in by this point but I was staying over regularly. Nothing to do with the proximity to my workplace, but rather the fact we were now joined at the hip.

There was one amusing incident around this time I'd like to tell you quickly about, even though this one probably *should* remain private. The company she worked for were putting on an open day in a nearby countryside park. I was more than happy to volunteer myself for one of the stalls, especially as Kerry would not be available to help on these; no, her occupation was to dress as a giant Snoopy and roam the grounds as children's entertainment. To the kids this went down as well as anyone could have hoped, but to poor Kerry it was no laughing matter. For an autumn afternoon the sun was beating it down, and this Snoopy ensemble was a furnace. This meant that in downtime, Kerry would not hesitate in shedding it for an hour's refuge, which required my assistance in one of the disabled toilets. These toilets had a particularly awkward lock on them, and, well, guess the rest. I thought I'd locked it, and about half-way through the saga that was getting her out of the thing, the door suddenly swung open to reveal Snoopy from the waist up and thong from the waist down, to three young children, a bemused mother, and an *amused* father. Although like here her identity was preserved, it was an excruciatingly embarrassing moment, and it took some time before we were able to laugh about it. But once we did, I don't think we ever stopped.

A month or so later, I officially moved in, and things were serious in a good way. In fact, a month or so after that, we were looking for a new place together, and the process went by in a flash. As we were in a small house and her ex had spent time there himself, it seemed all too exciting to find a new place entirely of our own to forge a new chapter. I'm fairly certain that it was the first house we viewed that we ended up going for, barely a mile away in the same estate. We had it all mapped out in terms of where possessions would go, and the spare bedroom would combine our musical instruments (she had a couple of her own), and we'd be in there in time for Christmas.

I even remember the process of submitting our character references to the letting agency. I wanted the following for mine but it was cruelly intercepted:

"Charming, witty, sophisticated, Mr Hughes is of a rare breed. A mere flicker of his eyebrow can melt the coldest of hearts, and strike fear into his enemies. He is exemplary at keeping a property".

Moving house is supposedly the seventh most stressful thing in life. But I don't recall it seeming that way. We did the classic things like painting the spare room together. One thing I've neglected to mention is that I also hosted a radio show at the time. A world-leading internet radio station for metal and, in particular, unsigned bands. I would attend and review gigs, as well as having early access to and reviewing albums from some of my favourite metal bands. I even got to interview one of them: Cult of Luna. If this wasn't enjoyable enough, every Friday night I would co-host a two-hour show for thousands of listeners across the globe. I remember Kerry and I painting the spare room whilst playing back a recording of the show I had done the night before, in which I had doted on her – unbeknownst to me – after she had fallen asleep. This meant that playing it back for the first time was a wonderful moment, though.

And for a short while, these moments would continue. We had our first Christmas together, and spring. Back on day one all those years ago, we had established a sense of humour between us, and our pillow talk was at times ridiculous. I remember an occasion where we went through the alphabet like a game of tennis, naming a band or film that started with that letter, then the next, and so on. We then turned to animals, then foods, and I distinctly remember getting to the letter R and she went for *"Rennies"*. I don't think I'd ever laughed harder in my life. You know when you can't control how your laugh comes out and it resembles more of a demented gurn…? It was the way she said it.

But there was by now an undercurrent of trouble brewing, and it was largely down to financial problems. My monthly outgoings were too much for my incomings, and I was petrified to broach the subject, especially as it was something I had known about for some time. I was still paying off the car, but also a couple of other loans, and my wages weren't enough to handle these on top of the utility bills. The cats weren't cheap to look after either, and, although the two I mentioned before were Kerry's, by this point we had a third *and* fourth which had just gone on her credit card. Why didn't I stop us?! If she had known about my struggles, she would have known I couldn't compensate and it probably wouldn't have been an issue. I just didn't have the courage. And there was me a few pages ago saying it's all about trust. Though it's no excuse whatsoever, I was petrified of it jeopardising things between us. All I wanted was to see her happy. I was too stupid to realise that the longer I kept this under the carpet, the more it could threaten to ruin everything.

So, I talked about weeks in my life rather than days. Here's another. Let's start with the good, as there were two things that week that were overwhelmingly positive. I had handed in my notice at the NHS for a new application support role. There wasn't much of a pay increase, but it did represent an exciting new opportunity. The NHS even by this point was well in the process of being dismantled and privatised, and there was the sense I was fleeing a sinking ship and no mistake.

Brentford, after years of languishing in leagues one and two, were about to be promoted to the championship. It was a tense final day; we did our bit and beat Preston 1-0, but were reliant on the Wolves vs Rotherham result, and that game was carnage. After 90 minutes it was 4-4, and our promotion wasn't guaranteed, but a late flurry of action from Wolves in some ten minutes of stoppage time saw it finish 6-4, which sealed our promotion with them. I went through the roof. I would have said *"see for yourself"* as there is a lovely photo of the moment, but sadly I can't really include it. It was of course Kerry that had taken it, and when I look back on it with what was to come that week, I still have mixed emotions. But I'm glad it exists. You could even see one of the cats failing to recognise the occasion.

Speaking of the cats, by this point I had finally given in and opened up about the extent of my struggles as well. Naturally, she hadn't taken it well, but we were working through it. We knew that the current outgoings weren't sustainable if we were ever going to get out of the situation, and outside of the bills that couldn't be avoided, it was obvious where all the money was going. And though emotionally devastating, it was one that was quite quick to sort out.

We put three of the cats up for sale; the two we had recently bought between us, and one of the original two Kerry already had, and within about 24 hours they were effectively sold. Saying goodbye to the recent two hadn't been quite so bad, but saying goodbye to one of the originals that Kerry had, was, and there's no way of emphasising this enough, dreadful. Think of the Shame & Guilt assignment in rehab, when I cried for the first time. Though I did shed a tear over other moments during that assignment, this was actually the one in particular I was thinking of. Although I was emotional in the therapy room in retrospect, I held it together here at the time, whereas Kerry didn't, and understandably so. I was so naïve I didn't quite realise just how much this moment was the start of the end. Perhaps unsurprisingly, it happened the same week.

Kerry came home from her mum's, her sunglasses concealing the state she was in. As soon as she removed them and said *"We need to talk"*, there came the crushing realisation that this was probably about to be a break-up. It turned out that it wasn't quite... but we did finally have the conversation that needed to happen over the issue of trust, and the fact I had concealed this for so long. Though I had done it with "honest" intentions, and truly out of fear of losing her, it just didn't feel that way to her at the time and I can still understand this. We were on eggshells, and though the start of my new job represented a small increase in incomings, it just wasn't enough to tip the balance after what had just happened with the cats. And we were never quite the same again.

Within this same seven-day period, on the Monday I began my new job. Now, back in Chapter 5 I said that starting this job coincided with some personal trauma, and that it was a miracle I got through my probation period there.

Day three of said new job. The previous night we had both been tossing and turning somewhat and neither of us had a particularly fruitful sleep. She too had changed jobs not too long ago and required a much earlier rise than me, and she said first thing that morning she didn't feel up to it and would be calling in sick. There's no way I could have done the same so early into my new job, and so I got ready and set off a couple of hours later. And a couple of hours after that, around 10, I realised why she had been tossing and turning so much.

I received a long text message saying she simply couldn't do this any more, and that she would be staying at her mum's overnight so that after work I could go over and collect all of my stuff, and leave no trace of ever having been there for the following day. She didn't word it like that, but that's how it was.

I couldn't move. My heart was racing though, and not long after I bolted out of the building. I quickly pulled myself together and went back in to explain what had happened, and it was almost as much of a shock to my boss as it had been to me. Just a few weeks earlier before I started, the company were celebrating a good quarter and had paid for everyone including myself to enjoy an all-expenses-paid jaunt to Alton Towers, with a stay in the hotel. On the coach there my boss had sat with me, given that I didn't yet know anyone. And I had been gushing to him over Kerry, and how I thought we were the real deal. If I'd been thinking properly, I would have seen the situation for what it was. As I was hurtling around Nemesis and The Smiler, she was moping around at work. That night as I was making new friends at a free bar, she was coiled alone on the sofa, quickly getting used to not having me around. The following morning as I was putting around the Mini-Golf course, she was putting an exit plan together. And three weeks on, it was her turn to board the runaway train, as I watched on from the station.

I can't remember if I replied to her text or not, but that evening I did as asked and managed to get all my belongings into the car in two or three journeys, leaving her the furniture, and I wrote a lengthy letter pouring my heart and soul which I left on the stairs along with my key. No reply. Despite all of this, and the cut-throat manner in which it had been delivered to me, it was not technically fully over, and I still had hope. It had been called a short break and hiatus, while she got her head together. I may have been devastated, but I got on with it, and was suddenly back temporarily at Mum's.

Days went by, which turned to weeks, and it was still as it was, left open for the possibility of reconcile, provided she got the space she had asked for. I was in a quandary here, as it had been clear from when she had been on the market before that she was desirable. I wanted to give her the space she had requested, yet at the same time I felt I hadn't done enough to emphasise just how much she meant. One night I couldn't help it any longer and messaged her, and was surprisingly invited over straight away. I was barely inside the door before I was in pieces, and it must have been clear at this point just how much she really did mean to me. She still had all the photos of us up in the lounge, and she even came out with a couple of in-jokes, especially one which hinted that some of the disdain over previous events had cleared, and that we might be OK.

What I didn't realise during this visit, was that she was already seeing someone else.

As was her way (remember before we got together), blocking was a go-to defence mechanism and done almost without thought. If I logged out of Facebook, though, and searched her name, I could see her profile again, and then suddenly (as would repeat itself years later with Amy), there she was in the arms of someone else. To make matters worse – much worse in fact – this was someone who's name I recognised from her profile – someone who had always been replying to her posts, but whom I'd never held in any suspicion. Not in my nature, or at least wasn't before that moment. Now suddenly I was questioning everything – *"clearly they're together now – how long has this been in the works? Was it whilst we were still together? Why did she keep it a secret? When was she going to tell me? **Was** she going to tell me?"*. I was already emotionally spent, with this hiatus coinciding with the start of my new job (apparently the 4th most stressful life event) and, as I obsessed overnight as to how this might have unfolded, it became too much for me, and again, I snapped.

With Amy, it was predominantly out of anger and hurt pride, and despite the stupidity of what followed, I was thinking with a strange clarity. This time (and this was the first time I had ever had any kind of emotional melt-down), it never crossed my mind to in any way go after Kerry, or her fella. No I just had to get out of the house, with the most dominant thought in my mind being to kill myself, and how best to do it. By this point Mum had woken up, and when she came in to see if I was OK, that was when I truly lost it. It somehow validated that this was real. I threw my phone at the wall, put my fist into my digital piano, and sprinted out of the house in a fit that most infants would find pathetic. Had anyone truly understood just how broken I was in that moment, I'm sure they would have taken it a great deal more seriously.

I knew I had to act fast and, before Mum could chase me to the end of the path, I was in the car and flying out of the neighbourhood. 'Luckily', there was a shop around the corner that was open at this ungodly hour and I remember buying a litre bottle of whiskey and tearing away, trying to figure out what on Earth I was going to do. The reason for buying the drink... well, in that moment I was sure in my mind that I wanted this, to put this suffering to bed, but – pun not intended – I wouldn't have had the bottle. As I drove away, something reminded me of a cul-de-sac in a neighbouring village which had a fence that led to a train track. "Better" still, it was sufficiently distant between stations so that any train would be coming sufficiently fast.

By the time I had thought of this and parked up there, I was thinking more clearly. Strangely, I remember being even more concerned with doing it. I thought back to our first date and the Radiohead song the band had played for us. In the back of the car, I had a small plaque with the lyrics of that song and our names against it, that had been custom-made for us. It was of course one of the things I had scooped up when I was collecting everything from the house, and it had stayed in the back of my car, with me not knowing what to do with it.

As I went back to the first date, thought through everything, I remembered that this was in the car, and I ripped the bin-bag open, strewing everything else across the back seat, and laid it on the bonnet as a suicide note if you will.

I traversed the fence with the bottle of whiskey stuffed in my jacket pocket, and sat on the tracks. It was about 07:00 by this point, and suddenly everything was still. All the noise had been in my head and for the first time I seemed to have a minute to myself. No one had seen me pull in, and I sat cross-legged on the tracks for nearly an hour, swigging and reminiscing further. I turned to the factors outside of Kerry, my friends and family for example, the other things I loved in life, and whether it was worth throwing all of that away over this.

I heard a train approach and could tell it was at full speed. My heart didn't race, if anything it made me calmer. Cool as you like, I got up and sidled towards a bush where I probably wouldn't be seen, let it go past, then returned to the same spot. Not long afterwards though, as I got half way through the whiskey, emotions were starting to get the better of me again, and I felt ready. I would have another thirty minutes at least before the next train arrived, and each passing minute presented a great deal more danger. There was an elderly lady walking her dog, who managed to see me from the fence where I had jumped over, and called to me. Something made me go over and talk, presumably the drink, and we had quite a long chat about why I was there. Now that the alcohol was in my system, I was happy to be open, but at the same time I remember trying to wrap up the conversation so that she would disappear, hopefully appeased with the impression that I was fine.

I have always had a certain way with people, and even

in the state I was in, it seemed that I had talked her round by making her think she had talked me round, and she left back up the road. The bottle was still half full (or half empty at the time), and I grabbed it and resumed position, this time further down and away from view of the fence. This stranger, as valiant as she was, had sadly done nothing to talk me out of anything. It felt like a good twenty minutes since the last train, and soon enough, all the pain would be literally buried.

Ten minutes later, I had virtually the entirety of the bottle down my neck, and there was no doubt in my mind that this was going ahead now. I can tell you, I don't think I would have chickened out or seen sense at the last minute. I had lost proper awareness of my surroundings, and so I didn't hear a car pull up behind mine near the fence, nor did I hear two people climb it and approach behind me; the first thing I knew about it was when I was being dragged off the track. It must have been the combination of my mum alerting them that I was missing, and the stranger at the fence alerting the police of a man with dark thoughts that matched their description, and they got there in time. Two or three minutes later, as I was coiled on the ground next to their car in tears, the train flew past that would have taken all of this away, and my destination was a psychiatric ward for the day instead.

*

Not much humour to be had in that story, eh? It wasn't Kerry's fault – she had every right to move on – but the secrecy over it, especially with the ambiguity over us having a second chance, was devastating, and likely the reason for so many issues that

I carried right through to the end of the decade.

When I started rehab, the incident with Amy was a month old, whereas Kerry was five years young, and I imagine you can see why she formed more of the basis of my therapy than Amy did. I never stopped loving her over those years and never fully processed the events of that day, or indeed the weeks that led to it. Whilst I spent my first nights in jail, in May last year, it was funnily enough Kerry that came back to me and whom I couldn't shift. In fact, the prison pillows were so bad that I had done away with mine, and had resorted to folding my jumpers instead. This made the pillow an awkward lump, and the next thing I was clutching it to me as I went to sleep. Rather than thinking about Amy and where it all went wrong, my mind was cast years back to the events of this chapter, where my life really started going wrong. I cuddled Kerry to sleep every night I was there, and by the time June and rehab came around, she was much fresher in the memory than Amy was.

Getting back to rehab briefly then, I'm sure you can also see why it was so important that I finally processed and buried everything that had happened that day. Kerry's name did appear once in my exit plan, but it was right at the very bottom of the priority list and would only ever be a message of apology. In the 12 Steps of Alcoholics Anonymous, Step 8 is as follows: *"Made a list of all persons we harmed, and became willing to make amends to them all"*.

Step 9: *"Made direct amends to such people wherever possible, except when to do so would injure them or others"*

Though at no stage was I or any other client expected to follow the 12 steps, these two did resonate with me, and it felt right to at least send a proper apology at some point. But the thing is, Kerry and I had actually spoken since that fateful day.

I never fell out of love with her and because of that it just didn't feel right getting into another relationship any time soon. I slept around over the following year, again not particularly in my nature, but it probably did help to some small degree. But knowing that Kerry was nearby (I was soon living very close to her again for work purposes), it had been impossible not to fantasise about seeing her and how it might pan out. She knew the extent of my breakdown, I'm sure it must have been traumatic to hear, and as such I hadn't heard from her. Nor did I particularly want to in the aftermath. Presumably, there was the communal hope that it would all wash away, and that, after time, it had never happened. I knew it was inevitable I was going to bump into her sooner or later, and finally in early 2018 it happened, in a McDonald's. She had changed jobs again, just down the road, and I was about to begin my foray into the theme park industry. It was a short chat and caught me completely off-guard. Any dialogue that I had ever planned out in my mind was slapped away just like that. Thankfully, it was a reasonably amicable chatter over some ten minutes, and we wished each other well for the future. She especially wished me luck for the upcoming theme park job, and I was quite happy to leave it there, until a week later when I started. In terms of job inductions, I have never experienced anything quite like this one. Here are some highlight quotes:

- *"Mind the goose turds."*
- *"Check out my award-winning sock puppet."*
- *"The guns are easy enough to figure out; you'll see."*
- *"Karen, could you bring the kittens in please?"*

The latter, in particular, had made me think of Kerry. It was less than a week since I'd bumped into her and, as if I wasn't already thinking about her enough when I should have been focusing on the job, seeing kittens brought it all back again. You'd think that this subject would have been especially touchy, but I took a photo of them and sent it to her (I was unblocked by this point), and as I expected she loved it.

Fast forward another year… almost to the day. Amy and I were in bed, when I received a random text from Kerry – the first time I had heard from her since – to say that tragically her beloved cat which she had kept when we sold the others (the adorable goblin and my favourite too), had died in most horrible circumstances. Hearing this, and thinking of the poor thing, affected me more than hearing from Kerry itself did. Despite the reason for the message, Amy did not take kindly to this exchange. She did know her name and the full story, but I don't think she quite ever understood the gravity.

These two brief conversations were all it had been since we separated though, and I felt a proper apology was due in trying to bury the hatchet. But that was one of the lowest if not *the* lowest priority in my exit plan. In terms of reconciliation, family and friends like Loz were much higher on the agenda, and in terms of any prospective new romances, I knew that was something that would happen naturally and not be rushed. In fact I hadn't made any plans around that at all; the only reference to it was in the Hopes & Dreams assignment, where I remind you I wrote *"Someone chilled, someone who seems to genuinely appreciate who I am. Someone with a creative flair… the dream scenario would be a fellow guitarist, or singer."*

10

Megan

So, back to day 28 of rehab. Keeping with the exit strategy, pretty much all of my plans had been centred around the following month only, for the simple reason that I had my court date and sentence looming, and there was still the very real possibility of going back to prison.

Once I ticked off the new Plaid album, I cracked on with contacting friends to let them know what had happened. I'd been missing from social media for about five weeks by that point, and whilst the notifications themselves were hardly important, checking my inboxes was. My thoughts then turned to the recurring priorities. Seek out local AA meetings and find at least two a week, and continue with healthy eating and exercise. I kept up the smoothies and salads, and joined the local gym and would go three times in the first week, and then four or five times onwards. The weight fell off, and this along with the confidence from rehab and AA gave me a real glow inside and out.

A couple of weeks later, I was to revisit the magistrates court, but not for judgement day yet – rather to meet probation for an assessment of eligibility for a community sentence. This lasted over three hours and required talking over Amy in great detail. Although, as I said, I don't particularly feel any regret over the event, that's not to say I haven't truly considered how it affected her, and I'm not saying it out of spite. What I mean is I wouldn't go back and change anything, for it was an event that sadly needed to happen. I can't remember whether I made this point then – probably not – but I do remember stating I believed Amy was the type of person to embellish any kind of victim's statement, in an attempt to maximise the punishment. Though I still believe this to be true, it is ultimately my assumption, and naturally this assumption found its way into my final assessment report. I would not learn of what was in the report though until my sentence a couple of weeks later.

I also spoke at length about what rehab had done for me, and my newfound eagerness to be the best I could be in life. I was still sober and had no immediate plans for alcohol, and was starting to make new friends at AA. Life was good again, great in fact, and it must have shown.

On the way out, there was an elderly gentleman struggling with his zimmer frame down the stairs to reception. As I held the door, he said he didn't recognise me and I explained I was there for the first time. His reply, and I'll never forget it: *"Cunts"*.

I continued my exit plan through the next fortnight – gym, AA, friends and family, and with each hour loomed judgement day: July 15th, which soon arrived. I was reacquainted with my solicitor, who remarked on how well I looked, before giving me the good news that the probation assessment on the whole had been very complimentary, and was proposing a community order rather than further custody of any kind.

After another agonising wait, it was time to go in. I did not recognise these particular magistrates, even though it was something like the fifth time I had been there that year over everything. I did recognise the prosecution, and it was very much déjà vu as he read through the report of the fateful day's events. He then went into something that was new to me but that I was expecting, and made my heart sink the moment he announced it... the victim's statement. As I said, I may have only met Amy that year, but I knew her well enough to predict the manner in which it was given. Although I do not believe the extent of what was told and wasn't surprised to hear any of it, it certainly didn't make for good hearing and I gulped watching the magistrates as it was read out.

This concluded the prosecution, and the magistrates turned to my solicitor to announce *"We believe this crosses the custody threshold, so you might want to change your approach"*. It's got nothing to do with the fact they were all female, though at the time I foolishly did wonder. It was stiflingly hot in the courtroom, especially the dock. It was mid-July and there was no air conditioning, and having just heard what the magistrates said, I was having hot flushes regardless.

I knew the case that was about to be made for my defence, which was relatively quick and simple to deliver in comparison.

The magistrates retired to make their decision, and some 15 minute later returned for the verdict:

10 weeks custody, suspended for 18 months.

A wave of joy and relief, as it meant that, after consideration, they had agreed with probation and my defence that I was suitable to serve punishment in the community after all. This must have been largely down to my stint in rehab, and the progress I had shown. Really it was a huge opportunity for me to hit CTRL+ALT+DEL, clear the cache, and open a new window.

There were conditions. An indefinite restraining order with Amy, and I would have to meet with probation once a week to monitor my progress. Two conditions notable in their absence, were any unpaid community work, or any kind of tag. My parents had been at the back of the courtroom, and when I got to see them outside there was huge relief all round. I'd been given a lifeline, a big one, and I wasn't going to muck about with it. I made a huge thank you to my solicitor, who thankfully I would never see again.

July danced into August. The relief from judgement day, along with my newfound health drive, had me in better mental and physical shape than ever. In six weeks I had lost almost two stone. And I wanted to show it off. I put up a post on Facebook about the journey I had been on over the last two months, to an overwhelming response. I had clearly not lost the love and respect of most of my friends; on the contrary, it was higher than before. It was after this that I decided maybe it was time to think about dating again. It was sooner than I had planned, but it felt like it tied in naturally with this fresh new start. And I had worked through my feelings over past relationships now. It was time.

I opted for a different app this time round, and pretty much immediately started getting matches. Like before, one profile in particular stood out straight away. I mentioned certain boxes being ticked; with Kerry it had been the rock chick element, and with Amy it had been cricket. Things like this were always more important to me than aesthetics. With Kerry the physical attraction *had* been there, whereas it wasn't quite so much with Amy, and I wouldn't say it was particularly here. But two much bigger boxes were ticked off from one of the photos instead:

- *Guitarist*
- *Singer*

Not in occupation, but for a hobby. But that was more than fine, and my heart leapt again. I had remembered her name, and each time I was notified of a match I was praying for it to be her. And this time – hallelujah – Megan appeared. As much as it was a relief to see the name, it was what was written below that stood out the most though… a thousand miles away. Somewhat outside my preferred radius.

When she opened dialogue, however, it became clear this wasn't a bug in the app; she was currently on a short break in Barcelona, and actually lived in Stratford-upon-Avon. We would chat over the next few days, and more boxes were ticked. If Amy was full of emotion, unpredictability, a bit fizzy in general, then Megan was the total opposite. She was affable and more considered. It did mean the conversation ticked along without maybe the same excitement, but somehow felt so much better for it. The real problem was at my end not hers, as at some point, as soon as possible, I both wanted and needed to tell her about my year so far. It was obviously the right thing – not least because a condition of my order was to notify probation of anything like this happening, who would then want to check with her that I had given the truth and full extent. But more so than that, I just wanted it off my chest.

Things had moved nice and slowly, but as each minute went by, I was twisting more and more. After all it was not just a recent situation but a current one, given I now had a criminal record. Eventually, whilst out for a drink with Loz, I had the courage (not of the Dutch variety) to go for it. Really this was a poor choice of moment though, as it meant my attention was taken well and truly away from Loz. I had to take time to convey this to Megan correctly, as it would have been a jarring piece of information at the receiving end. I had already mentioned her to Loz and he had noted the glint in my eye, and I think understood how important this was.

With her response came another big box ticked, two in fact; caring and understanding. She recognised the difficulty in opening up so early when it might have turned most away, and she remarked on how well I had done to get through and beyond it. She also recognised that as a human being I would not be defined by that fateful day, but rather how I bounced back and learned and grew from the experience. As with fitness, everyone tires, but the barometer is in the recovery period. I was mentally and physically fit now though and, thank God, it commanded her respect.

As we continued chatting, we learned that we had some other huge things in common besides the music. She was another Vic and Bob fan, in particular *Shooting Stars*, which

I had not missed an episode of since its inception during my school days. This meant she also had an affection for my random and at times warped sense of humour. I'd had an output for this down the years; on Facebook there was and still is a secret group of around twenty members, of which the purpose is to deposit, as and when, whatever kind of random sketch is in our head. I've submitted plenty down the years, and they will remain in the group, however, there was one that I had decided to share to the wider Facebook audience for some reason, and now her, which she loved.

Whilst perhaps not my funniest, it is one of the more accessible ones, and maybe the one that sums me up the best.

If the above didn't work, try "Scott Hughes poppadom" on YouTube. Sending her something like that was an equally calculated risk, but I thought it would go down well and indeed it did. By this point she had got back from España, and Saturday was touting itself for a potential first date. This was agreed, and I couldn't wait. Thankfully to quell the nerves, the day before this was a trip to Warwick Castle which had been arranged some time ago with the family. A lovely day, and our first all together since the recent turbulence. I had been there before as a nipper, but far too young to appreciate any of the heritage.

Eventually, Saturday came and we decided on the meeting point; a pub/restaurant not far from where she lived, at 12:00. No boat festival this time and hopefully no pineapple incident either. Of course I had just lost my driving licence, and so it was a First Great Western train that got me into town at 11:45, with a 15-minute walk to get there. Perfect.

Now, this mode of transport meant, obviously, that if I wanted to have a drink, then I could. I'd had nearly three months without, and with the newfound clarity of thought, I had looked back on my relationship with alcohol as a whole, ahead of this potential new relationship with Megan. There had never been a problem with the social side, or on my own at the right times, and I had known even before rehab that if it was kept this way then I was safe. And the decision was made, by myself alone, that I would see how this went for a period of time. Ahead of the date, I had been to the pub on one occasion and had two pints, with my headphones in, and taken my first step towards proving control.

Noon was of course very early in the day to start drinking, and this was on my mind as I walked through town. We hadn't set an end time; we would simply see how it went. And if we did have a lunchtime pint, then we would counteract this with, you guessed it, lunch. I don't know whether it was my newfound confidence, but as I approached the pub I had a powerful sense in my mind that this was destined to be.

Amy had proved to be stormy waters at the best of times, and Megan, still on paper at that point, was the rainbow. And as I walked in, there she was, at a table in the corner.

The word that leaps to me is radiant. Not least for her floral dress. She was more or less the same height as me, with very short dark hair heavily gelled aside. She had also lost weight recently, and seeing her there in her dress, smiling as she was, was a better moment than I could have hoped for. She shone every bit as brightly as the rays of sun kissing her through the window. And again, as with Kerry, something told me I had to kiss her. I don't think I even said hello.

It could have been seen as some sort of party trick, but, thankfully, I don't think she saw or felt it that way. To me it just felt natural, comfortable and right, albeit a risk. I made some quip that *"I greet everyone like that by the way"*, and the ice was well and truly shattered.

We talked for hours. As you have experienced, I do love a tangent, as does she, and it meant it took at least two hours to get through our careers. Again, most comforting, not least because conversation was flowing, but also that it was the preceding years of my life that were of more interest to her, and which to her shaped the person opposite.

The day continued in similar fashion; we moved to other venues, and as the evening came there were no intentions of separating. As if by fate, we happened upon an intimate backstreet acoustic gig, and stood there in the audience, hand in hand, in a quite brilliant moment.

I was later invited back, and did not dither on my response. She shared a house with her sister on the outskirts of town, and I was forewarned of her being rather socially awkward, and not to be offended if she withdrew herself upon our entry. As we tiptoed upstairs, there was no sign of anyone. Going straight to her bedroom was not for reasons you may think, but rather for a lounge, leaving the communal downstairs one available. The last thing I wanted to do was make anyone feel uncomfortable in their own home.

We got the laptop out and had a joyous remainder of the night browsing comedy on YouTube; certain Vic and Bob sketches, and those hilarious out-takes from *Extras*. One thing that had slightly marred the tranquillity, was a message Megan received from her sister, which without intending to I had seen and partially read over her shoulder. She had a migraine and was going straight to bed. I was looking forward to meeting her and hopefully making a good impression, but equally I didn't mind what seemed like her excuses to delay it. It struck a chord if anything, as exactly the sort of spurious reason I have given at times in my life to get out of something. Megan's reaction all but confirmed it, as she locked her phone and cast it to the bedside table without reply.

We put on an Athletico Mince podcast and spooned as we went to sleep. As far as I can recall, this was the first time I had ever been comfortable enough to drift off like that with anyone. Although things had moved carefully enough to this point, it notched up a gear that day, and again after having slept on the situation… as by 10:00 we were in a relationship. And this one did go on Facebook, as we were both proud of it. The publicity was in stark contrast to how it was with Amy, and the reaction we got was touching. In fact, the same day, I would be taken just minutes round the corner to meet the folks. We had been sensible with our drinking the night before and so I wasn't ropey for the occasion. I could have a shower, but would have to remain in the same clothes. The plus-side of this, though, was that I still looked smart/casual in a white T-shirt (the pineapple one from the self-portrait) with a grey blazer over the top, a pair of smart jeans which I think Amy had initially gifted to me, and, come to think of it, the same white converse from that photo with her too.

Megan's parents were as gentle and warm as she was. Though this must have been a swift turn of events for them, they were happy to welcome me in so early, and as far as I can recall the Hughes charm was there from the door. It transpires, they both had past addictions of their own. Megan told me of this on the walk there, perhaps to make me more comfortable, but she hadn't yet decided to tell them about my issues. Even if she had though, I doubt it would have changed a great deal, as it seemed as if, on the whole, placidity ran in the family. Music clearly also did; her father had an expansive vinyl collection including many of my favourite records, which made beautifully for another ice-breaker. He, like myself, was into progressive rock of the 70s, so I must have impressed when I waxed lyrical about my favourite band of the era and genre: Gentle Giant. Forget Genesis, Jethro Tull, Yes, even King Crimson; GG were the pantheon for me. Just listen to the album *Free Hand*, or their opus, *Three Friends*.

Back to Ricky Gervais and *Extras* though for a second. On the walk over I had also been forewarned rather comically that her Dad looked just like him, which had been somewhat of a running joke in the family. Although he had the classic Brent goatee, I didn't especially see any more. But as we sat down over a coffee and I looked to Megan, I suddenly saw it slightly in her. Only mildly, but her smile in particular now reminded me of his trademark grin, circa 2004 when he'd lost the facial hair. It didn't help that she had the *exact* same haircut too. At first, it didn't bother me in the slightest, it was just something of note, and was as quickly forgotten as it was observed.

A week passed with a second date the following weekend, and much like the second one with Kerry, it was every bit as enjoyable as the first. I remember we were on the phone in location of each other in the town centre, and as I turned a corner suddenly there she was again. A different radiant dress this time, but the same radiant smile. And I wasn't thinking of Ricky, thankfully. Our embrace must have looked soppy to drivers by, but who cared. It was so good to see her again. We enjoyed another evening and night, I met her sister this time albeit briefly, and the following day it was Megan's turn to meet the parents.

We had a Sunday roast with Dad at the local, then got a lift into the neighbouring town to meet Mum. Both took to her. It would have been hard not to; she was so gentle. A bit of a chameleon, but that's OK, right? An eagerness to please. Playing it safe. There was a sense all round that I'd finally met the rainbow as I'd hoped. After Mum's, we took a walk through a nearby nature reserve under the autumn sun and moon, and returned with a nice collection of photos of us. I thought back to Amy, and how illicit that one picture had felt, and it was so refreshing to be back to normal with someone. I wanted to show her off, and this time I could.

Further weeks passed, and we were learning more and more what we had in common. There was an issue, but I'll get to that later. Bizarrely, one topic that had come up was controversial movies. She had seen *A Serbian Film*, a quite notorious piece of cinema, and was fascinated by it in a non-perverted way. Equally, I had seen a film called *Irreversible* and this gave me an opportunity to talk about it with someone who understood, which was really quite cathartic. In fact, *Irreversible*, to this day, remains host to possibly the most uncomfortable scene I have ever witnessed, and arguably the most graphic and visceral death ever put to film too. Instrument of choice: fire extinguisher. There's much more to the film than these two moments of course, and much beauty by the way. And as we talked of these moments, there was no sense that either of us were depraved for our interest. It was above all a passion for the arts, and for daring to be bold. Controversy not for the sake of it.

Naturally, we were talking more and more about music too. With us both being guitarists, we were a duet waiting to happen. Also I wanted to push myself to see whether I could sing confidently. There is one song in particular that stands out as the anthem of 2019 for me, which she was keen on covering when I played it to her. I had heard it fittingly soon after the Amy ordeal, and although they're not one of my favourite bands, it has to go down as one of the best pop songs of all time. That one about not crying for yesterday, finding an ordinary world again, learning to survive. You know the one.

We began adding songs to a hypothetical set-list, and the above seemed destined as an encore. It was all too perfect. What on Earth could, or would, mess it up?

11

Kerry: Part II

Let's rewind a smidge again. Before I had met Megan – before
we even knew of each other in fact – I had decided it was time
to drop Kerry a line and apology. *"To make amends with those
we had harmed"*, but no more. Like the last time I had to some
degree planned for a conversation, but that one happened out
of nowhere and this one ended up happening on impulse. No
script to work off, and perhaps this bolstered the sincerity of
the message, as she replied almost immediately and thanked
me for the heartfelt apology. I still wanted to deliver it properly
in person though, and she was surprisingly receptive of this,
too. There was nothing between the lines for her to read into.
A meeting was agreed loosely for sometime in the future, but
before anything was ever finalised, Megan and I had matched

and opened dialogue, and it looked like falling away.

But a week or two after Megan and I were officially together, Kerry messaged again, quite sporadically it seemed, proposing a meetup the following weekend. She had seen Megan through my Facebook, but I don't know how much if at all this had factored into her message. I assumed it simply reminded her that there was an apology to get in the diary. She still lived in Malvern, but would come to the town next door to me for a coffee. Again, in the full interest of transparency, I told Megan that I was meeting up with her, how important this was to my recovery, and she was in unwavering support.

The day arrived, which rather randomly coincided with a major cycling event passing through the town. Absolute bedlam. All the main streets were cordoned off, parking was non-existent, and it took twice as long as the drive itself in order for her to find a space on the outskirts. This meant, strangely like with Megan the previous week, that we were on the phone trying to locate each other. And again, like Megan, I turned a corner and there she was. The same rock chick as ever, sporting a black hoody and backpack dotted in glossy silver stars that competed valiantly with her eyes in the shine of the September sun, and lost. An amicable hug, and in tandem: *"So where the hell are we going to be able to sit down?"*

We found a quaint cafe that I had never been in before, with just a single sofa available. Straight away this threw my plans into the ether; I had not wanted to get too physically close at all, barring a hug at the start. I wanted this professional; for the distance to match the disparity. We took our iced cappuccinos and sat side by side, knees together, and again in tandem: *"So where the hell do we start?"*

I don't remember how long it took, but I told it all. Every unflinching detail. Though I did mention the drama over us, Amy ended up being a topic she was much more interested in, and again I was somewhat shocked to be sympathised with, a reaction I still don't think I necessarily deserve. And all this time we were right in each other's eyes again. Rather than conjuring any moments from our relationship, though, it brought back the first time we met, as friends, which was comforting and encouraging. We moved to the park and chatted for another hour before she made her way home. This wasn't all one-way; I learned of what had changed in her life, and a lot had happened there, too. We clicked like the best of times, but it never felt for a second anything more. Yes, I still fancied the pants off her, but I waved that away, waved her car away, and thank goodness, it had gone well. We had put any past issues to bed it seemed, and it looked as though we were mates again. I can't tell you what that meant.

Usually after a first date, one would thank the other for a *"lovely time"*, even if no intention of meeting again. I don't know where that sits on the courtesy ladder. This *wasn't* a date, but 30 minutes later when Kerry got home she did drop me a text, and after words to the effect of *"thank you for today; good to see you"* etc, she dropped the mini bombshell that she hoped we could have stayed together forever, but that I seemed happy with Megan so no worries…

In some ways a throwaway comment, but I clutched it in disarray. She had been the love of my life, and for five years, I had dreamt of this. I hadn't expected it though, nor oddly did I particularly want it. But suddenly, here it was, and I was at sixes and sevens. I did eventually brush it off though, after all

268

I *was* happy with Megan at the time, and I was *not* going to throw that away.

Kerry and I continued to chat, but nothing like the same density of correspondence with Megan, which was of course just how I wanted it. Yes, this had given me a minor jolt, but I had replied stating, truthfully, that I was happy with Megan and that I was just glad that Kerry and I were friends again. And that relaxed the conversation thereon.

Another family event was about to happen, this time a week in Devon. This had been booked the previous year, before any of the madness, and as we convened for the drive it felt like everything was back to the serenity of years gone by.

Although I had touched base with alcohol again, this had only been on two or three occasions, and I was happy to give it a wide berth over this week, not just because I didn't need it, but also because it was a simple way to demonstrate to everyone that I could live both with and without it. Unfortunately I couldn't contribute to the driving, but the convoy of Mum's car and my brother's was sufficient, and off we set for the rolling downs of Exmoor. Mum had been born in Tavistock, and her uncle lived nearby, so this was not just a retreat to the country, but a mini pilgrimage of sorts.

We had a beautiful cottage to ourselves, with a hot tub. Refuge from just about everything, including phone coverage. Although there was supposed to be Wi-Fi in the cottage, there effectively wasn't, and so I was having to take mini walks up the lane in order to be able to contact Megan. Sometimes there would be a message from Kerry, too, and each and every time I strolled up the lane, they would both be alternating in my thoughts. It was almost like having Megan in the passenger seat, but Kerry in the wing mirror who just wouldn't overtake us. Perhaps the first *real* sign of worry.

We had a week there in total, and the conversation continued down both lanes. My thoughts were still predominantly with Megan though and no mistake. The seaside had always been close to her heart, and I took this coastal break as a nice opportunity to pick out some special gifts for her upon my return. Her birthday was also coming up, and I would plan for that too. One day in particular, two ideas presented themselves, and Kerry would be all but banished from my mind for the remainder of the trip. Megan messaged to say she had dropped another dress size, and as she delivered the news I happened to be in the nucleus of a giant shopping centre. Though I had virtually no money, especially compared to my salary at the start of the year, all I wanted was to spend every little thing I had on her. And as I perused the shops, items left right and centre were singing far more angelically than any AA Jaffa I can remember.

By the end of the afternoon, I had spent two thirds of my spending money for the entire trip on various clothing in her new size, each purchase more exciting than the last. But they weren't enough. What else could I do? More-so than anything money could buy, I hoped I could melt her heart by scouring the beaches and picking out a collection of items to go in a personalised jar; something that could sit on a shelf in her room perhaps. The next five days were spent lovingly scanning thousands of shells and sedimentary stones, with a pinch of sand, and eventually I had a jar's full which I would ribbon-tie and wrap with the other presents. I bought two snazzy gift bags – a large one for birthday clothes and a smaller for the holiday gifts – and as I went to bed they remained in my peripheral on the table, tokens of how much I really *did* care, and a growing excitement for getting back the next day to present them. We had already planned to meet in the evening.

About half way home, we stopped in a service station, and rather than a conventional comfort break I instead took the opportunity to send a quick video to her, fraught with all the silliness that was my style, saying I would be back within a couple of hours and that I couldn't wait. As we rejoined the motorway I received her reply, followed by another message from someone else – a message that stopped me in my tracks, sent my heart rate through the sunroof... and, believe it or not, it wasn't from Kerry.

Remember back at the end of Chapter 2, when I received a random message from Amy's new boyfriend later in the year? Though I didn't recognise his name (Tom), I most definitely recognised his face from that photo I had stumbled upon mid-bail and mid-binge. He didn't look too happy then, and he certainly didn't appear happy now... enquiring as to how she had treated me during our relationship.

Again, I both could and couldn't believe what I was reading. Whilst my behaviour back on that day had been appalling, I assumed that by now she had dined out many times on the fact *"I tried to kill her"* when she as well as the magistrates and I knew that wasn't quite the case. And he was certainly questioning it. I knew, though, that replying to this message was perilous for a couple of reasons, and this plagued the drive home. For all I knew, she could have put him up to this, or was even sending it herself from his account. But it appeared to be Tom, and because of that, replying directly to him would absolve me of any potential breach of the restraining order. And after all it *wasn't* meant for her; I just wanted to help the guy. That might seem rather in contrast to how I had first felt about him, but it's not. Seeing his face back in June may have been a shock, but I never had issue with him, rather the publicity of him. Plus, time-wise, the poor bastard was at the same stage I was when things really started going south. It was a case of *"Could I help?"* before *"Should I?"*

After two hours of deliberation and getting nowhere, we arrived back in the village and I popped my head in the pub two doors down, where I knew I could spend further time on this without anyone poking their nose in. It was all I could think about. I eventually decided that I would reply, but would state in no uncertain terms this was a direct response to him, and first asked for him to confirm he understood this and that none of these messages would be seen by her. He replied and confirmed, and so I composed a long message, trying to get it all out in one and be done with it.

Though I captured it as succinctly as I could, it felt at least 30 minutes to type and send. To compound this, Tom was showing as online and I knew he was watching intently throughout... not only could I feel it, but the moment I hit send it flagged as *'read'*, and a few minutes later a reply came back saying he felt the same about where things were headed for him and them. I replied to another question, and the conversation ended, which really should have been the end of it. But this remained on my mind for the rest of the evening, which was of course about to involve seeing Megan again. And I had just broken my sacred rule of *"knowing when not to start"*. I'd only had two pints, but I hadn't had them in the right frame. I called into home to quickly change and collect the bag of goodies for town. The urge was strong to bring something from the larger birthday bag, but I resisted. The small items were special enough to me.

Though I had lost control with Amy at the end, in anger, that was just not in my nature, and had been a moment of madness. Put simply, I had turned into someone else. The contents of Megan's gift bags – the small one in particular – very much represented who I *really* was in a relationship; I have always been overly soppy and tender, and I love to agonise over the small things. My mum and brother would attest to the fact I obsessed over these items whilst I was there, often at expense of family time. I couldn't wait for her to see them, but equally I couldn't shake off what was happening right now between Tom and Amy.

1) It was none of my business, and 2) why *should* I care anyway? But having been through it myself I was picturing the sorry scene at his end – deleting my messages before she had the chance to go through his phone, hurriedly relocating items in the dishwasher, Crystal Maze and all that, before being shown the same engagement ring online. Anyway, *"bollocks to Amy; I've done my bit to hopefully help Tom, and I should be thinking about **Megan** right now for Christ's sake. We've had a week apart and here I am with a bag of treasures I can't wait for her to see."* And with that, I scooped them and my backpack with my overnight items and set off. We had decided we would meet back where we did for our first date. The same table.

It should have been so perfect, but something felt wrong from the get-go and I couldn't put my finger on it. It wasn't just the back of my mind, but it felt like perhaps there was something at the back of hers, too. The relationship may not have had much in the way of intensity, but it had still moved quite quickly again. Despite chatting for weeks prior to the occasion, we were still technically in a relationship within just 24hrs of having properly met each other. I had already met her parents, she had already met mine. It had gone through the gears. Though she was to all intents and purposes a lovely soul and spirit, one thing had been chiselling at me.

With Amy, the emotion had always been there, whether virtuous or not. And with Kerry, though she struggled sometimes with conveying how she felt, it was still there in her eyes, and I understood. With Megan, however, it just wasn't there, perceivably, at all. We'd had meaningful discussions about things, but whenever it came to *us* it just felt like she was always paying lip service. One could be forgiven for thinking that everything she said was a lie, or at the least teeming with uncertainty. It didn't mean I didn't love her, but I never quite knew how she felt back.

In fact, on one very distinct occasion in my memory, I said *"I love you"*, and in return got *"I love **you**"*. Now what's wrong with that you ask? Well remove approximately 100% of the conviction and picture it again. Honestly at times it was like talking to a Furby.

And when she started unwrapping these gifts that I'd poured my heart soul and wallet into, again there was just an absence of anything. Yes, a smile and a thank you, but little else it seemed. She had never really had much to say, but I suppose this is the first time it really bothered me. Yes I had abandonment issues from Kerry and from Amy, but I am not blaming them, nor am I blaming Megan. It just struck me that if I didn't feel any love from her right now, would I ever?

She worked her way through the presents, as we worked our way through cocktails, and given I'd had a couple of beers before I even got here, and after the emotions of messaging Tom, I was already spent not just financially. We did get a photo together that night, a photo that I look back on right now, and it would hint that everything was fine that evening. But that picture does not begin to tell a thousand words.

We continued to another bar, and by the end of the evening, I was, for the first time in about 4 months, drunk. It was entirely my fault, I make no excuses, but I don't think Megan realised how drunk I actually was. We fell into a taxi to hers, and the next thing it was morning. Once more, something didn't quite feel right, and Megan asked where my backpack and her gift bag were. No sign. I had no memory of where I had put them when we got in. Had I even got in with them? *"Bollocks"*.

Bollocks indeed. After 10 minutes, it was clear I had either left them in the bar at the end of the night, or the taxi. The fact it was me carrying her gifts around could tell you something. We started making calls to different taxi companies (we had hopped in one at a taxi rank – I could remember that – which meant we had no record of which company we'd used). We tried the bars we had been at, even Police lost and found. Nothing. As you can imagine, frustrating. But that's the key word… to me at least, frustration was all that it was. For the first time I did see some emotion in Megan, maybe just embarrassment, but it didn't do anything to change the fact that for me, the overwhelming negative was that I'd lost my overnight bag. And that was the turning point for me, and us. All I could think about was my beloved Brentford jacket, and my MP3 player from rehab and what Dad would think when he learned it had been lost in a drunken stupor. Even trivial things like my gym card were bothering me. *["That'll be a fiver to get that replaced".]*

Not much time for Megan and I to discuss the situation, as later that morning I would have to leave for home. Thankfully, I still had my wallet and, as I boarded the train, it was suddenly Kerry back on my mind. *"Is this a sign? Does this mean I don't love Megan after all? Why am I not bothered about her gift bag? Is this from her lack of reaction to them, or part of a much larger underlying issue in me?"* It was torture. Sadly that week would only go on to be more torturous for myself and for her.

The previous night was not just a turning point for the relationship between Megan and I, but also my relationship with alcohol. Though I had plenty of ammunition from rehab to address these warning signs, I am ashamed to say that I all but disregarded them, and opted for the old familiar approach of two doors down the road. The main thing I was grappling with, was how to broach things with her. I *had* to tell her. I hadn't lost my sense of decency over any of this. What was happening in my head was explainable, given how big an impact Kerry had had on me. I didn't know how on Earth I would do it, but it was the right and honest thing to do, and perhaps discussing it together would help me understand how she really felt about me. That's the other thing I had been grappling with: *"How does she actually feel about me, or anything? Does she even know?"*

Eventually my conscience got the better of me, but the manner in which I told her was a complete mess. And I didn't treat it with the weight it deserved. I just slipped it into a long message, casually as you like, that I was still in love with Kerry, and probably always would be. After dropping a bombshell like that – which had ultimately been the right thing to do – what followed was completely the wrong thing to do, which was to step away from almost all correspondence with both of them.

I had already taken a step back with Kerry while I tried to figure this out, but stepping away from Megan in the same manner must have really put her through the mill and I am ashamed to look back on it. Guilt too. She was finally starting to show that she cared, and for the first time I saw some assertiveness as she tried to force a meetup for as soon as possible. It must have seemed like suddenly I was the one that didn't care, at all, and I wish I could have seen it that way at the time. I didn't know whether it would make the situation worse or not, but it did need to happen, and a few days later she came over. By the time she arrived, it was clear that I wasn't mentally well. She was holding it together valiantly but, clearly, she wasn't either.

We would actually have a pleasant evening together; we did very little other than relax and watch some of the comedy that we did back on our first night. I wanted to give one of her birthday presents in advance (we were now in October with both our birthdays looming within a week of each other) and I knew which one I would give to her, which was perfect for that evening, and as far as I could see it did go down well.

Perhaps all of this would prove to be the ultimate blessing in disguise. The next day I would stay over at hers, and though again it was a pleasant evening, I was starting to lose the battle with my own inner demons, and it would be the last time we would ever see each other. Neither of us knew this at the time, but, in retrospect, it should have been clear that the end was at least in sight.

As I got home, another increasing problem was remembered to me. Not only was my relationship with Megan deteriorating, but so was the one with my father. I still lived with him after all, in very close proximity, and he was seeing me make old excuses to be out of the house on a daily basis, to return only to put myself to bed. It was obvious I had relapsed. Not only this, I was starting to fabricate reasons for needing money, in order to do it. I was too pathetic to face going straight home on the day, so I called in at the supermarket, bought a 4-pack of beers, and sunk them on the walk home. It wasn't long after that we reached breaking point, and I was essentially told I was homeless. I had alcohol coursing through my veins and, though I did not snap, I did text Megan to tell her what was happening, and that I didn't know what I was going to do. She was perhaps an hour or so into her day at work, and I didn't expect much conversation from her, nor did I particularly want it, but I thought I needed to at least tell her.

She did reply, I asked politely whether I could be left alone and given some space, she replied again, and before I knew what I was doing I had blocked her. I did explain what I was doing as I did it, that I had asked for some space and had not got it, but it turns out one thing Megan and I truly did not have in common were our views on blocking. As far as I had ever known she just agreed with everything.

Now I have since changed my views on blocking, but at the time, I was used to being on the end of people like Amy or Kerry, who were both quite cavalier about it. It's just what I knew, and I had never been overly bothered with it whenever it had happened to me. Confused? Sure. Poor Megan, I later learned, did not take it well at all, and assumed the relationship to be over there and then. I had not explicitly said this, nor did I actually want the relationship over, I just wasn't making any progress in my head and was desperately trying to find the way to do it.

Some 6 or 7 hours later when she had finished work, I went to unblock and apologise for my behaviour and look to take the somewhat more adult steps to trying to sort this mess out. And as I did, I saw she had set herself to 'single', and removed every single photo of us online; anything that hinted we had ever even met. I had no idea that she might react in this way, but then I don't think I ever really knew who she was, so in hindsight it's less of a surprise.

Also, in retrospect, I still don't technically know who ended the relationship (I'm not putting the vote out on that one either, and it hardly matters anyway). Although we were both to blame in progressing the relationship so quickly in the first place, this was 100% my fault. I had sown the seeds again, and, though I didn't want this to be the end, I can have no complaints that it was.

My reaction wasn't great either. I replied with something like *"I hope you realise this enables me to get back with Kerry, and alleviates any guilt I may feel over it"*. Yeah, that's the person I was becoming again. And just imagine how that must have gone down.

Talking of going down, I will assume I have just done so in your estimations. But that's OK. I deserve it. I'm certainly not writing this book to be popular. I want to tell you the truth and, as such, I wouldn't sugar-coat here or skimp on detail there. It's right that you know what happened.

Back to the title of the chapter, then.

The funny thing is I had barely thought about her until that moment. There had been other more immediate matters at hand. I was still in a relationship or so I thought, and my father and I had tipped over the edge. After he learned of what happened with Megan, he softened slightly, and I would at least remain at the house that night. And by the end of the night I had all but forgotten that Megan even existed, as she had spent the day doing with me. I told Kerry what happened, and though she feigned sympathy I knew what she was thinking, and I knew she knew I knew.

We did arrange to meet up a couple of days later, but it was still only going to be as friends at this point. It turns out there was something incredibly important to discuss about our past that I didn't even know was on the agenda. I wish I could tell you more about this, especially as I just said I wouldn't skimp on detail, but I am going to have to keep it brief for publishing's sake. Basically it transpires that Kerry thought I had cheated on her towards the end of our relationship, with one of my old housemates (we'll go with Charlotte), who I had lived with approximately 6 months before Kerry and I got together. That shared house was, for a time, fab. Three lads and three ladies who did everything together. The Midlands' answer to *Friends*. Charlotte moved in a week after I did and we clicked straight away. It didn't take long before we were housemates with benefits. I wanted it to be more, but she was very forthright and indeed respectful about it only ever remaining casual, and the whole thing became a badly kept secret.

Kerry was later aware of Charlotte, in fact they met on my birthday, and I don't recall them exactly hitting it off. During the beginning of the relationship with Kerry, I would still occasionally call in at the old house and catch up with everyone, as they were near to work and en-route to Kerry's. I never really saw Charlotte at this point though; it had become awkward by that stage, and the last thing I wanted was for any feelings to come flooding back.

Anyway, when Kerry and I split up 5 years ago and all the mayhem happened, I had apparently told one of her friends that I had slept with Charlotte again. I have no recollection of sending this. But when it was mentioned to me, I found her friend's name way down in my Messenger app from years ago, and sure enough there it was. I was mortified. I can only assume the reason I sent it was to try and hit back in some way, especially as I had wondered whether she had been cheating on me.

There was no hiding the shock in my face when Kerry brought this up, and why would I? I didn't realise how big a deal this had been to her – I had no idea it was a deal at all – and when she mentioned it, in the same park where we had sat last time, I can't tell you the emotion as it was cleared up. I have never in my life cheated on anyone, or thought about it.

As this all came out, every granular feeling that we ever had for each other came back in that moment. I've mentioned Kerry's eyes many times already, and I don't want you to think that they were ever a Venus Fly-trap of sorts for me, but as the

Charlotte ordeal was cleared up and I saw what it meant to her, I realised that I *had* still been madly in love with her all this time. The eyes are said to be a window into the soul and, as I looked at her, I really felt that I was looking into her. That I knew who she was. That she meant what she said. She knew I was being honest about Charlotte, and the hug that we shared is another moment I'll never forget in my life. It was a hug that undid all of the stress we had held on to for five years, and a hug that seemed to show we were the ones destined to be after all.

We walked arm in arm back to her car, but we were not back together yet; no no no. It had been quite an afternoon, but I was never for a second going to lean in to kiss her like I had done on our first 'date'. I had only separated with Megan days ago. And as Kerry and I parted ways that day, as I waved her car off again, I really didn't know how long it would be before we would next see each other. It turns out, it would be later the same day! A quick soft drink at the local, as she had band practice at a studio not too far from me. But over this second meeting, as fleeting as it was, it became clear this was already something again.

My birthday was two days later, and it did offer ample opportunity to reflect, not just on the recent events, but my life in general. This past year had been beyond eventful, I hadn't intended for any of it to be, but here I was, and where would I go from here? I was almost back with Kerry again; I had never for a moment anticipated that. Where would that lead? Would it be as perfect as it had felt last time? Slow down, Scotty, we're not there yet.

I had assumed I wouldn't hear from Megan on my birthday, even though I knew she had already got me something, and I was glad to be proved correct. Kerry had bought me a pint of Pepsi a few evenings ago, jokingly for my birthday, but all things considered this was the most incredible thing to be on the receiving end of. And the next time I saw her, the stars would realign once more.

I was invited to her mum and step-dad's, who were currently abroad. I should have known that by being invited somewhere like that, there was the underlying feeling that this was beyond merely lending a hand with the housekeeping. Afterwards we sat with the TV on, knees together on a sofa once more. Still as friends… until she told me that she was suddenly nervous; that it felt like there was ice to be broken all over again. She went to make us a coffee, and minutes later I followed her in, tapped her on the shoulder, wrapped my arms around her and we kissed, just like the very first time. Disney magic. We just felt so right in each other's arms again. We both had our issues, and a history of not dealing with them in the best way, but they were entirely forgotten in the electricity. Yet another moment with her that I'll never forget for the right reasons.

Despite this, it didn't mean that I wasn't still thinking of Megan. Her birthday was two days away, I still had all her presents, and I wasn't thinking of anything other than to still get them to her, whether it would go down well or not. Because of this, I knew exactly how I would approach it – I would send them recorded delivery with a short letter trying to explain everything, that I hadn't initiated nor wanted a break-up, and to include all of the receipts to potentially get herself something else instead. I didn't mind that she knew the monetary value of each item; what was more important was the thought or reason for doing it, so that she could swap or refund everything if she wanted to, which I assume she did.

I didn't hear back, but I did want to know that they had arrived, so I decided to ask a friend that I had introduced her to whether she had received them. Sure enough I got a reply to say that she had checked with her and that she had, and appreciated them. (No, I didn't think to check the delivery ID on the Royal Mail website. We've established I don't always think things through). I don't know what she finally did with them, and ultimately it isn't any of my business. But I was at least comforted by the fact they had got there. I had spent all of my money on them, and an additional £20 that I didn't have on the recorded delivery.

By now, Kerry and I were unofficially back together. I met up with an old friend of hers who I had seen many times during the previous relationship, and that in itself was a wonderful moment. She was a lovely soul, as was her husband. They were a month away from getting married when Kerry and I had split before, and I remember seeing the photos of an angelic looking Kerry at their wedding when I was in pieces over the breakup. I also met Kerry's mum and stepfather again, which was rather surreal, especially given we had rekindled in their house just days earlier. There was the amusing reprisal of old chestnuts, given Brentford had now pinched Walsall's manager and two of their best players, and were well established in the Championship whereas Walsall had dropped to League Two. But no hard feelings – not even over what happened with Kerry. Things were strangely back to normal straight away. Something else felt strange, though, and I couldn't put my finger on it. Did I deserve this? Given our respective insecurities, were we already on a knife-edge again? Could the slightest thing unravel this all before it even got off the ground?

A few more weeks would go by, and the time together was every bit as it was before. I had forgotten some of her bizarre but lovable traits. Do you know anyone that puts ketchup on their prawn crackers? The time apart was different though. The issue of trust may have been addressed over my behaviour, but we had never really spoken about what happened at her end, and how much that had destroyed me. There was an unspoken feeling that it was all in the past now and that we were on a clean slate. But perhaps I hadn't fully let go. I was still on my anxiety medication at this point, and I unfortunately had to wait a couple of days before collecting my repeat prescription. This caused an immediate sense of panic that I remember to this day. I didn't want to admit that I was dependent on them, but I certainly felt I was back then. The day before I was due to collect my prescription, I was chatting on WhatsApp with Kerry, who was at work. I call it chatting; I would send a reply promptly from my end and then wait up to two hours for hers. No drama in that alone; she was after all at work. But I had time on my hands and, due to a separate group-chat, I was buried in WhatsApp the entire day. Kerry had read my message – the ticks had gone blue and each time I reopened the conversation, she was showing as online, but not *"typing"*.

"If she's at work, how come she's spending so much time on WhatsApp, and why isn't any of that being spent with me?"

She'd disappear offline, online, off, on, countless times over the next hour again, and still nothing. With what happened in the past, definite cause for concern. Though I had anxiety issues, I believe I had every right to still have trust issues. We weren't *officially* back together yet, but it's safe to say we were 'dating', or 'seeing each other', whatever you want to label it, and my mind started running riot again with who she might be talking to. There was no alcohol at play yet – I was at my friend's in town – and as I mentioned this predicament she agreed it was a little suspicious to say the least. The last thing I wanted to do was let this eat away at me over the course of the day, even the week, so I decided I would broach it there and then. But again, the manner in which I chose to do it was poor, and too abrupt. *"What's going on?"*

And, as she replied, it was instant discord. She had apparently been talking to her boss who was out of the workplace, hence the need for spending so much time on her phone at work, and she didn't take too kindly to the way I had defaulted to suspicion over the matter. This had plunged everything into doubt for me – I couldn't bear losing her in the same circumstances as last time. So this effectively put us on 'hiatus' again, whilst it was me this time that took some time to 'sort my head out'. I didn't know whether to believe her, I really didn't, and sadly I did everything but sort my head out that week. I had resorted once more to alcohol to deal with the stress from this and the panic from the medication, and it snowballed rapidly. And each sight of my father was enough to send me over the edge, even though he was largely the one financing it. Though he loves me very much and knows how much I love him, too, being so close to him in the house was the worst possible thing for me at the time, and was not the rest and recuperation I needed.

We fell out heavily once more, and off I went into the night with nowhere to stay, and really I could have ended up anywhere. After wandering the streets, I heard back from a friend nearby who let me stay on his sofa. Although I was very grateful of a place to stay, the night would prove to be almost unprecedented turmoil for me, and once it literally dawned on me that I wasn't going to get any sleep, I decided I'd put Kerry to bed instead. I sent a string of messages, getting everything off my chest, and that I never wanted anything to do with her again. The first signs of trouble had brought all of this back up again for me, and I realised I just wasn't willing nor able to deal with it this time.

When she woke an hour later I was predictably blocked, but finally I felt relatively clear again and at peace. I knew exactly what I was going to do with the day too. First things first, it was the Rugby World Cup final, and I was missing that for nowt. We had just dismantled the All Blacks in the semis, and there was a unified sense this was our year again. As it was hosted in Japan, it kicked off at something like 08:30, and well, it wasn't the start to the day I hoped for. We were dismantled ourselves and can have no complaints with the result. Thankfully, rugby is a sport of respect and honour, and so there wasn't any sense of ill-will afterwards, rather the acknowledgement that we were beaten by the better team. Congrats again to the Springboks.

It may not have been the best distraction, but it had at least served as one. Afterwards, I did what I had planned since the night before, and took a little stroll back to the train tracks where it had all happened the first time. There was no sense of uncertainty as to whether I was going to do anything, though; I knew that I was *not*. I hadn't slept, but at least this time that's all it was, physical fatigue. Mentally, I felt strangely OK. I just wanted total separation from human life, to return to where it happened before, and hopefully get a much needed sense of perspective on my own and where it was headed again. I didn't sit on the tracks this time but walked alongside them, for a good mile, through nature, and can honestly say it helped me a lot. This had all happened in such a short period; I had spent five years thinking about whether we would meet again, before I knew it we were back together, and as soon as it had happened, we had gone our separate ways again, for the best.

And I still know it was for the best. Whether she was being truthful or not, the damage had been done those years ago, and though it had been discussed in rehab, I clearly hadn't yet processed the trust issues. I don't think Kerry is necessarily a bad person, but like all of us she had her ways, some of which were potentially virulent. That doesn't make someone or something inherently bad; if a box jellyfish or a dart-frog could apologise to a human, I'm sure they would, albeit too late. I still don't think she knows just how much of an effect she had on me. As much as it seemed like at times we were perfect for each other, that clearly wasn't the case, and no one has ever had both the positive and negative effect on me that she did. I say effect rather than impact, as I had the bigger say in the impact.

I'll say it again, and I cannot state this enough; I do not blame Kerry, nor Megan, nor Amy, nor a lack of medication, for any of my actions. Nothing in this book is an excuse for anything I did, but hopefully an explanation as to how and why I arrived at the end of each of these chapters. And I knew before typing this one that it would have little-to-no-humour in it, and I'm glad I was right, as it means I told it properly.

And if I am to command your respect by the end of this book, it will likely be though my honesty.

This type of incident was waiting again, and I'm grateful that it happened as early as it did, as perhaps if we had been together as long as we had done before, then I would have walked those tracks with different intentions, and would not be here to tell the tale I'm telling. And I'm not done yet.

12

Megan: Part II

Sigh, and spoiler alert: before things do hopefully reach a happy ending, they're about to get a heap worse I'm afraid.

Let's forget Kerry for now if we can, as I more or less had done so at the time. I'd been through the dress rehearsal years before, and though this wasn't quite as bad, it didn't mean I wasn't still in shock. Foolishly though, my distraction technique was to attempt to open a line of communication with Megan again. It was barely a month since we had split and December was fast approaching, which should have brought enough distractions of its own.

Sadly, another thing that was all-but-forgotten at this point was rehab and everything that I'd learned there in terms of coping strategies. I had dealt with Kerry relatively well in the immediate aftermath, but I just couldn't find a sensible way to deal with being back at Dad's. He had offered me another lifeline, and although I was grateful of this, the whole situation felt poisonous there too. I needed the personal space more than ever, and in a village with a myriad of walking routes, it was a good marker of just how much I'd deteriorated that I was opting to further poison myself at the pub two doors down instead. If there had been an AA held in the building between, I don't think I'd have had the sense to go. (Mind you, not a practical place to put one).

And as Advent began, it was already looking to be a white Christmas if you catch my drift.

I'd say *"what was I thinking"*, but I wasn't thinking. And this brought back the old familiar routine of caring what had happened with past relationships one minute, then killing it synthetically the next. I was hell-bent on trying to make amends with Megan – not necessarily looking to get back together, but to at least apologise in person and go from there in terms of friendship. I should have known this wouldn't go down well; I'd already had a big clue from the birthday letter and lack of reply. More time had passed though, and perhaps it might be different.

I couldn't contact her through WhatsApp or Facebook, but I could certainly reach out to any mutual acquaintances and see if anything came of it. Whilst there had been friends I had introduced her to, it was predominantly hers that I had met over a music festival that I decided it would be best to try. They would have been closer to her throughout all of this, and I hoped they would take any message from me on merit and at least pass it on to allow her to decide what to do with it.

I did this, and not long afterwards – it may have even been

the same day – I received a message from Megan's sister. Now it was her passing a message on. The contents of this will remain private out of respect, but it should have been enough for me to know not to pursue any of this any further. Sadly, I was on the verge of being someone else again before I even read it. There was still the emotion in me to feel devastated for having caused the upset that I did, but the rational thought had gone, and I somehow believed that things were still salvageable. I poured out to her sister, but I should only ever have expected it to go literally one-way. She did respond though, very sensibly telling me to move on, as anything initially romantic could quite easily become construed as harassment. I don't believe her sister ever liked me (she certainly wouldn't have after how it ended), but something was telling me that she was pouncing on another opportunity to nurture a dependence upon her from Megan. Not just house-mate, not just big sis, but a second mother. This may well be the case, I don't know, but to her credit this reply to me did appear to be with both our interests considered.

At the time I truly believed that if I could speak directly to Megan, then I might be able to go some way to explaining everything, and not least address the confusion around our breakup, for closure. There was a way I could do it… through a separate Facebook profile she had. And, well, this is where 'not knowing when to stop' applies. As each message went 'read' without reply, I became more and more obsessed that I hadn't worded it correctly, that I hadn't quite conveyed my point. I was drinking more and more by the day, becoming more and more clueless as to what was happening, and eventually, I turned to the one contingency I felt I had left; the final way perhaps I could force a conversation.

I asked my father for a lift to Stratford, under false pretence that she had agreed to meet and that there might be possibility for reconcile. For some reason he didn't question this, even though I was in a bad way. Not long after he had dropped me off though, he clicked what was going on. (I had asked to be dropped half a mile away from Megan's, conveniently near a convenience store. Amazingly I couldn't see how suspicious this must have been).

Although I was about to embark on another drinking spree, I was *not* about to do anything like I had with Amy; let's quell those fears immediately. However, as the beers went down and I walked the streets, I circled her neighbourhood, increasingly ill, increasingly drunk, and eventually turned into her road, having already made her aware that I was nearby. I still had no intention of knocking her door, but the state I was in, I thought the intimation of it might finally force a reply. But no. Each message still 'read' though, and although I would have been presumably seen from the window, I continued as planned down the opposite side of the road, into a park and once more out of sight.

But, sadly, like a shark, I was always going to circle back around. I am appalled with myself to say that the whole thing was – and there's few other ways of saying it – psychologically predatory. In my selfishness, I didn't realise the extent. And by the time I did circle back around, eight pint cans were in my system. I turned back into the road, and to my surprise immediately spotted the car that had driven me into town. Dad, once he recognised, had messaged Megan to check if everything was OK, and had been invited over. I'd been on the phone to a friend, but once I saw the car I made a stop and terminated the call so I could speak to him instead. And as I did, I saw another familiar vehicle, a blue and yellow chequered one, roll on to her drive.

This was to be a formal warning, and nothing more. They did appear to understand to a degree why I was there, and provided I could give them a place to go, they would drop me there with no further action. My friend (that had relayed receipt of her birthday gifts, and who was nearer to home), was thankfully available for a cup of tea and a chat, and so I was dropped off at hers, well away from Megan's, with no intention of ever speaking to her again.

We chatted quite animatedly over the next hour or so; I was clearly inebriated which was distressing enough alone to her, having been there for me at times over the past year. She's a candid one and there was not for a moment any ambiguity in how she felt about what I was doing. Yet another person's respect that had been won back in spectacular fashion earlier in the year, had just been tossed further than ever before.

I left hers in a foul mood, and deserved to – she had brought to light much of the absurdity in what I was doing, and rather than facing it head on I shamefully went straight for the pub, now effectively homeless again. I had no anticipation or plans for what was about to happen though.

[1] Unread: **Tom**

I had completely forgotten about him and Amy; it had been almost two months since the last contact, which had been minimal. It turns out nothing had changed, and, unlike myself, he'd finally had the sense to end it with her. Like I said it was the third successive relationship for her that had ended due to mental health at the other end, in a year. He was looking for some closure, and it may not be the best example of doing a good deed to feel better, but it did represent a good opportunity for me to do so. Anything I could do or say to help again, I would.

I knew this would be best done with a phone call, so I rang and we chatted for the rest of the hour, exchanging stories, and offering each the validation that the problems weren't ever *really* with us. I may have had my issues particularly over the last year, but I can safely say I wouldn't trade any for Amy's. And I'm pleased to say I have conquered them; mine and hers. Although Tom wasn't in a good way at the time, this was probably the first time either of us could laugh over any of it, and it must have helped.

Ultimately, for good reasons or not, it perked my evening up, and suddenly I felt clearer again. It was now quite late, and naturally my thoughts turned to where the hell I was going to stay. I had on one occasion slept in an alley between my parents' homes, but I was 10 miles from there, and hardly dressed for the occasion. Again, rather selfishly, I contacted another person who I care deeply about, another person who did not for a second deserve to be dragged into any of this; my brother. He very kindly put me up for the night – once I had eventually found my way to his house. I'd run out of phone battery and had to negotiate a rather sketchy park in total darkness, but eventually made it and curled upon his sofa with the cats. Were things going to be alright from here?

I had probation in the morning, and I knew if I didn't make this my suspended sentence would be invoked and I'd be back to jail. As soon as I saw my probation officer's face I knew she already knew everything. It's not like I wouldn't have told her, but it did at least get the conversation started straight away. I was hungover, and that much would have been clear as I hadn't had the chance to shower or get a coffee or breakfast. I said quite truthfully that I had no intention of contacting Megan, her sister, or anyone involved with her again. I can't remember how I got home.

Sadly, yet another opportunity to get my shit together was wasted, and the rest of the week was cloud. There was a final message with Tom, a thank you for helping to provide closure, and a mutual good luck for the future. I haven't heard from him since, and I take that as good news and that he has moved forwards in his life. He seemed a good chap and, wherever he is right now, I hope it's where he wants to be. Sadly, I was moving backwards, rapidly, and the relationship with my father was now virtually irretrievable. You may remember that at its worst at the end with Amy, he had stayed in a hotel to give us both the space we needed, and the same thing happened again now.

A few nights before, while I was wandering the streets, I had made numerous phone calls to my dad, and my behaviour was frankly disgusting. They say that in order to achieve a long-term recovery then you truly have to hit rock bottom and recognise that you have done so. I weirdly never quite felt that I had done over the Amy drama, but there was an increasing sense that this time I really was at rock bottom. Not just over that day when I turned up at Megan's, not just over the way I spoke to my father, but that I was still somehow capable of doing more. He was only in a neighbouring village, and I was back in the house again, and with a small amount of his money to burn. Well, it was not long before I found myself at the pub again, and it was not long after that I found myself messaging Megan again.

Like I had done on occasions with Amy and Kerry, this time it came out in a weirdly controlled barrage; I got everything off my chest, in the best possible way I could, and as I hit 'send', I sat back, knowing, accepting, and awaiting my fate.

The next day I was back in court, my suspended sentence invoked, with a further 10 weeks added for Harassment.

13

Isn't this where we came in?

"I travel, not to go anywhere, but to go".

*"I'm going to WALES; that's the fucking **worst of it!**"*

Two different quotes from two somewhat different folks, back on page one. Here's one from page two:

"For me, these journeys were the best opportunity for reflection on exactly what I did to get myself there. I've done that to my satisfaction, but don't worry I shall do it here for your exposition."

And I hope I have. It's been a bit of a journey to get to this moment, hasn't it. The main thing, though, is that I recognise how I'm here, why I'm here, and accept both in full understanding. Which I did. This was fair. This was deserved. This was justice. And, already in that moment as the bus crossed the border on December 12th, this was different. I felt a sense that this had to happen, and that this time I really would learn my lessons.

I also feel I may have lost my right to quip about prison life in the same way as before, and should perhaps show a little more humility, but that will hopefully find its way in naturally, if I've really learned it. I would rather be consistent in tone, and frankly, after the last few chapters, you deserve a break more than me.

It seems a heck of a time since we were last inside, and, well, that's because a heck of a lot happened between. If you remember we checked into reception (and checked out our tobacco), got our ID, our clothes and equipment, had our medical, then our phone call, met a listener, met our pad-mate. Then we nailed our English test (and almost failed maths), created a CV, and picked our education or employment options. We visited the library, pondered a gym instructor, and packed everything up to move from the induction wing to a proper one, and we've just done it all again. Well done, us! We must be hungry.

Food

A rudimentary strand of prison life, and life. And we're to have a rather mixed time of it here, until we learn what is produced to edible standards and what isn't. There is always variation, and so if you're fussy you're not going to suffer over choice quite as much as you might have thought. Whether you go on to like your choice or not is a different matter, but, hey, you'll get what you're given. And hey, you asked for it in more ways than one. We'll go through a hypothetical menu, but before that, the word of the day, ladies and gentlemen, boys and girls… carbohydrates.

Tomorrow's word: carbohydrates.

Bread, pasta, rice, potatoes. Nice and cheap, nice and filling. Whatever menu option you go for, you will ultimately wind up with over half your plate consisting of one of the above. Then another when they slap a couple of slices of bread on top. Of course you can choose no bread at all, which was essentially my choice each day, as although I did collect it I bagged it up to keep it fresh and then stored it as currency. Yes believe it or not bread holds some cards in the prison economy. It may be small change compared to the likes of vape capsules, but always carry change on you.

Even if you don't eat the bread, you're still going to end up putting on weight in here, for three reasons. The portions are surprisingly big, they will pretty much always involve carbs, and then there's very little to do afterwards other than lie down, as you're immediately locked up once you've brought your meal back to the pad, which is how it works. Before I ever came here, I always imagined something of a canteen environment, but canteen means something entirely different, as I'll later explain.

Right, what's on today?

Mains:

- **Water-pounder with Peas**: Double-stacked aqua-patties with 30% turkey, crowned with a lettuce leaf in our signature 'denture's peril' bread roll. No sauce. Potatoes.
- **Arctic pasta:** 10% carrots, 10% peas, 10% sweetcorn, 20% rice, 50% penne. Rested for 90 minutes.
- **Jacket potato:** No chilli, no cheese, no tuna, no beans, no butter. Extra potatoes.
- **Slop of the day: 'Find the Chicken' Jalfrezi.** Peas and rice.

Dessert:

- **Sponge**

What did you go for?

Although that's a fairly typical selection, there was a good rotation of other things too. There were also three culinary traditions that I'm pleased to say were in some way honoured, even in Wales:

- **Friday night:** Fish & Chips
- **Saturday morning**: Full English Breakfast
- **Sunday lunch:** Roast Dinner

Let's address each in turn. As much as I love fish and chips, I don't have it every week; far from it. Possibly the last one I'd had was in rehab, which I regaled for you lovingly. This one (and I wasn't complaining), underwent a different method of preparation. And the result: an 80% grease 20% haddock fillet (battered…) with "hench fries" (overcooked thick cut chips), and with no salt, vinegar, mayo, or ketchup. Oh and garden peas. A myriad of 'em, as with everything here.

And as I said before, I never feel more patriotic than when I'm eating a cooked breakfast or a Sunday roast. There's a lot going on, but if you mix it all together in one forkful then surely you're doing it wrong. The beauty of a full English and its components is that there are perfect marriages:

- Sausage and beans
- Sausage and tomato
- Fried bread and beans
- Toast and beans
- Bacon and fried egg
- Bacon and scrambled egg
- Hash browns and ketchup

Go with the above and you're enjoying yourself. They're not all always together to begin with on the plate, but hopefully will end up together on the fork. It's the culinary equivalent of *Love Actually*, as I see it. Then there are the items best enjoyed on their own, such as mushrooms, or black pudding. (I'm a late convert to black pudding. I admit the idea of it freaked me out until I eventually tried it. We're alright now).

For me with a Full English though, the two key components are the baked beans and orange juice. Call me a simpleton, but baked beans are just about a perfect marriage with an*ything*. Scrambled egg and beans on toast in particular makes for an excellent breakfast of its own. And it's always prudent to have orange juice to hand for this kind of meal, because nothing cuts through to the spot more than a glass of cold orange juice, to cleanse and reset the palette. Or a Sorbetto al Limoncello, dopo cena.

Prison does not have Limoncello sorbet, nor orange juice, or the vast majority of the above. Their idea of a Full English is sausages, hash browns, baked beans, and that's it. Again, though, I didn't complain. In fact I looked forward to Saturdays.

With roast dinners, you also have your classic pairings, like lamb and mint sauce, beef and cranberry sauce, the gravy pairs up with the roasties or the stuffing, as do parsnips, yada yada. I've waffled enough. In fact I won't describe prison roast dinners at all yet, as surely the king of roasts is Christmas Dinner, and I'm about to be locked up over Christmas. We'll review it then.

So, to end again with the word of the day. Above any financial factor, I think the main reason the prison system is so intent on loading everyone up with carbs is that it tends to knock them out for the afternoon and evening and keep them quiet. It's so easy to fall into that trap of saying yes to extra rice, potatoes or bread, then collapse in a bloat and sleep it off. Subsequently, it's just as easy to put on weight. Pretty much everyone does, especially heroin addicts who are just getting their appetites back. They'll take every slice of bread they can get, then they stretch their stomach and suddenly it's a very different kind of viscous daily cycle.

We've had our evening meal then, and conked out in front of the TV, and next we know it's another day.

Meds

As I said, this is a big deal in here. Depending on what you're on, you'll see the nurse twice a day, first thing in the morning and in the evening after dinner. And the queue for the meds counter is a very different queue than what you're probably used to. Heroin addiction is no laughing matter and it's never less funny than when you're sandwiched by two people with the shakes, picking at their skin waiting to get their methadone. I learned that methadone comes in a liquid, and once your GP attests to the fact you are in opiate withdrawal, you are prescribed and have to use a fingerprint scanner to authenticate yourself. Amazingly, some people pretend to swallow it, then walk back to their pad and spit it out into a cup, and "sell" it to other inmates. Yes I saw that happen. For me, my only medication was anxiety tablets, and though recently coming off them for a couple of days had led to the end of things with Kerry (not *caused*, but led to), I took this trip to jail as an opportunity to come off them for good. I was tapered down, and by the time I was discharged I was officially med-free, and thankfully still am. I really, really don't miss them.

Of course there are many different kinds; a lot of people are on sleepers, for example. Then there are the ones that fall outside of NHS and HMP protocols.

Drugs

Like I also said before, they're everywhere too. And prison is no exception. Most people, I assume, conceal them inside themselves when they come in, but there is an easier way of bringing in a certain drug, one that prevails above all others here, and that is Spice / Mamba.

This stuff, though I've never tried it, is utterly horrible. Ketamine, if you don't treat it with respect, has the capacity to sedate you to a jelly, I believe heroin does the same, but there's nothing that zombifies someone quite like a hit of Spice. And the way it's brought in? Paper. This stuff is supposed to be synthetic cannabis, and I do vaguely remember when it was legal it also mimicked cannabis in its appearance, but nowadays it comes in liquid form, which can be applied to blank paper. And there's no way of testing it apparently, meaning that no matter what wing you're on, in any jail, it's going to have found its way in there. And it really is the worst kept secret.

"How do people smoke it in there?" you might ask. During my stay with Windsor I saw it first-hand. A 'Viva' milk carton is emptied, with small holes punched into it to make a gauze. The spicy paper is placed on top of the gauze, with a small amount of toilet tissue to make it more flammable. And the flame itself comes from a doctored vape, with part of it removed so the coil that creates the heat is exposed. Honestly, if these people had applied half of this ingenuity elsewhere in their lives, then they wouldn't be here.

Clearly people manage to smuggle weed inside too, as on several occasions I could smell it on the wing. I'm sure other things find their way in as well. If you prefer not to indulge in any of the above, and would rather spend your day in better general health, then there is usually an option each morning to:

Exercise

It's not quite the plethora of options you would have available outside, but it is at least *outside*, and one of the few times you will get to breathe any natural air. Exercise is usually called in the morning after meds, and all it really involves is a walk around a yard. You also should have this option available if you're in a police station for the night. Rather than the exercise yard being for exercise, though, it's predominantly used to exchange insults with the wings that surround it, through the windows. Only once did I bother with the yard, once I experienced this. Not that any of these insults would have been levelled directly at me, but it's a strange sensation going out for a communal walk and having something like *"PAEDO!"* or *"CRACKHEAD!"* aimed in your general direction. I prefer Hampstead Heath or St James's, put it that way.

You do of course have the gym a few times a week once you receive the timetable, but again you're in a smog of testosterone, and so if you *really* want to exercise in peace, while you're in jail, you're better off having a routine in your own pad, of sit-ups or press-ups or burpees or whatever you want to do. One pad-mate in particular did this and he was one of the first I ever shared with, in my first stay back in May. And he's just as worth telling you about as Windsor.

It was my first ever time inside, and I'd only experienced one wing up to that point, during induction (with cuddly Clint). I was then moved to Block 1, and all kinds of things were running through my mind. *"Does the fact it's the first block mean anything? Is there a system, and a reason people go to Block 1? If so how am I categorized?"*

I didn't know what to expect when I was shown to my cell, but I thought I did when the door swung open and I met Bert. Not a name that went with his appearance. He was black with a classic afro tied back with the comb poking out, a large cro-magnon jaw, and muscles up to his eyeballs. He seemed friendly enough, though. He was clearly a man of routine and order; you could tell not just from his physique, but the way in which the pad was decorated. And after I unpacked my items and got my bedding sorted, I joined him watching TV. He was very affable, and again one of those people who could make you laugh without even saying anything. And his laugh was as infectious as it gets. Slightly maniacal, and often for no reason whatsoever. He was also not without a high degree of intelligence. We had a whale of a time dissecting the adverts. I remember watching one of the Trivago ones, and we discussed how effective it was for its simple and shameless word association. If I say *"Hotel?"* what's the first thing that comes into your mind. Exactly. These things stick. If someone whispers something to me, they will always get the same reply… *"Secret Escapes"*. I'm not bored of it yet.

I must admit, as much as I do have a begrudging respect for Trivago's marketing, I have grown weary of the Aussie woman in their adverts, and this was discussed, too. It seems that above any enjoyment of her actual stay, she loves nothing more than to loiter around the foyer and make smug remarks on how others have been fleeced. Imagine holidaying with her, Christ. The trade-off would be the discount, of course.

These sorts of discussion continued and, honestly, he was as well-informed about how the human psyche can work or be led as anyone I've sat in a product meeting with. The first couple of days went the same, and we seemed destined to be another perfect pairing. Then things got weird.

On about the third or fourth evening, he started talking. Not at me, not at anyone. He just started talking. And he proceeded to chat away to himself well into the night. Half the time I couldn't understand what he was saying. It was not an angry muttering, but it naturally put me a bit on edge. Then the 'conversation' did get progressively more hostile. I assume it was his way of communicating with someone in his past, perhaps someone with whom he held a grudge. There were certain phrases that I could pick out, such as *"Psssh"*, *"It's one'a them"*, and *"I'm a SLAP you, mate"*. And as he started talking less and less to me, and more and more to himself or whoever this was, it only became more and more disconcerting.

As I was on the bottom bunk, I would lie there watching TV, with him on a chair to the right of the desk, in my full vision. And one evening after about three hours since any communication between us, and maybe 40 minutes of rambling, out of nowhere he slowly turned to face me, with a most threatening look in his eyes, and said *"Did you just **spit** on me, bruv?"*

Of course I hadn't – I don't know where he got the idea from – but it sent a chill down my spine, and I spent the rest of the night coiling in fear as to whether he was going to act on this accusation. It was the last time I think I actually spoke with him, and the next week or so had an incredible air of unease about it. Much more-so than Windsor. Imagine being locked up in a small room with someone like that for a long period of time, in silence, after something like that. I'm not asking you to sympathise, I'm simply saying imagine yourself

in there. Again, in hindsight, most amusing. At the time...
mental.

And you really don't know who you're going to wind up
with. Over this particular Christmas stay I was paired up
with someone *"from the Valleys"* with an almost impenetrable
Welsh accent. The only thing I could make out clearly was the
tattoo on his upper back which read *"Hunting is in the blood –
fuck the ban"*. Delightful.

Association

As if your pad-mate wasn't delight enough, there is usually an
hour in the evening when the doors are unlocked, and you
can exchange pleasantries with the rest of the wing's clientele.
Association is a peculiar one, as there's not exactly much
you can really do, yet everyone is flying around in different
directions. It could be for a drug deal, or exchanging bread for
teabags, as was my enterprise. The screws will patrol and make
sure everyone is behaving themselves and this represents an
excellent opportunity to speak with one of them and ascertain
anything you need to know, or request anything you need to
request. If you have built up a level of respect with them, then
it's much more likely they will end up acting on the little note
they have just jotted down.

Most wings will have one or two pool tables at the bottom,
and good luck using one if you even want to. You might think
you're first in line, but if a 7 foot brick presents themself at the
last minute, you're not.

Showers

I'm one of those people that likes to stand aimlessly in the shower just because it's warm. But we're on a time limit here, and plus who said it was going to be warm. Not that you'd particularly notice the time limit, as you've got the whole of association to take one, but why would you want to hang around anyway. The thing with the showers is, they totally vary depending what block you're on. Some are surprisingly private, with their own saloon door, and others are just as you were imagining them. I was dreading the moment; I'd heard all the horror stories, but of course it's complete bollocks, at least from my experience. If you're sensible, you'll wear your boxers in the shower, and like I said you won't dither in there. Not because of any soapy shenanigans, but rather because while you're in it your belongings are at the mercy of everyone else. In some wings it's not possible to lock your pad when you're away from it, and if you want to secure the safety of all your possessions, you'll have to potentially offer up your popularity by asking the screws to lock it after you each time. It's worth it, though, for peace of mind.

And these are all the things that make up a typical day inside, over the first week to two weeks. Thankfully, more options then become available.

Work / Education

Yessss, some purpose. We were getting sick of lying in bed watching *Ramsay's Kitchen Nightmares*, right...? Oh, fair enough. Now we chose music did we not, but let's remind ourselves of some of the other options:

Work

- Kitchens
- Cleaning
- Maintenance
- Recycling
- Peer work
- Laundry

Education

- English
- Maths
- Art
- Family matters
- Mechanics
- Music
- IT

There's plenty more, but these are the typical ones I imagine you'll see almost everywhere. Each has certain perks; for example, working in the kitchens allows you to eat when it's as fresh as it will ever be, and as much of it as you want. Working in laundry gives you access to bedding and clothes when they're as fresh as they'll ever be, and on a more regular basis. But I didn't care about that, I just wanted to play guitar and/or drums.

My experience with music was not on this stay, but in the much larger jail earlier in the year. There had been a slightly longer wait, but eventually my name was called in the morning and off I went, no idea what to expect. There were only 4 of us, and looking around the gear in the room, it was about as to be expected. Three or 4 very basic Yamaha acoustics (absolutely nothing wrong with Yamaha as a brand, but these ones were at the shallow end). In fact, perhaps HMP have some sort of deal with Yamaha, as I saw their name on the electric drum-kit too.

The lessons consisted of some basic theory, followed by the practical side of things; jamming and learning songs. Two we learned were 'Every Breath You Take' by The Police, and 'Three Little Birds' by Bob Marley. Although I was whiling away the time, and earning some money by doing this, it didn't stop it from getting a tad tedious after a while. The real joy that came from these classes, was learning in discussion of some of the bands that the music teacher was into, and then better still, discovering the full extent in his crate of CD's in the back office.

You know of some of my favourite bands already. Some of these weren't to be found in here and I was expecting that, but what I was not expecting was to find many of my other favourites in his collection, which included the following: The Mars Volta, Oceansize, Cardiacs, Avishai Cohen, Sigur Rós, Karnivool, Björk, The Dandy Warhols, Porcupine Tree, The Cinematic Orchestra, Kate Bush, Tool, Neil Cowley Trio, Mogwai, Jorma Kaukonen, Max Richter, Seal, Tommy Emmanuel, Demians.

*"You know **Demians**?"*

He even had my favourite album of all time: *Laughing Stock* by Talk Talk. Oh how I wish I could go into this record. But I haven't the time or space.

No sod it! This I have to digress for.

*

Talk Talk made a name for themselves in the 80s with synth-pop such as *It's my Life*, which, if you're my age, you'll remember No Doubt covering in the 90s instead. After *It's My Life*, in 1986 they released their most commercially successful album yet *The Colour of Spring*, and were given practically a blank chequebook and unlimited time for their next release. That release would be the seminal *Spirit of Eden*, an album that was nothing like anything they had done before, on the surface extremely indulgent and pretentious, and unmarketable… in fact they couldn't even tour it. The record label were flabbergasted. Rumour has it their manager was in tears, for one because of its raw beauty, but secondly because he knew there and then that it was a commercial lead balloon. Radiohead would go on to do a similar thing at the turn of the millennium with *Kid A* after *OK Computer*, though they could at least play that live. And *Kid A* was their masterpiece, along with *In Rainbows* (yes I'm rather opinionated I know).

Back to Talk Talk and *Spirit of Eden*, rumour has it that they hired a string quintet, at great expense to the label, and the only thing that ended up making it on to the record was a mistake by the cellist. I so hope that's true. When you hear the album, you'd understand how it *could* be, but I still don't think it sounds pretentious. It sounds, above anything, organic, spiritual, gorgeous, and the album they always wanted to make.

And then three years later, they followed it up with their swansong, and zenith, *Laughing Stock*. In much the same vein, but this time an even more minimal approach, and somewhat jazzier. Mystical, magical, wonderful. It just feels, how can I put it, alive. I don't think I've ever heard anyone else create a record that actually sounds like an entity of its own, almost as if it created itself.

Microphones were set back from the drums for a more ethereal and distant sound, hours and hours of guitar improvisation were meticulously cut and pasted together. A truly unique approach, and I don't particularly like the term *"ahead of its time"*, but 30 years later it still is. It's certainly not a background record; it requires your full devoted attention as to not miss some incredible nuances all over the place. One of the highlights, which to be fair you wouldn't miss even in the background, comes from a solo in 'After the Flood' – a banshee's wail from the feedback of two saxophones, that spans well over a minute. I've never heard an instrument sound like it's dying before. It may not sound like a highlight, but my goodness it's jarring in a marvellous way.

It's the space between the notes though that you notice just as much throughout. It's a sparsely arranged record at times, and the silence is most definitely an instrument too. Mark Hollis once said: *"I get on great with silence. Before you play two notes, learn how to play one. And don't play one unless you've got a reason to play it."* A genius, and I don't throw the word around lightly. He died recently and believe me when I say it was one of the saddest moments of the year. Listen to *Laughing Stock* is what I'm sezzin'.

*

You can imagine the discussion that followed in light of the discovery of these albums. I doubt he had met many inmates who were willing to discuss whether Kate Bush's *The Dreaming* was her best or too indulgent as she produced it herself, or whether Oceansize and Karnivool are two of best bands no one's heard of. Hopefully I brightened his days as much as he brightened mine.

Anyway! The point of work or education – above just spending your time and having some purpose – is to earn money and induct yourself into the canteen system.

Canteen

So this word actually means your emporium for groceries and extra toiletries etc. Think of it as a poor man's Tesco delivery, literally, as you'll earn around £15 per week whatever you do. Most of this will immediately go on vape capsules, but if you really wish to splash (again literally) you can opt for a shower gel that doesn't come in a sachet. Or some chocolate. Or, depending on your pad-mate, air freshener.

The single most important thing, though, that you can purchase through the canteen is phone credit. If you really want the time to pass in prison, then it's speaking with your loved ones that will do just that. Of course it's mixed emotions doing so, but it's certainly what mattered to me above anything else.

Usually you'll submit your canteen form on a Sunday and receive it the following Friday. And there's a strange feel in the air on Fridays, the one night everything goes quiet. The night where people finally have what they want or need, and will blitz through most of it that evening.

There's one thing that beats a phone call though, one thing that has to be requested from outside rather than from within, and that is a visit.

Visits

Remember how herded we felt going through reception and induction? There's only two other times you'll feel anywhere near as bovine; one is on the way to or from work/education, and the other is now. Again, your surname is called, and you are filtered like *Lemmings* through the corridors and back to near reception, before being locked in a holding room for what feels like an hour. In fact, even though you've no real concept of time, it must be about that. You're then searched, before being handed a bib that will thrust you back to those rainy Tuesday nights, jumpers for goalposts and so on. Here though, there's no physical exercise, but rather the mental exertion of scanning a huge hall of chairs, tables and people, to eventually lock eyes with the one(s) that you love and haven't seen for potentially weeks.

Imagine the elation. Probably not so much for them, for it's not as if by being in here you're the only one suffering. And, on this rainy Tuesday, making that first eye contact is likely going to rain down the emotion for them more than it would for you. You know that you've been finding a way to get by, and that things are OK, but for them, they may well have created and contemplated all manner of horrors between the lines.

You'll get roughly an hour and you will be monitored fiercely as you do it, but that's to be expected and accepted. This is a prime opportunity for smuggling after all. As a result you will go back through metal detectors and be gloved up and down again, before back to the cattle pen, and eventually back to your wing and pad, emotionally drained, but fulfilled. Now they hopefully know that things *have* been OK. Because your eyes should say more than your words ever can.

And that's more or less it in terms of what you can expect in a prison day. There's a few other things, such as a visit to the chapel on Sunday mornings. I never went myself, but I always found it amusing how certain inmates would parade around, saying *"gimme a bit of that"* like they're God's gift, and then visit God every Sunday to renew their redemption. I don't think it works like that, sunshine.

So, with everything we've learned, here's how a typical day's routine in jail might pan out. I'll exclude work/education, as sometimes that won't come to fruition before you've actually left, and it won't happen at weekends either.

- Unlock
- Meds
- Bang-up
- *Frasier*
- *Undercover Boss*

- *Ramsay's Kitchen Nightmares*
- Unlock
- Lunch
- Bang-up
- *Flog it!*
- *The Big Bang Theory*
- *Brooklyn Nine-Nine*
- *Tenable*
- *The Chase*
- Unlock
- Dinner
- Bang-up
- *Pointless*
- *The Simpsons*
- *News*
- *The One Show*
- *MasterChef*
- *Film 4*
- *Film 4* again

Dominated by the box, and that's how they like it. Entertained and contained. Prison, we are told, is about reform, but frankly if you live a day like the above then this is not nurturing reform; far from it. Ultimately, *of course,* it is possible to reform yourself if you have the right attitude. I'll tell you about mine, but before that here's another example.

There's someone else I met during my recent stay in Wales. I had been ushered from the induction wing to my new one – the wing where I would be staying over the festive period – and just as I had unpacked and set my bedding, I heard voices outside as the other inmates returned from their day's occupation. And the flap on my door swung open to reveal a face I never thought I'd see again. A face I had only just stopped seeing in my nightmares. Nathan Windsor.

I kid you not. Like me, he had reoffended and, also like me, found himself this time being ferried over the Prince of Wales Bridge for his sentence. My blood ran cold as you might imagine, but as my door was unlocked later that evening for association and we got to have a chat, I found he was an altogether different being. Gone was the man who would steal, wheel and deal for his own gain, and in its place a person intent on bettering himself in every possible way, hopefully never to return. I was initially flummoxed, but as the days went by I saw that this was genuine, that he was really trying to turn his life around, and that it was paying dividends not just visibly for me but more importantly of course for him. He had enrolled in an art course, and as he showed me his work, I was genuinely taken aback by not just the care and love he had put into it, and indeed the quality, but the love he was getting back out. Woah. I never thought I would see him again; I certainly didn't think we would become friends in there like we did, but I have respect for him now. We took an interest in the football over the hectic Christmas period, and did our own accumulators, and that passed Saturdays in a flash.

Nathan Windsor, well done mate. And there are a lot of Nathan Windsor's in this world; those who fell on hard times, descended down a dark path, might have seemed inherently bad, but never quite lost the spark within themselves for change, found the change, and found peace to a degree. I can tell you, it's thanks to them.

Prison does not promote rehabilitation. It might ostensibly, but it doesn't. They want you calm and quiet and not for the right reasons. It ain't the staff's fault. The system will offer you a shred of help out of obligation, but if you want to reform, it really has to come *entirely* from within *you*.

That's how Nathan did it, and well, here's how I did it.

14

Ebenezer Hughes

That might be a little over the top. I've not been the best of myself at the best of times, but I have always felt love throughout. And it's usually been in the right direction. We can't help where we put our love a lot of the time. But that's almost the beauty of love. You don't choose your favourite film or band, it chooses you. And you don't choose who you fall in love with. I do have a habit of falling for people too quickly, and never was it more to my disadvantage than last year. That is no fault of Amy, Megan or Kerry. It's not mine either. It's life.

What I can and will blame myself for, though, 100%, is what happened at the end of those relationships, and afterwards. If I was going to learn anything this time and sort my life out, I had to recognise this. And I had to take my time recognising it. No more distractions; I had to face it head on.

Back in May and June, in the Amy aftermath, I just hadn't processed everything by the time I was released. I knew I was being punished, but there was too much going on inside both my head and the facility itself. It was not a friendly place; I've told you about Bert and Windsor, but that was little compared to what else was going on in there.

A few days into one of my stays, during association time, I heard talking outside our cell, followed by banging, followed by shouting, followed by the most piercing scream I have ever heard in my life. Going to check whether our door was locked, we noticed the flap was still open, and through the window both of us saw a man running out of the cell opposite, steam pouring from his body. He had been kettled.

Kettling might sound like a quaint Cumbrian village fête competition, but in jail, it's the tradition of launching the scolding contents of a kettle at someone. And this poor man was howling in agony, his face already blistering and his shirt fusing with his skin. I don't know what he had done, but there must have been reason for it. It was clearly a coordinated attack. What I found the most horrifying though, was that his cellmate had been attacked too, with a black eye already forming, and two teeth broken. Just for being his cellmate. That could have so easily been me.

And as the bus took us to Wales this time around, I thought back to that incident, and to my time there in general, and asked the question I really should have asked myself months before: *"Is this the life I really want?"*.

The first time round, if I'm honest I didn't know who was the real victim; me or Amy. Yes I'd been subjected to months of mental anguish, yes she wasn't a particularly nice piece of work, but I could have walked away at any time, and didn't. There's no question that on that fateful day, she was the victim, and that overall she was the victim, and I deserved what followed. Now that I'd had 6 months to process everything, I realised that I had perhaps been lucky to have got away with a suspended sentence, too. It just felt overwhelmingly right that that was now being invoked.

Not to mention the 10 weeks added on for Megan. Harassment typically wouldn't carry 10 weeks – that's the absolute maximum I believe a court can impose, but because of my suspended sentence they added it in full, and I didn't have any disputes. It initially seemed strange that I ultimately got more time for Megan than I did for Amy, but that was not down to the severity of the crimes, rather the order of them. But then I realised, forget the judicial system for a second, overall I undoubtedly hurt Megan more than I did Amy, and I was glad that this had been accidentally factored in.

I would be serving 18 weeks, down to 9, although I'd already served several of these earlier in the year. So I knew in my mind that I would probably be doing around 5 weeks, out mid January. I was going to be spending Christmas and New Year in here, but I felt strangely good about it. Justice was happening, and I felt something within me that I hadn't felt up until that moment (even after leaving rehab). I'm no mechanic, but it felt like a new spark plug.

Subsequently, I went in with a plan. In terms of my spare time, I would look to spend it more productively than just watching endless TV. Yes, of course this would still feature – it was Christmas after all. But I wanted a sense of purpose. What would I do? First and foremost, I'd write letters. Every day if the paper was afforded to me. I wanted to show my family that I had somehow already changed, and I wanted to walk with them each step of the way. Would I write anything else, too? I didn't know at that point. I had joked at times throughout the year that *"I could write a book on this someday"*, and maybe this was time to get cracking on it. Either way, I just knew I wanted to write, and write.

I also wanted to enrol for work or education that was sensible over fun this time round. This was my first experience of this prison – I had only ever visited one other before – and so I had no idea where the crossover would be, and what would be different. Once I got through my induction and could make these choices, I signed up to recycling and laundry, which had the shortest waiting list and to some degree would keep me physically fit. And, in terms of education, there were evening courses that counted as extra that appealed. As part of my suspended sentence, I had been placed on the waiting list for a 'Building Better Relationships' course, and by the time I had gone through Kerry and Megan, this course was still nowhere on the horizon. Now that my custodial sentence had been invoked, I knew this would wipe this relationship course from being a condition and that I would not have to attend when I came out on licence, but that did not mean I didn't still want to try something like this and see what I could learn. Something similar appeared on the application form, and I've never ticked something so fast in my life – it was even remarked upon.

To have the energy to keep this up, and not fall into the TV trap, I would have to eat as well as I could this time around too. This meant choosing options on the menu that I don't particularly like, but that I wouldn't be weighed down by. The irony is that despite my surroundings I felt that I was for the first time in a long while, unchained. And I didn't want diet holding me back.

A week went by, and I was sticking to the plan wholeheartedly. I was still on a waiting list for the job and courses, and Christmas was complicating this further, but I had at least signed up, and could do what else I could in the meantime. Despite my relationship with my father being at an all time low, he still saw something in me, the capacity to still be able to change, and so priority number one was to write to him every day. This was helped a great deal more in this prison than it had been last time, as emails were processed much more promptly and also had the option to reply, so I could simply write on the back and they would scan it and email back for me. Far quicker than posting a letter, especially to another country.

Emails were flying back and forth, and yesterday, before starting this chapter, I asked for all of these to be sent across so I could re-read and re-live them. I'm not going to share any of those – it's between my father and me – but I shed a tear, as I could read them as being from *me* – not a surrogate writing what they felt should be written and read. These emails continued in the build-up to Christmas, and as families up and down the world prepared to be together, I felt an ever-growing sense of contentment that I was where I needed to be. Previous spells in jail had been up to a fortnight, but I knew I needed longer, and the festive period would strangely help this along. Sadly, the courses I had enrolled for were yet to present themselves, but I'd had my first canteen form, and I had decided that I would ration my vape so that I could use the money I did have to purchase a notepad, and well, that notepad got this book started.

I had no idea at the time how I wanted to convey my story and journey, I just knew I needed to get it down – to just make a start and see where it took me and indeed where I took it. It began initially as just a diary of prison life; I did not intend at the time to go into too much detail as to what brought me there, but as you've read, that since blossomed, and the new word of the day, ladies and gentlemen, is *honesty*.

Amusingly, the first chapter to be written and completed in full was *Chapter 7: Windsor*, while he was only 3 cells down the lane. Little did he know. Chapter 1 was then penned. The most notable thing for me though, that I wrote during my time there, was a Christmas diary, which I hinted at before, and would be delighted to share with you now:

Christmas Eve

Watched "The Day The Earth Stood Still" last night, and forgot how good it is. Ironic how the message was "When we're on the precipice, we change". Also, the perfect role for Keanu Reeves, as he didn't even have to pretend to emote. My cellmate had work in the morning, and there was no association for anyone else so I'm currently locked up on my own. To utilise the time, I fixed the curtain around the toilet, then celebrated with a crap, then watched the Gallagher Premiership (rugby) equivalent of Match of the Day. *Forgot how awful the Warriors are, as are Brentford's soon-to-be housemates, London Irish. By the time* our new stadium is ready we are much more likely to be in the top flight than they are. I'm trying not to watch much TV, and currently it's nothing but things like Kung Fu Panda. If something like that can get commissioned, then I have every chance.

In fact, I had an idea for a cuddly children's animation of my own. It's about a Labrador in Africa that becomes poisoned from the oil and plastic pollution in the Niger Delta, and mutates into the ultimate rabid killing machine. The Nigerians must turn their guns off each other and work together to survive, so it's really all about the power of teamwork over indifference, an important value for infants. Also, there is actually more piracy in the Niger Delta then there is off the coast of Somalia, so it would be educational. Not to mention "don't pollute". At this moment I'm unsure if I can secure the rights to the name DOGZILLA, so I'll set to work on a backup. Wow, I wasted a lot of space for that.

Lunch was a chicken leg with korma sauce, rice and peas, followed by a staple dessert of any jail it would seem: plain sponge soaked in yellow water (they insist on calling it custard). I actually thoroughly enjoyed it, but I think that had more to do with the fact my ulcer is finally disappearing.

Just had association and chatted to others at this end of the wing. Here they're a non-threatening bunch, and we have a group of 7 or 8 or so that convene and chat football etc. at the end of the day. Now locked up again watching Frozen for the first time ever. Like Game of Thrones I enjoyed being in the minority for so long, before pounded into submission.

Christmas Eve banquet just arrived: a coronation chicken baguette, a mince pie, penguin bar, and a packet of curry *flavoured instant noodles. The wine was a choice of Barollo or Chateux Margaux 1787.*

I've written some more of the book, and about to watch The Wrong Trousers. *I've seen approximately 140 adverts for* The Tiger That Came To Tea, *which is on later. As Paul Whitehouse is involved I feel I have to watch it. Then* Die Hard 2. *Perhaps a few festive "Yippeekiyay's" will ring around the corridors.*

Watched both, off to bed.

Christmas Day

Woken up several times in the night. Lots of banging and shouting – mainly people just messing about on the wing, but it sounds like it may have kicked off in another one... anyway, not my problem. Cornflakes and croissant for breakfast, then we submitted our football predictions – my notable ones were Bournemouth 1-0 Arsenal, Man U 1-2 Newcastle, and heart said another Brentford win over the current neighbours Swansea. Right, Christmas Dinner is served!

Cold turkey slice. Cold ham slice. Cold beef slice. Rolled up together. It looked like someone's windpipe. Accompanied by roast potatoes, the world's most sorry-looking Yorkshire, and some parsnips from the local supermarket's 'Impenetrable' range... I fear a filling has literally bitten the dust. Topped off by a rectangle of Christmas Pudding in the signature yellow water. I really don't know if there's any custard in there at all; in fact it's not even a proper yellow – if anything it looks like it's been siphoned from the toilets. That would bring a whole new meaning to the term Christmas number one...

Now watching Mr Bean *posting himself some Christmas cards; infinitely more tragic than any of my predicaments. It's the original* Christmas Bean *episode from around 1992. I grew up with those different coloured VHS cassettes and this is probably the most enjoyable thing I'll watch today. Didn't bother with The Queen's Speech, but it sounds like the royal family's year has drawn some parallels with my own: "bumpy", and with perception at an all time low.*

Just been given our evening food in a plastic bag, and now locked up early for the rest of the day, presumably so staff can leave early. That's fair enough. BBQ chicken baguette, steak slice, salt and vinegar crisps (bastards), but at least followed by the best thing I will open on Christmas Day this year: a fun-size bag of Minstrels.

Watched Home Alone 2. *In that exclusive group of sequels that trumps the original (many thanks to Trump's cameo). It's really made me want to go back to New York; my favourite city along with Budapest. Perhaps one day I'll return for a book signing event. Gotta dream.*

The Great Christmas Bake-off followed, then Gavin & Stacy's *return after 10 years. The ending paved the way for a new series, but, honestly, I think it ran its course in series 2. Onto* Jurassic World *now… another solid sequel. Judy Greer is so gorgeous. Stop it, Scott.*

Trying to treat today just like any other day, rather than wondering what everyone's up to outside. I still maintain I needed and almost wanted to come here, and that it's for the best both short and long term. Feeling very positive, but missing everyone like crazy.

Boxing Day

Slept well. Association was good as I got my solicitor letter scanned and it looks like I might be out earlier than I thought. Nothing on TV so I'm just re-reading emails and my notepad.

Lunch: chicken and chips and sweetcorn. Guess the dessert. The Simpsons Stonecutters *episode was just on.* **Attach the stone of triumph!** *Then watched another episode, the one about Maggie being born. The plaque in his office at the end… I completely forgot about that, and shed a tear or two, quietly obviously.*

Wrote some more of the book, then retired for Cool Runnings. *"A gold medal is a wonderful thing, but if you're not enough without one, you'll never be enough with one either". If that film doesn't warm your cockles, there's probably something wrong with your cockles.*

Ended the day with Richard Osman's World Cup of the Decade. *Most amused to see* Wolf of Wall Street *voted the 2nd greatest film. Perhaps for the country club scene alone. (*Toy Story 3, *since you asked. Still not seen it.)*

Ending the day again with a feeling of love rather than loneliness. I'm so grateful to have the family and friends that I have, and I'll see them soon enough. They all know the love that I have, however, perhaps not the extent of it. But they might know how I feel about Busch Gardens, Opeth and The Office, *but do they know how I feel about* them?

And that's Christmas. Never thought I'd be in this position during one, but here I am, and I almost feel better than I ever have. A few weeks more and I can show it.

Before I knew it, NYE came to pass, and we were in a new decade. Though I never heard back regarding the relationship course, or my job, I did hear back from the OMU department regarding my sentence, which had been recalculated correctly, and I was to be released the very next week, January 6th: Ascension Day.

15

2020

Like rehab, I left with an exit plan. Except this time, I wasn't asked to create one. And whilst it may not have been quite as comprehensive as before, I feel it was very much all killer no filler. The immediate priorities were to see my family and have a second Christmas of sorts with them. Very mixed emotions there, as I didn't have any presents of my own to give, but I think that was understood. I certainly felt the love in the room regardless. Hopefully over time I can give back to them everything they have given to me over the years. I love them all so much.

Though he wasn't present for the above, what I said of course includes my father. Though he and I had patched certain things up by now, there were still loose threads aplenty, and one of my other immediate priorities had been to sort out housing for myself. I had actually been declined early tag release by probation, on the grounds that they didn't think my father's was a suitable address. This was a blessing in disguise, as it meant I stayed as long as I deserved to stay and could also thrash out a proper exit strategy. Although probation couldn't stop me going back there on my release, they were absolutely right, it wasn't suitable, and sadly that showed within a week of being back there.

It's not my father's fault in any way; if anything we're too similar, and we were right on top of each other again from the get-go. Remember I didn't have a bedroom of my own; I had been on a pop-up bed in the dining room over the past year, which was never great for my mental health (though just to stress one final time, I was always grateful to have it as an option even if I didn't always show it). And it certainly wasn't great for his mental health either. Even if I was saying and doing the right things when I came out, it was far too early to have built up any level of trust, and there would always be that niggling doubt.

Though I hadn't factored alcohol into my exit plan on paper, it had visited my thoughts once or twice, and I was comfortable with the idea of a quiet pint on my own sometime later in the week when I got back. To take a bench by the river, in its reflection and my own, and look to the new decade. Control. I did this without telling him where I was going though, in fear of a bust-up. And that's probably what caused the bust-up when I came back. It was about as calm as one had ever been between us, but it did thrust my housing plans right to the very front, as this time, on mutual agreement, I was properly homeless.

I immediately made a call to the local council, and registered myself officially. One of the biggest ironies was that I was sent a link to complete the process on a system they were trialling, a system I had been loosely involved with through a previous job. Now I was an end-user. But any embarrassment was swiftly reconciled. I would do whatever it took this time. I had started the process of turning my life around over Christmas, but by no means was I anywhere near it yet. This was a gradual process, which continues today. And this sudden homelessness was not a bad thing at all; in fact it hadn't de-railed my exit plan either; just re-jigged some of it.

I did have a place to stay that night, on the floor of The Salvation Army. It was not where I had imagined I would be a month earlier, but it was still somehow a firm step in the right direction. The Salvation Army are a wonderful organisation; please do think about donating to them if you are ever asked. They're not like certain high-profile charities with 6-figure wage bills, they are as honest as it comes and they do amazing work, and I was so grateful. I was given a camping mat, a sleeping bag and a pillow, and as I curled up that night in the corner of their main hall, mid-January, I smiled. Many are more deserving of that floor than me, and I was going to make the best of it.

Tea and toast in the morning, followed by an interview with a housing officer, and incredibly 4 hours later I had a phone call asking whether I could get to Birmingham the following day. I had qualified for a shared house, under supported living. Another night would be spent on the Salvation Army floor, and, as I collected my bag and myself the following morning, it felt like I was truly on my own path now, even though technically I wasn't. It certainly didn't feel like a step backwards; in fact I don't believe there is such a thing, as long as you're still looking ahead. I was very fortunate to have housing provided so promptly for me, and I made haste for New Street, met with my new landlords, and was taken to the charming suburb of Quinton.

Birmingham as a city does not hold the character of London, Bristol or Manchester, but the further out you stray, the more any of these cities could be the other. Quinton is your typical outer borough; anodyne and pallid, no identity anywhere you look, but always a barbers or off-licence. Please note anything I say about Quinton is firmly tongue-in-cheek; I was genuinely thrilled to be there at the time.

We arrived, and after a quick guided tour of the communal areas and the signing of a few papers, I was given my keys and left to my own devices. My bedroom was on the ground floor, and really was better than I could have hoped for: a single bed in the corner with the wrapping still on the mattress, plenty of space, and crucially, a lock. I didn't have any bedding yet; all I had was a waterproof jacket that would serve as my blanket that night, but, honestly, I still felt like the luckiest man alive. This may have been supported living, but it was just the level I needed to be at in order to discover what I needed to and get everything into perspective, and to start from again.

And what I discovered and how I continued into the year is I suppose is where we reach the crux of things, and many of the reasons for publishing this. If it ended at this moment, I probably wouldn't be happy as a reader. I don't think I'd be satisfied that any resolution had actually been reached yet. So what have I learned, really? If I was a fictional character, what would I have learned, typically? Though this isn't a work of fiction, I suppose I have managed to somehow play both the protagonist and antagonist. If anything my life has been a work of *friction*, and I certainly hope to be moved into Non-Friction here on. Wow that was cheese.

Let's just carry on and see if I've learned anything. I made arrangements to collect my belongings from my father, including bedding, and started to decorate the room. I got everything unpacked the same day, everything in order. All the little things. Then I met my new housemates. Two twins upstairs, same age as me, and a pleasant enough duo. One I learned was heavily epileptic, which brought back my first school teacher from Chapter 5. Again, that's a hardship I am most fortunate to be without.

Tragically, as I complete this final draft, I add that he passed away upstairs a couple of weeks ago.

There was another housemate in the room next to me downstairs, and again he was welcoming enough. I've always enjoyed being in shared houses; it's nice to know there are others under the same roof to talk properly to anytime, but equally nice that I still have my own space.

I propelled myself into action, and chapter 2, 3, and continued in order up to where I am today. In terms of working from home, I had always enjoyed this in my career, and for the most part had exemplary discipline. There was one role where I am amused to recall setting a timer every 14mins to literally flick the mouse and prevent my little Skype circle from turning yellow (it almost became ceremonial)… but other jobs I took a little more seriously. I do consider this work, though I have no idea whether it will actually make any money. I intend to charge as little as I possibly can for this; I am less interested in making a profit and more interested in reaching people. As I write this we are into lock-down, and though my past problems don't seem any less significant, I have made a lot of time for thinking about the journey we are all on, not just through this pandemic but in life. We're all in it together. Or most of us. If I'm honest, I haven't suffered that much over this pandemic at all, especially compared to 2019. I have kept myself compliant, safe, and in decent physical and mental health. I have still managed to put on weight like I believe others have. But that's cool! I can look at myself in the mirror and be comfortable again now, as I was back during the self portrait. A comment that kept coming up in rehab was *"learn to love yourself"*, and I never fully understood it then, but something has clicked and I do now. I can take pride in myself too, for getting through everything that I have and coming out as strong as perhaps I'll ever be.

I always had the PlayStation for downtime, and I found some rather amusing ways to keep myself entertained on YouTube as well. For example, I would watch episode after episode of *Architectural Digest*, to be shown round the luxurious digs of celebrities. It might have sickened many others in the current climate, but I wanted the stark contrast to where I sat watching them, hunched over my phone by the window (the only place I can obtain a 4G signal). Maria Sharapova's home in particular is sublime. And I must mention Lenny Kravitz's farm in Brazil. As if my aspirations didn't need fuelling already.

I also enjoyed the irony of joining a *Rate my Plate* group on Facebook and seeing some of the culinary masterpieces being whipped up on there. You might associate *Rate my Plate* with culinary car-crashes rather than masterpieces, but in the group rather than the page the majority of the posts are of dishes lovingly prepared, and to salivate over. More often than not, I was eating a car crash of a dinner whenever I saw them (I have whipped up the odd signature salad while I've been here, but I'd be lying if I said I haven't enjoyed the odd microwave meal or pizza, too. (I haven't posted in the group)). Again, it was my little way of finding humour in my current status. Though I do not have the appliances or equipment to create some of these wonderful dinners, I can certainly digest some inspiration to create them whenever I next can. And I've been saving recipes to my new favourite YouTube playlist.

Talking of appliances, and the house in general, I should describe the rest of it. I started in the kitchen so let's continue there. Plenty of cupboard, fridge and freezer space, but the microwave and oven leave something to be desired. Clearly the other household members have not quite figured them out themselves, as I can't tell you the amount of times my writing of this book has been disrupted by the smoke alarm. A quick check to make sure everything's OK, only to see a sheepish grin leaving the kitchen looking like a Rammstein concert had just been held in there.

Then there's the bathroom. And back to the old chestnut of a simple lock on the door. This took me straight back to prison, as sadly there wasn't one, and still isn't. For some bizarre reason there is a large reclining chair in there, though, almost like an art installation, and so the obvious hack is to push this against the door. I still laugh every time I use the facilities. It is what it is. There wasn't even a working light in there until recently, but again, a first-world problem and nothing the torch on my phone couldn't solve.

The garden is also a sight to behold. Talking of art installations, two shopping trolleys just chilling. Haven't asked. And a clump of human hair, where a housemate had shaved his head and for some reason chosen there as a receptacle over the bin. Overall, I'd say it's about as you'd expect from supported living and, I've said this many times now, I'm not complaining. If it hadn't been for the lock-down then perhaps I would have already moved on, but here I am and there's no sympathy to even think about asking for. These things are good for me; they're grounding, they remind me on a daily basis of how far I have yet to go, and they're a better source of inspiration than anything else I can think of.

Talking of grounding; this was a technique taught to me in rehab, which I have finally started using now. If you ever feel overcome and that things are getting on top of you, simply stop and focus on something else, in extreme detail. For example, picture a room, maybe the one you're in. Observe every nuance, the placement of the furnishings, the scuffs on the wall, the screws on the door-handle, all of it. This also works for films or music; think of something you know off by heart and just let it run. It may be no surprise that *Laughing Stock* is my go-to here. And I can get as far as I need to before I'm feeling cured. The other one I sometimes use is Pink Floyd's *The Wall*, which I managed to reference earlier in the book without a tangent for once. Gold star if you spotted it.

Grounding is essentially a form of meditation, and one key discovery I have made this year – one I feel must get a mention – is a man named John Butler. I happened upon a long interview with John on YouTube, and almost immediately I knew that to have found him was to be a revelation in my life. John is a man who like me has suffered with depression, and also grappled with theology and the idea that there is so much more in the world than we know. Although as I said before I am agnostic and have been for some 15 years now, I definitely sit more with faith these days. But how can anyone know for sure? Surely we are all agnostic at the end of the day? Atheism is, after all, also a belief system. Built on logic, yes, but no more verified by empirical evidence than any of the religious institutions. I do believe that, spiritually, there is to some degree a higher plane of intelligence, a force of love, and light, that exists within the universe. How anyone can claim to truly understand the universe is beyond me, really. I'm so glad there are people like John Butler that exist within it though, to help me to focus on the here and now, the things within my control, that I *can* understand, and that are within my influence to make this existence on Earth a happy one, and a successful one.

And surely, happiness is conducive to true success, in life. As John suggested, is success when there are no more questions? Some deliberate irony in that being a question, I suppose. But surely that's where we all want to be. He also says many times: *"To make whole, be whole"*. Well, that's the new journey I am on, and the meditation is definitely helping with it so far. John is nearing the end of his journey after 83 years, but has found peace and love through meditation. He has written many books, and has a fantastic YouTube channel. In particular his 'Discovering Stillness' interview gives a fascinating insight into a much more fascinating life than you have read about here. I strongly recommend you check him out, especially after a bad day. He also has the second best voice in the world, after Michael Holding.

340

Talking once more of lock-down, I hope you have found things OK. I may not know your face, or your name, but you have read what I have to say and I consider you my friend. Things have quite probably been harder for you very recently than they have for me, and I'm sure many others are the same. Although I've had my issues with ex-partners, it hasn't stopped me thinking fondly of those out there who are currently in loving relationships and feeling great for them, but also how hard it must be for them if they live apart during this lock-down. Wow that must be difficult.

Rate my Plate and *Architectural Digest* were good for light entertainment, but I have supplemented this with more profound viewing, too. I watched an excellent new series called *DEVS*, which is to some degree about pre-determinism. I may have felt at times like I was on a predetermined path, or that I had been sent off-course beyond my control, but with a proper head on my shoulders I look back on all the moments where I had the power and the influence to change my direction and I just didn't take them. Does that mean I regret those moments? Again, at risk of my popularity, I can honestly say that I don't regret a single thing I did or said last year. That doesn't mean I don't have guilt or shame, to return to the assignment again. Of course I am truly ashamed of some of the things I did and said, and yes of course I feel a deep sense of remorse, but should that mean I regret them? If I could go back and change anything, I wouldn't. It was all necessary in the grand scheme of things to get me where I am today, metaphorically and physically speaking. There was an upside in everything that happened. *Everything*. It just took a clear head and a little time to make sense of some of it, and

I'm grateful of the experience. Consider that a final word on Amy I suppose.

A final word on Megan. Every time I see Ricky Gervais now, I see her. And given how much I revere and re-watch some of his shows, it feels like a strange sense of karmic justice. I haven't watched *After Life* series 2 yet, but it's nothing to do with that. Sticking with justice, I could have had my driving ban cut by 5 months if I'd attended a course this year. However, long before the pandemic, I made the decision that I wanted to ignore this and serve the full 20 months. It's the right thing.

A final word then on justice. By far the biggest punishment in all of this for me, is that on paper now I am classed as a domestic abuse perpetrator. My god that hurts the most. It may be in the past, and it may have "only" been text messaging, but that *doesn't* matter, it *was* abusive, I deserve the label and will fight with everything I have to ditch it, as I am not an abusive person by nature. I couldn't be further. I have such love for things I can't tell you, even though I've tried over these pages. Sadly, on more than one occasion last year I turned into someone else. However, it's *me* that deserves the label and, as much as it does currently hurt, well that's justice, isn't it? I'll swallow it and move forwards with my life. I'm certainly not looking for any relationships at the moment. I'm focusing on myself first and foremost, and family and friends. I'm sure I'll meet someone who I fall for because of the right reasons and in the right amount of time. There's a Dawn or a Pam somewhere out there for me, but not before I'm more like Tim or Jim.

A final word, most importantly, on the relationship with my father. We have, of course, spoken at length about everything that happened, and though I struggle to emote sometimes, he knows how ashamed I am in particular of my treatment towards him. I hope he knows how much I love him too. I am delighted to say we are in a good place these days. What needed to happen happened, and though I haven't been able to see him much recently for obvious reasons, we remain in close contact and I am delighted to say I am moving much closer to him soon.

And a final word on Kerry. I will likely always have certain feelings for her. A recent dream in which she appeared reminded me of that. However, I'm glad that, in my own time, I have arrived at the realisation that I just don't want or need someone like that in my life. In fact it was surprisingly simple to let go second time around. I'll never know if she was honest or not, on either occasion, but despite my disposition, I don't feel like I need to. And that shows, to me at least, the strength I have now compared to before. Perhaps the biggest thing I've learned over this past year is that I need to work *with* my feelings rather than against them. And if I can continue to do it, then I'm gonna be fine. A year ago I would have run from a dream like that, but I like to note my dreams down these days, and I had no reticence in adding this one to the list. I can can recall all of my dreams vividly when I read them back and it's hilarious and fascinating; you should try it!

Talk of Kerry and of frothy psychoanalysis brings me nicely back to Frasier. You may remember that in my very first visit to hers, I saw the box set in her collection. There are 11 seasons in total, and we got up to #10 before things ended. At the time, it put me off finishing the show for life. How would I ever be able to detach it from her? However, I had managed to watch the first seven seasons of *Game of Thrones* with Amy and then enjoy the final one without her almost immediately, and during the lock-down, I finally got round to watching the final season of *Frasier* without Kerry. And it was a joy from start to end. Definitely up there with *Curb* as one of the best American sitcoms.

Talking of American sitcoms, one of, if not the most famous of all, is one that I have mentioned a couple of times throughout the book and have to one final time, as I recently watched two episodes that were as profound as anything else I've seen this year, and that told me I have the best of my emotions back.

I have always known what my favourite *Simpsons* episode ever is; it's always been head and shoulders above the rest, and that's Season 2 Episode 20: *War of the Simpsons*. Back in the early days, The Simpsons was as full of morality as anything else on television. There were no cheap jokes, in fact rarely were they interested in even ending on a joke. If they'd tugged the heartstrings, job done.

A quick synopsis of *War of the Simpsons*:

After watching a drunk Homer ogling a neighbour's breasts at a dinner party, Marge concedes their marriage is at breaking point and has been for some time, and in a last ditch effort to save it, enrols them for a couples counselling weekend at a nearby retreat. Homer begrudgingly agrees, but is immediately distracted on arrival by the local fishing lake and the legend of General Sherman: a huge catfish that has been sighted and once photographed, but never caught. Failing to recognise the deep water their marriage was in, Homer can only think of Catfish Lake, and he sneaks from the cabin overnight to defeat the general and write his name in folklore. Before he can leave to catch him though, Marge catches Homer, and he aborts the operation. Instead he takes an honest walk to clear his thoughts and focus his mind on the real matter at hand, to be a husband.

He innocently picks up a fishing rod to return to someone who had just walked off without it, and is suddenly and vehemently tugged into the water by General Sherman. An epic battle ensues, between man and catfish, and man and conscience. After hours of struggle, they both lay semi-conscious in the boat, with Homer's name almost up in lights. The only other person to witness the struggle? Marge, who heard the commotion and has come to confront her soon-to-be ex-husband at the waterside.

Homer sees her, and himself and what he has become. The general is laboured overboard, and almost in that instant their marriage is saved. The closing monologue by the bait shop owner is a wonderful moment.

Why have I just told you that? Well, the protagonist had lost the ability to control himself and demonstrate the love for his family. Thankfully, a family member stepped in and offered a glaringly thin lifeline. Whilst taking the lifeline, the protagonist did not seize the opportunity but rather conceded all-too-easily again to greed, reputation, and the wrong type of self-respect. Thankfully, at the last minute, he realised the error of his ways, on his own, and used every last bit of his energy throwing every last morsel of his ego into the water.

The other episode, is actually the very previous one, S2E19: *Lisa's Substitute*. Lisa develops a crush on her substitute teacher: Mr Bergstrom. Though he is only there on a short term surrogate basis, an amazing friendship and bond is quickly formed. Suddenly Mr Bergstrom has to leave his post and town, and poor Lisa is distraught. Life isn't worth it. As they embrace for a final time on the train platform, he hands her a note and says *"Whenever you feel alone, this is all you need to know"*. And as the train rolls away in a shroud of steam, Lisa opens the note through the tears, to read: ***"You are Lisa Simpson"***.

Talk about tugging the heartstrings. On more than one occasion lately I have felt like that, and that all sense of meaning had gone up in smoke, but this episode reminded me who *I* am more than anything else. It's funny how I haven't always just had issues with my personality, but used to have a thing about my name, too. God knows why. But I've learned to love it. Because that name is me. Someone once told me it sounds like a reporter's name… *"Scott Hughes, News at 10, Quinton."*

I've talked about my favourite album of all time, mentioned one of my favourite films, and I can tell you now that the *Simpsons* was comfortably my favourite TV show that ever was. No other has been written that was funnier and that had more pathos.

And knowing who I am is what this is all about. To me it really is the meaning of life as best I can grasp it. I have myself back now, and I missed myself a lot. I am enough for me, and so I am enough. I forgot how much of a release it is when one can smile and laugh again, especially at the little things. Case in point, just yesterday I saw someone walking down the street with an NCP umbrella. How did that come about? Umbrellas are usually as simple as it comes with no branding. Who designed one themed to National Car Parks and, more importantly, who bought one?! How I chuckled. The same day I overheard a lad in the local shop seemingly trying to woo the girl he was with, by saying: *"You're smart, d'ya know what I mean?"* A quite charming oxymoron there… emphasis on moron.

Whilst we're here, a final word on Loz too. I'm delighted to say that we are tighter than ever these days. In fact we've started a podcast: ***The Scott & Loz Show (Two dicks talking bollocks)*** – available on Spotify and other platforms (including my YouTube channel which you may have accessed for the poppadom sketch).

But just because things like this are happening it doesn't mean I can get complacent. I have worked at this, to get back to where I am, but I can't drop off. I will be diligent. I was never a particularly spiritual person up until attending rehab and AA, and though I don't visit AA meetings at the moment (it would be wrong given I am not in total abstinence), that's not to say I can't remember all the things those meetings taught me. And what rehab taught me, in particular those morning sessions, was how one can set up their mentality for the day powerfully with a few simple thoughts and reflections.

Those readings were predominantly concerned with gratitude, and for good reason. I have been given a life, and numerous chances at it, and I should never forget it for a second. Finally, I'm putting what I learned from rehab into proper practice. Every morning now I do three things: a series of breathing exercises, meditation, and I practice gratitude. It sets me up for the day better than any cup of Gold Blend has done before. I sometimes have a cup of Gold Blend after, though, just to be diligent.

I've also been listening to Max Richter's album *Sleep*, often while writing, and often overnight too, rather aptly. Nearly 9 hours long, it has helped no end. It's the unofficial soundtrack to this book as far as I'm concerned. As I return for the final draft, I am listening to his excellent new album *Voices*. I need things like this and always will; like I said, I am not the finished article now and never will be. I still get depressed, I still ponder my worth, and I have to work at it full time. Thankfully, I know people like John Butler are out there doing it too.

If I think back to the jigsaw, I feel that somehow by doing what I've done over the past 5 or 6 months, I have placed the final few pieces. Not in terms of completion – it will always remain unfinished – but the last few pieces that I can actually place. In that sense maybe it is completion. This book has felt almost like writing my own clean bill of health. I am not still without my anxieties, but that's OK. I would rather recognise them and deal with them myself, rather than by medical assistance that only affects other things. In my wallet, I have a slip of paper I wrote on which is far more important to me than the one Mr Bergstrom gave to Lisa, and it's another one I learned from rehab and have finally put to use:

Stop,
Observe
Breathe
Evaluate
React

There's no irony in the above – yes, I do enjoy the odd pint now and again, and it's because I know now when I can actually enjoy it. With recent events I have not enjoyed one for some time, and it's not the thing I miss the most. It's way down the list. I mean *sober* in a different sense, and that's how I use the mantra, for my anxieties. Here's a fairly recent example and perhaps the best I can give in terms of what it's like to live with social anxiety.

I mentioned that not long after my recent release I met up with my family and we had a second Christmas. I already felt slightly tense that the focus was on me, opening my presents, and that I couldn't do the same in return. After unwrapping the final one, I collected the wrapping paper and ribbons etc., as well as the envelopes, and as someone passed me a recycling bag I simply said *"straight in the bin"*. It's obvious what I meant; we were putting any detritus tidily away, but suddenly in my head I went through a gauntlet of terror. *"My **God**, do they think I was just talking metaphorically about the present itself when I said that? Do I say anything? They're not looking at me, but are they thinking it? Do they think I would be capable of such a callous comment, or thought? Do I say anything? Do I say anything?"*

I didn't have the courage to say anything, which would have put any paranoia straight to bed, I'm sure. But these are the typical over-thoughts that can happen, and, when all's said and done, I can live with them easily enough compared to other troubles in the world. I'm still learning about myself each and every day.

Here's a more recent example of my social anxiety, in which I demonstrate I believe some significant progress in dealing with it – better perhaps than a lot of people without anxiety might even have done. The height of lock-down, in the queue for Tesco in Quinton. Classed as a 'superstore', you presumably know about the queuing protocols. I was mid-queue, minding my own business, when all of a sudden, I inhaled, and something caught, and I was inexplicably into an uncontrollable coughing fit. We've all done it. Just at better times. A simple breath and we're suddenly spluttering and gasping for water. Our voice is shot to ribbons for the next 10 to 15 minutes and we don't quite know how it happened.

Well, it's especially fun when you're out in public, during a pandemic in which everyone is acutely on edge about anyone with respiratory or bronchial issues, and also when you have no access to a quick glass of water to try and kill it off. Naturally, I tried to hold it in, which led to a series of weird convulsions and noises, as the body's requirement to cough was far stronger than my vain urge to contain it. I couldn't have looked more shifty, and I certainly couldn't have been looked at with more contempt. Eventually, after I'd say 5 minutes of learning how to control my breathing to minimise the coughing and indeed my heartbeat, I settled back into where I was, about 5% further up the queue. I knew I was healthy and that this was a freak incident and I knew these people would probably never see me again, and in a eureka moment, I was able to take that logic with me to the end of the experience. Yes, I was more than a little self-conscious, as I venture anyone would have been, but it didn't consume me to the point of doing anything. I didn't try and laugh it off and potentially make it any worse with anyone, I just fought with all of my energy, swallowed it, kept my place, did my thing, and we all moved on.

Talking of vanity, I have a tattoo on my right arm, which I had pretty much as soon as I turned 18. It's a demon skull design, behind strands of skin, giving the illusion that it's underneath. I only had it at the time because I thought it was *"gnarlsberg, dude"*, and I could quite easily have it removed, but I have decided I want to keep it and get it touched up, as at least it's allegorical now. He is to some degrees my inner demon, who wreaked havoc on so many occasions, but these days I have kept inside on a leash. I am no longer subservient to him, and I don't mind having him there or even giving him a sleek new paint job when I can.

I don't want to rely on other people's quotes in this chapter, but back in Chapter 2, before we met Amy, I used one from Steven Wilson in 'Song of Unborn':

"It's not the wage you earn,
It's about the things you learn,
And the love that you feel."

That was worth saying again. Here's another quote from the same song:

"Don't be afraid to die,
Don't be afraid to be alive."

I hope that doesn't come across as pretentious or trying to be prophetic. None of these quotes define me, but they do resonate with me, and I share them in the hope that they resonate with you too.

And I hope everything else has resonated, I really do. My aim has been to take you on this journey with me, and as such I hope my asides to you haven't come across in any way as patronising (patronising means to talk down to.)

It has been a true journey for me. The writing of it has also been somewhat of a journey, in re-living it all. And in my downtime, when I should have been chilling, I was on another journey to try and finish *Dark Souls*...

Where we left off, I had conquered Blighttown on the way down to buxom-spider-woman, then had to conquer it all over again on the way back up. My reward was the unlocking of a fun-house known as Sen's Fortress. A place that revels in trying to kill you. Narrow pathways with a perilous plunge either side, and, just to hit the boost button, pendulous blades to dart between, whilst also being shot at. I actually enjoyed it.

But then I unlocked and visited a grandiose and opulent city called Anor Londo, and met an infamous duo named Ornstein and Smough. This is where I hit the wall again. And after god knows how many attempts, I knew I couldn't and wouldn't get past them. Did it anger me this time? Not particularly. I knew I just wasn't good enough, and I was OK with that.

But I wasn't ashamed about asking for help, when I needed it.

I summoned someone online and we took them down, and I'll never forget the moment, as sad as that may sound. What was especially satisfying is that Dad was there at the time to see it (I can't get Wi-Fi at home, and had taken the PlayStation over to his one day). How nice it was to bring a good fight to the house for a change. Many people have reached this point in the game and bowed out. Many people probably with more patience than me. But I stuck with it and did it. **Bonfire!**

And things got a bit easier from there. The next boss that caused anywhere near as much trouble was a tower of bones named Gravelord Nito, not because of him but rather getting there through a section called Tomb of the Giants, in which I had to traverse total darkness with giant snarling skeleton dogs that got the better of me goodness knows how many times. I could quote Chumbawumba here.

Before I knew it, I'd unlocked the final boss in the game: Gwyn. However, as I owned *DS: Remastered* it meant I had access to the DLC (extra) content, which was entirely optional. It was also renowned as being by far the most punishing section of the game, for only the hardcore. I thought I'd give it a whirl.

I met a foe named Knight Artorias, with a backstory far more tragic than mine. He had completely succumbed to mental anguish and was crazed beyond any repair, and, boy, was he a fight. But after many attempts, I was the victor. Then the two absolute toughest bosses in the entire game: Black Dragon Kalameet, and Manus: Father of the Abyss. These names might mean little to you, but to anyone who's played the game, they're serious business. But by this point I was so strong both in-game and mentally, that it was a simple case of learning and recognising the warning signs and the damage, and slowly through trial and error, finding ways to get round them, without the online assistance this time. KO. KO.

And the 'walk' to Gwyn's final arena was something I won't ever forget. If it didn't already represent my journey, it really did now. Thankfully, the developers gave him and I the build-up we deserved. Once more, one final time, after learning what he had to throw at me and my strengths and weaknesses, I engineered a plan and pulled it off with the final swing of my Zweihander, and he was dust. The game was dust. I lit the final bonfire, and sat back for the credits. I had not finished *Dark Souls*, but *beaten* it, and more than that.

The *Dark Souls* journey technically doesn't end there, as there's always the option of New Game +, where you start again with the same equipment and strength, but stronger enemies, and maybe I'll do so with it someday. Either way I'm satisfied. In terms of my own journey, this isn't an end either. It's a start. I'm also on NG+, and bring it on. There will be the proverbial nettles, but at least now I carry a dock leaf. Wow that was even cheesier. I can't end on that.

Thanks for reading. I don't quite know where it goes from here, but that's exciting. I was going to add a somewhat frivolous final poll on what to do next with my life. But I don't feel like I need to know the outcome of that, really.

If you have a story of your own, be it concerning mental health or anything else you may share with parts of this story, do share with me, in complete confidentiality of course. I can't guarantee that I can help, but I can promise I'll reply, and hopefully understand.

Here's my email: **scott-a235-hughes@outlook.com**

If you wish to join me for the remainder of my journey, here's my Instagram. It features many photos throughout the timeline of these events, in fact.

@scottalexhughes

Oh, and don't forget The Scott & Loz Show!

Now if you'll excuse me I'm off for dinner at Bob Cratchit's.

UPSIDE IN

3rd party content attribution

Pages 15 and 351: "It's not the wage you earn, it's about the
things you learn, and the love that you feel."
- Artist: **Steven Wilson**
- Song: **Song of Unborn**
- Album: **To The Bone** [2017]
- © All rights reserved by Steven Wilson Productions Ltd.,
  under exclusive license to Caroline International.

Page 16: "Hearing without listening"
- The Sound of Silence
- Words & Music by Paul Simon

Page 21: "Those who don't believe in magic will never find it."
- Author: Roald Dahl
- Title: The Minpins [1991]

Page 80: QR code
- Artist: This Will Destroy You
- Song: The Mighty Rio Grande
- Album: This Will Destroy You [2008]

Page 116: QR code
- Artist: Midnight Oil
- Song: Bakerman
- Album: Red Sails in the Sunset [1984]

Page 191: "God, grant me the serenity to accept the things I cannot change, the courage to change the things I can, and the wisdom to know the difference."

- Author: **Reinhold Niebuhr**
- Title: **The Serenity Prayer** [1951]
-

Page 202, AA Step One: "We admitted we were powerless over alcohol and that our lives had become unmanageable"
-

Page 250, AA Step Eight:"Made a list of all persons we harmed, and became willing to make amends to them all".
-

Page 250, AA Step Nine: "Made direct amends to such people wherever possible, except when to do so would injure them or others"
-

Page 330: "A gold medal is a wonderful thing, but if you're not enough without one, you'll never be enough with one either"
- Film: **Cool Runnings** [1993]
-

Page 344-346: Synopsis of *War of the Simpsons* and *Lisa's Substitute,* including the quotes: *"Whenever you feel alone, this is all you need to know",* and *"You are Lisa Simpson."*

Page 351: "Don't be afraid to die. Don't be afraid to be alive."
- Artist: **Steven Wilson**
- Song: **Song of Unborn**
- Album: **To The Bone** [2017]

If you are still reading I do hope you check out all of the above, which are simply wonderful pieces of work!

For exclusive discounts on Matador titles,
sign up to our occasional newsletter at
troubador.co.uk/bookshop